PrincetonReview.com

THE ANXIOUS TEST-TAKER'S
GUIDE TO CRACKING ANY TEST

BY THE STAFF OF THE PRINCETON REVIEW

Random House, Inc.
New York

The Princeton Review, Inc.
2315 Broadway
New York, NY 10024
E-mail: bookeditor@review.com

ISBN: 978-0-375-42935-4

VP, Publisher: Robert Franek
Editor: Laura Braswell
Executive Director of Print Production: Scott Harris
Senior Production Editor: M. Tighe Wall

Printed in the United States of America on partially recycled paper.

9 8 7 6 5 4 3 2 1

CONTENTS

How to Use This Book

Tests are a ubiquitous part of modern life. As children, we are subjected to a barrage of different tests that measure what we know, what we are good at, how we learn, and what we should be when we grow up. As adult students, the pressure to prove our mettle is often much greater, and the stakes, in most cases, even higher.

The goal of this book is to give everyone—high school students, adult learners, parents, educators, and other interested parties—a 360-degree view of testing so that you are better informed and better prepared for those moments in life (and there will be many) when your abilities and knowledge are measured. We start from four simple premises:

1. **Good test-taking skills can be learned.** Taking a test is a skill in and of itself, separate from (though connected to) the content and worthy of study and practice. Even the writers of some of the largest and best known tests acknowledge that proper preparation can help you increase your score. The more you know about a test, the more you can use its unique qualities and structure to avoid mistakes and score your best.

2. **Not all tests are created equal.** Different tests do different things, and thus should be prepared for appropriately. Additionally, there is a pretty wide spectrum of quality when it comes to tests: some are less valid and more poorly constructed than others. We'll take a look at the traits of specific tests and discuss general principles that should be applicable to nearly any test.

3. **Understand the test writer, understand the test.** Throughout this book, we will talk a lot about how test writers create tests, particularly how they create trap answers. Tests are written by people. If you can get into the heads of the test writers and become familiar with the distinct idiom of a particular test, you can get a lot better at avoiding traps and develop a keen eye for what makes an answer better than all the rest.

4. **Test takers have rights.** In the game of testing, the test taker is not a powerless victim. You have the right to have your knowledge and abilities measured in a fair, accurate, and valid way. You have the right to know what you are to be tested on and how your score will be calculated, as well as how those scores will be used. You have the right to be tested under conditions that allow you to perform to the best of your abilities. We'll talk more about what a valid testing experience should look like, and what you can do to exercise your rights when the testing experience doesn't quite go as well as it should.

It is only by reaching for something more that we can grow as learners and as people. Imagine a test as a wall standing between you and the next place you want to get to in life. There are number of ways you could approach the wall. You can stand there staring at it. You can bang your head against it. You can yell at it, telling it how unfair you think it is or how badly it is measuring your abilities. You can walk away from it altogether. The problem with these approaches is that none of them help you do what you need to: get past it and move on to the next thing, whether that is the next test, the next grade, college, graduate school, or a professional certification. Nearly any test is an opportunity for you to reach for something more, to challenge yourself, to risk displaying weakness, but possibly to reveal abilities you didn't even know you had.

In the end, preparing to take a test involves more than just memorizing information. At its core, it should be a combination of developing good habits, a positive attitude, an awareness of your own strengths and weaknesses as a test taker, content mastery, and a smart approach to testing that allows you to show the world what you can do.

To help you improve all these things, this book will take you through each aspect step by step.

Chapter 1: Introduction

Why are tests there? How are they constructed? What do the test-makers claim your scores mean, and what do they really mean?

Chapter 2: Testing and Learning Differences

Test performance is mitigated by a number of factors, *including* the unique way that each person learns most effectively. We'll talk about the different styles and how awareness of your ideal learning modality can improve your ability to prepare for and perform on tests. We'll also review the basics of learning disabilities.

Chapter 3: Study Skills

We have lots of advice to offer about how to approach a test, but that advice assumes that you know your stuff. Lots of students simply never learned good study habits, so we'll talk about how to take better notes and learn more effectively.

Chapter 4: 360-Degree Preparation

There are easier and more successful ways to prepare for a test. We'll take a look at all the academic skills that can be improved upon to make you that much more ready on test day. We'll also review the kinds of preparation resources that are out there and which may be best for you.

Chapter 5: Tackling the Test: Tips for Any Kind of Question

A survey of all types of tests, information on the major standardized testing programs, and advice on how to perform best on every kind of test out there.

Chapter 6: What to Do (And Not Do) on Test Day

What to do (and not do), what to bring (and not bring), and how to perform your best, no matter what.

Chapter 7: Specific Test Information

A list of major testing programs at the pre-high school, high school, and college level and basic information about test structure, costs, and how to contact the testing programs.

We hope that you find this book useful, and that it enables you to step up to any test with confidence. Best of luck to you!

1

Introduction

HIGHLIGHTS

- Testing terminology
- Tests in a historical context
- Testing errors
- What scores really mean

WHY TESTS EXIST

Let's be honest. If there is one thing to say about tests, it is this: taking tests kinda sucks. Tests are hard. Tests are scary. Tests to make us feel bad about ourselves, or at least make us feel like losers in comparison to that smug kid in class (and there is ALWAYS a smug kid in class, isn't there?) who barely studies, finishes first, and ruins the curve for everyone. Many tests cost money and, depending on the test, can keep us from getting things we want in life.

So why, why, *why* does life seem to be an endless array of tests? Because the world can't take your word for it that you can correctly solve for *x*, make a birdhouse, fix a radiator, explain the fall of Communism, conjugate the verb *estornudo*, identify the principle according to which electrophoresis separates substances, and explain why the author refers to "tasty snack-pack pudding cups" on line 47 of the passage below. For good or ill, our educational system is astonishingly varied in terms of the quality of the learning provided. This is true to such an extent that magnet and independent schools, graduate and professional schools, and colleges need some uniform yardstick by which to compare applicants and to measure those applicants' abilities to excel. And in school, we certainly can't expect our teachers—or the government in the era of No Child Left Behind—to just trust that we have mastered the content we've been taught. So we may not love the fact that we are tested to death in today's world, but we can certainly understand how we have gotten here.

TESTING IS ACTUALLY GOOD FOR YOU

As unpleasant as taking a test can often be, it actually does more than just tell others what you know: it can actually help you learn. Researchers at Washington University in St. Louis—particularly Henry L. Roedinger III, a professor of psychology there—have shown that students who are tested regularly actually learn more content and retain it longer than students who have not been tested. Frequent testing also has been shown to help decrease test anxiety. So look at tests as another tool to help you learn rather than an impediment to learning or an unnecessary burden. They are actually doing you more good than you may realize!

TESTING TERMINOLOGY: A PRIMER

Intelligence tests: Tests that are intended to measure one's capacity for learning.

High-stakes tests: Tests used to make decisions that have important consequences for individuals, such as whether one will graduate, move on to the next grade, or have access to special resources or programs.

Achievement tests: Tests that measure how much someone has learned.

Norm-referenced tests: Tests used to compare test takers to each other, with no standards set for what one should know or be able to do. Most admissions tests are in this group, as are course exams that are graded on a curve.

Criterion-referenced tests: Tests that measure how well the test taker has achieved a particular level of proficiency, i.e., does one pass or fail. Most state achievement and graduation tests are in this group, as are most course exams.

Psychometrics: The field of study concerned with the theory and technique of educational and psychological measurement, which includes the measurement of knowledge, abilities, attitudes, and personality traits.

Standardized tests: Tests that are administered and scored according to a set standard or procedure so that the content and interpretation of results is consistent.

Authentic assessment: A form of assessment in which students are asked to perform real-world tasks that demonstrate meaningful application of essential knowledge and skills. Distinct from traditional assessments, such as multiple-choice tests.

Rubric: A set of criteria and standards linked to learning objectives that is used to assess a student's performance on a subjective assessment such as an essay or open-ended project.

A LITTLE HISTORICAL CONTEXT

Using tests to measure people's knowledge and abilities is not a new idea, but the modern world of testing looks a lot different than it did 100 or even 50 years ago. Whereas scholars now argue over whether standardized tests are biased against certain groups of people and work to perpetuate social inequality, or whether high-stakes testing does more harm than good, there was a time when tests were looked upon in a much more hopeful way, as tools that would do more to help than to harm.

We aren't here to rail against this particular trend in modern society, since one of the first things one needs to do to perform one's best on any test is accept the fact that taking a test is sometimes a necessary evil; avoidance won't get you very far in most cases. Instead, we will help you meet the challenge that tests pose head on, armed with all the knowledge and skills that we can bring to bear. Like it or not, being a good test taker is a very useful skill and one that can open many doors.

BUREAUCRATIC APTITUDE TEST: ANCIENT CHINESE SECRET

China's Imperial Examination System, in place from 605 to 1905, was used to determine who among the male population would serve in the state's bureaucracy. Rather than just hire bureaucrats from the ranks of the nobility, China's system was meant to find the most capable. They are generally considered the oldest standardized tests based on merit. Candidates were quizzed on their mastery of music, math, writing, archery, horsemanship, military strategy, civil law, taxation, agriculture, geography, and the teachings of Confucius. And you thought the SAT was tough!

Intelligence Tests

Tests can be used to measure many things, and the results of those tests can be used in a number of different ways to fulfill a range of goals. Achievement tests are intended to measure what someone has learned, and the results of these kinds of tests can include determining whether an individual student is placed in a particular course or level of study, promoted to the next grade, or allowed to graduate. Results can also be used to determine raises or bonuses for teachers and administrators, whether a school or district is making adequate progress toward pre-determined learning goals, or even how an entire country's quality of education compares to another's.

Intelligence tests, on the other hand, are intended to measure what students are capable of learning. Intelligence testing was all the rage in the late 19th and early 20th centuries. The intent of these tests in many people's minds was beneficial: if science was able to measure intelligence, a country could identify the smartest people and harness the power of its best and brightest. Alfred Binet, a French educator after whom one of the most well-known tests is named, embraced intelligence testing as a way to find students who were less intelligent than their peers so that they could be given extra assistance to learn. However, Binet did not believe that intelligence was static and unchangeable. With proper instruction, nearly all students could become more intelligent.

Unfortunately, Binet's system of testing was adopted by American psychologists who used it for very different purposes: to find the smartest to help them advance and to find the least intelligent to limit their opportunities in life in various ways. Many of these turn-of-the-century psychologists believed intelligence to be immutable, a permanent characteristic that you were born with and that couldn't be changed. Following from this belief, intelligence testing was used in the early 20th century to justify limiting the number of immigrants from certain countries, their inhabitants deemed "too stupid" to enter the United States, and even to sterilize women considered "too stupid" to have children.

Thankfully, the more obvious flaws in early intelligence testing and the rather odious, xenophobic policies that followed from it no longer exist, but intelligence testing's ugly past still colors many commentators' perception of testing in general. While test makers claim their tests measure only what they are intended to, critics contend that many tests are biased, underpredicting the performance of particular groups including females and many minority groups.

The SAT

The SAT is a good example of a test whose history is, in many critics' eyes, irredeemably tainted by its intelligence testing roots. The SAT was first given in the 1920s, and was based in large part on the U.S. Army's intelligence testing program. The idea of the original SAT was hopeful: In the 1930s, an age when mostly upper-class white men in the northeast United States attended the best colleges in the nation based on their family connections, James Conant of Harvard University embraced the SAT as a test that could be given to students across the United States to identify high-potential candidates who would otherwise not be considered for admission. Of more humble background himself, Conant wanted to see students admitted based on academic merit and ability, not just family name and wealth. In place of privileges based on elite status, Conant wanted to see a "meritocracy" in which the "natural aristocracy" (an idea popularized by Thomas Jefferson in the 18th century) identified by tests like the SAT would rise the top.

MER·I·TOC·RA·CY (MER-I-TOK-RUH-SEE)

A system in which advancement is based on individual ability or achievement.

First coined by the British social activist and politician Michael Young in his 1958 book *Rise of the Meritocracy*, the term *meritocracy* originally had a negative connotation. The book was a satire depicting a future society in which formal educational credentials were the main determinant for one's place in society. The result was a system of discrimination as bad as the existing one for Young based primarily on class. However, the word *meritocracy* has since lost its original pejorative sense, and for most people denotes a just system that allows people to move up in society based on their accomplishments, regardless of their race, class, or gender.

Over time, of course, the SAT became the standard admissions test for the most prestigious colleges in the nation, and eventually for nearly all colleges and universities. But it also became clear over time that the SAT measured neither pure intelligence nor academic achievement. The SAT is also criticized as biased against females and minorities; while girls on average have higher GPAs than boys, boys tend to outscore girls on the SAT. The SAT also underpredicts the success of black, Hispanic, and other minority students at the college level.

SAT Scores as Crystal Ball?

Thanks to the magic of statistics, SAT scores are correlated with some pretty interesting things that have nothing to do with education. Here are just a few examples:

- SAT scores are strongly correlated to household income—the more money your parents make, the higher your scores are likely to be. Statistically, the connection between parental income and SAT scores is stronger than that between first-year college grades and SAT scores.

- A study of more than 1,000 hedge funds showed a strong correlation between hedge fund performance and the average SAT scores of the hedge fund manager's undergraduate school.

- Changes in average SAT scores at the school or district level have statistically proven effects on property values—if average scores go up, property values also tend to go up.

While the SAT opens doors for some students, it is just as likely to limit other students' opportunities. So why is it still such an important test, and why can't we find something better? Critics will continue to ask this question when so much rides on test scores and college degrees become more and more important to one's success in life.

NCLB & High-Stakes Testing

The rise of achievement testing as part of the No Child Left Behind and of high-stakes tests in general has a similar double-edged sword look about it. On the one hand, NCLB was intended to hold schools accountable for how well they educated students, and many high-stakes tests were put in place to stop the practice of allowing students to move through the school system and even graduate without actually having been given an adequate education. It also provided more comparability among students and schools. This all sounds good. However, the way these programs have been implemented has caused a host of other problems affecting students and educators.

In the end, tests are here to stay. They may continue to grow and change over time, but the need to measure educational achievement in the modern world will not be going away any time soon. We prefer to look on the ubiquity of testing as a good thing insofar as doing well on a test may provide advantages that otherwise may not have been available to a test taker. Worried about affording college? Good test scores can make you eligible for scholarship money. Want more than the education your school is providing? A good score on the right tests can open the door to gifted and other kinds of alternative programs, or even to transferring to a better school. Want to stand out in a sea of other applicants? High test scores help you float to the top and get noticed by admissions committees. Tests are a means to an end, not an end unto themselves, so don't let them scare you. Instead, look at every test as an opportunity to do well, learn more, gain skills, and generally show the world what you can do.

HOW TESTS ARE BUILT

Not all tests are created equal. Some are the result of millions of dollars and weeks, months, even years of writing, editing, and validation. Others were written this morning while your instructor was wolfing down a Power Bar and a grande caramel macchiato with an extra shot of espresso. Most fall somewhere in the middle. There is a pretty big gap between standardized tests and the tests you take in class that your teacher prepares, so we'll deal with them separately.

Standardized Tests

Standardized admissions tests are usually produced by organizations or associations that have a vested interest in the validity of the tests they create because they use the tests themselves. The LSAT is created by the Law School Admissions Council. The MCAT is created by the Associate of American Medical Colleges. The SAT is created by Educational Testing Services, which has a long-standing partnership with the College Board, which is composed of more than 5,000 schools, colleges, universities, and other educational organizations. When it comes to state achievement tests, they may be created by the state's board of education, an outside testing company, or even a combination of the two.

A standardized test of any kind needs to be both valid and reliable. **Validity** refers to the degree to which a test actually measures what it is intended to measure. Take this question: $2 \times 2 = $ ___ ? Most would agree that is a valid multiplication question, but only at a basic level. It does not, for example, demonstrate advanced mathematical knowledge. Put this on an English literature test and it would suddenly be completely invalid; knowing that $2 \times 2 = 4$ doesn't say anything about how well one knows literature! Re-write this question in words—"Two time two equals what?"—and its validity changes a bit, since now it tests not only basic multiplication but also reading.

Reliability simply refers to the consistency of a test or other measuring device. A test is judged reliable if the results of the same test applied more than once give, or are likely to give, the same results (this is often called test-retest reliability). Reliability does not imply validity. That is, a reliable measure is measuring something consistently, but not necessarily what it is supposed to be measuring.

In order to create a test that is both valid and reliable, data must be collected on the test questions by having a population similar to the test taking population answer the questions, preferably under real testing conditions. With major admissions tests, this is often achieved by including an experimental or equating section during a real test administration. One's performance on this experimental section doesn't count toward one's score—it is there only so that the test maker can gather enough data to determined the validity and reliability of the items. The SAT, ACT, LSAT, and GRE paper tests all include one of these experimental sections. On the GMAT, experimental questions are mixed in with the other questions: 11 of 41 verbal and 9 of 37 math questions—about one-fourth—are experimental. Other testing programs simply reuse test items from previously administered tests.

Both validity and reliability are very important on standardized tests. In the case of high-stakes testing, that test had better actually measure what it claims to. And every test taker's score on a given test must be comparable, so every test form had better be statistically equivalent. In other words, there can't be an "easier" or "harder" version of the SAT, since all students' scores must be compared to each other's.

Unfortunately, when it comes to achievement tests, test makers aren't always so thorough when it comes to building tests that are both reliable and valid.

The National Board on Educational Testing and Public Policy found that many standardized tests fall short for a variety of reasons, including:

- Those that purchase and give the test use the results in ways not recommended by, or even in conflict with the opinions of, the test maker.

- Those that purchase the tests demand that tests be created in such a short period of time as to make proper validity and reliability testing impossible.

- Testing companies are not required by any law to provide valid, reliable tests.

- There are no enforcement mechanisms or any federal agencies that oversee or audit the quality of testing companies.

- Testing companies either do not have or do not choose to spend the money needed to conduct proper and thorough testing.

(Source: Rhoades and Madaus, "Errors in Standardized Tests")

Scary, huh? While one may assume that a standardized test, particularly one that may mean the difference between graduating from high school or moving on to the next grade, one is given is valid, reliable, and free from errors, this may not be the case. Even scarier is the fact that even if a test's validity has been shown to be suspect, the test may still be used and student scores still used for high-stakes decisions. In the book *Standardized Minds,* Peter Sachs tells the story of how the Texas Assessment of Academic Skills (that state's graduation test), despite damning statistical proof that the test's validity was weak and that it was biased against minority students, continued to be used in that state. Why? Because there were no simply standards or laws to prevent it, and those in charge of the educational system refused to do anything about it. So if you think there is an error on a test you are taking, don't assume you are imagining it—you may be right.

TESTING ERRORS

The purveyors of standardized tests are not immune to errors, human and otherwise, and recent history is rife with examples of why one should not be afraid to question the test writers. The National Board on Education Testing and Public Policy's 2003 study titled *Errors in Standardized Tests: A Systemic Problem* (available online) unveils a rather depressing litany of errors in testing, both large and small. Even if one accepts that mistakes happen, there are still things to be unhappy about. As noted in the study, "Despite widespread use of testing in education and employment, there is no U.S. agency...that independently audits the processes and products of testing agencies." In other words, **organizations that create and administer tests are not accountable to anyone.** If errors come to light, the testing companies are not required by any law to inform those affected. It is left up to test takers to not only notice and report the errors, but also to take the companies to court to seek remedies in cases where errors have hurt the test takers. Test makers are also not required to share their data with outside organizations that may seek confirmation that the tests are valid, reliable, and align with appropriate standards. Such refusal requires outside organizations to sue for access to that data.

Errors in scoring tests or reporting data can have serious consequences, particularly as standardized tests become more ubiquitous. The NBETPP study describes many examples: students held back from moving on to the next grade or graduating, students forced to attend summer school, prospective teachers kept from becoming certified, and prospective lawyers kept from practicing law. More recently, other stories of testing errors have made headlines.

- In 2004, more than 4,000 teacher candidates received failing scores on the PRAXIS PTL 7–12 teacher certification exam (produced by ETS) as a result of a scoring error on tests taken between January 2003 and April 2004. Dozens of lawsuits and class action suits were brought against the test maker requesting damages for loss of employment, lost wages, lost tenure, re-testing costs, and psychological damages. Payouts to affected test takers have exceeded $10 million.

  (Source: www.fairtest.org, court documents)

- In 2005, more than 4,000 students who took the October 2005 SAT were affected by a scoring error that caused some students' scores to drop by as much as 450 points. The errors were brought to light by the request of several affected students who, skeptical of their scores, had requested their exams be hand scored. The error was discovered in January 2006 but not reported to the public until March 2006, too late for some affected students who were rejected for admission or scholarship consideration because of their incorrect scores. In August 2007, the College Board (which owns the SAT) and Pearson, Inc. (the company that scores the SAT) agreed to pay out $2.85 million to settle a class-action lawsuit brought by affected students.

(Source: NYT)

It Could be Worse: Truth-in-Testing Laws

The list above may be scary, but there used to be a time when none of these kinds of errors would be publicized at all because it was much more difficult to challenge the test makers or even know if an error had occurred.

The 1970s saw a surge in the size of the teenage population, making competition for college more fierce. ETS was seen as a gatekeeper which decided who got into college and who didn't. ETS's secretive monopoly on testing began to face more criticism from more powerful figures. In the early 1970s, a former ETS employee appeared on national television claiming that the SAT was biased against minorities. Consumer advocate Ralph Nader took up the anti-ETS cause, inspired by a book by Banesh Hoffmann entitled *The Tyranny of Testing* and by a Princeton student named Allan Nairn, who opened Nader's eyes to the inequal preparation for the SAT that students received depending on how rich their parents were. At the time, Stanley Kaplan ran SAT courses, mining his students' memories for questions they saw on the real tests, which gave his students an advantage. The anti-ETS movement wanted all students regardless of income to have the same insider access to real test questions. In addition, the anti-testing movement was motivated by frustration with test organizations like ETS and the total lack of oversight or accountability to consumers—considering how important admissions tests were at the time, many felt that there had to be a mechanism to allow people to challenge test makers in the case of error.

In 1978, California passed a truth-in-testing bill that was, unfortunately, pretty weak, not forcing ETS's hand in the way its supporters had hoped. It wasn't until 1979 when the tide turned. In that year, the Truth-in-Testing legislation sponsored by NY State Senator Kenneth LaValle, Long Island Republican and chairman of the State Senate's Higher Education Committee, finally passed (he had tried to get it in front of the senate for a vote for each of the previous two years with no success).

The NY bill affected college and grad school admissions tests, requiring the test makers to allow test takers to pay to get some tests and answers, and to see their responses on all tests. Even though this law was only enforceable in New York state, the College Board voluntarily made the provisions forced on them by the New York legislation available to all students nationwide. Other testing agencies followed suit, adopting some semblance of transparency and allowing students to challenge suspected errors.

So if you ever have the misfortune to find yourself haggling with the College Board or another testing program about a suspected error, just remember that once upon a time it would have been much harder if not impossible to do so.

What Can You Do if You Think You Are The Victim of a Testing Error?

If when taking a test, you feel that there is an error in a test question (more than one correct answer, no correct answer, ambiguous wording), speak up! All standardized testing programs allow you the opportunity to write to them if you think there is a problem with a test question. If a question turns out to be faulty, they will remove it from the test and recalculate scores for everyone. Information on who to contact and any deadlines for complaints is usually contained in registration information for the test. If you can't find any information, contact the testing organization. Most if not all have this information on their websites. Submitting possible errors can be done at no charge.

But let's say that during the test things were fine, but once you receive your scores, you feel that your scores are incorrect for whatever reason (faulty question, wrong answers, or problems with scoring). In these cases, you can do a few things:

- Write the testing program with your specific concern, which can be done for free.
- Request that your test be rescored by hand (if you feel that you are the victim of a scoring error resulting from either mechanized scoring or human essay grader error). This service is usually available, but it nearly always incurs some sort of fee.

K-12 TESTS			
Test	**Can you request score verification?**	**Deadline for Request**	**Cost of verification (as of 2007–2008 school year)**
ACT	Yes—you can have either your multiple-choice or essay scores verified	Request must be made within 3 months of your receiving your score report	$30 each for multiple-choice or essay score verification
AP	Yes—you can request to have the multiple-choice questions (and thus your overall score) recalculated. Free-response questions and Art Portfolios cannot be reviewed	Requests must be made by October 31st the year the exam was given	$25
ISEE	Yes	None specified	$25
PSAT	No—you can't request a rescore, but you can request a photocopy of your answer sheet	You have until April 30th of the year after your test to submit your request	$10
SAT	Yes—you can have either your multiple-choice or essay scores verified		$50 each for multiple-choice or essay score verification
SAT Subject Tests	Yes		$50 for multiple-choice score verification
SSAT	Yes	None specified	$20

GRAD			
Test	Can you request score verification?	Deadline for Request	Cost of verification (as of 2007–2008 school year)
GRE	Yes—you can have either your multiple-choice (on paper-based tests only) or essay scores verified		$30 for paper-based rescoring only (not available for online test), $55 score review for Analytical Writing Measure
GMAT	Yes—for Analytical Writing Assessment only	Requests for rescoring must be made within 6 months following your test date	$45
LSAT	Yes	LSAC must receive request within 60 days of test date	$39 for hand scoring
MCAT	Yes—you can have either your multiple-choice or essay scores verified	Requests for rescoring must be made within 30 days following your test date	$50 each for multiple-choice or essay score verification
TOEFL iBT	Yes		$60 each for Speaking or Writing Test rescore

Keep in mind that testing is expensive enough as it is—the last thing you want to do is add to the cost by requesting unnecessary rescoring services that may also delay the release of scores to programs you are applying to. On the other hand, if you notice a significant drop in your score (measured against previous administrations) or answers marked blank or unreadable on your score report (and you know answered every question), you may want to order the rescoring service to be sure your score is correct.

The 2005 SAT scoring errors affecting more than 4,000 students were discovered because two students requested a rescore, so you never know—you may help unearth a larger problem and help lots of other students!

Course Tests

The tests you take in school may not be created by teams of experts in far away lands, but they should still be fair, error free, and able to measure what you are actually being taught. Teachers in middle and high school are more likely to have been given (either when earning their degrees or as professional development once they became teachers) guidelines for how to write tests or at least how to create a rubric that clarifies for the students how their work will be evaluated. At many schools, teachers may work in teams to create tests, or their departments may provide tests for them to give, which provides some level of uniformity. At the college level, it is much less likely that your professors will have been given any training or guidelines on how to write tests or assess your knowledge, since college professors are far more autonomous than are teachers at the K-12 level, particularly public school teachers. As a result, college exams run the gamut from well made to pretty darned sad.

Why are we telling you this? To some extent, to burst tests' bubble somewhat and bring them down a peg. Tests are not infallible. Test makers make mistakes. Teachers and professors may have little experience in test development. Tests may be thrown together pretty willy-nilly and plunked down before you, ready to test your mettle, even if they don't seem particularly fair or well made. But mainly, we are telling you this to empower you. As a test taker, you should always be critical of any test that is put in front of you, especially those non-standard tests written by goodness knows who.

Think you found an error? Say something.

Is a question unclear? Ask for clarification.

Unsure as you how your test is to be graded? Ask your instructor for a clear explanation of the rubric.

WHAT SCORES MEAN

Different tests mean different things. Standardized admissions tests usually purport to predict how well a student will do in the program of study to which she is seeking admission. For example, the SAT, GMAT, GRE, and LSAT specifically purport to predict first-year GPA, though they do this with varying degrees of success. Other tests such as the ACT, SSAT, ISEE, or TOEFL are intended to generally assess a candidate's ability to succeed in the program of study by testing mastery of particular content and skills. AP scores reflect how qualified a student is to do college-level work in a particular subject area. Licensure tests such as the PRAXIS for teachers simply measure knowledge and skills considered important to the job of being a teacher. State achievement tests, equivalence exams, and other exams you take in high school or college courses measure how well you have mastered a given set of skills or learned a particular set of content.

HOW WELL DO THE MAJOR ADMISSIONS TESTS DO WHAT THEY CLAIM TO?

Admissions tests, generally speaking, are there to provide admissions committees with a single number that gives those committees some idea as to how successful an applicant will be in their program. Specifically, test makers point to the correlation between test scores and first-year grades. Correlations are represented by a number from 1 to 0—the higher the correlation, the stronger the relationship between the test score and GPA. Here are some correlations of major admissions tests.

Test	What does it purport to predict?	Correlation	Says who?
GRE	First-year grad GPA	.33	A 1999 study by the Graduate Record Examination Board
LSAT	First-year law school GPA	.39	A 2002 study by the Law School Admissions Council (LSAC)
SAT	First-year undergrad GPA	.47–.48	College Board

GMAT	First-year grad management program GPA	.51	Graduate Management Admission Council (GMAC)
MCAT	GPA of first two years of medical school	range from .615 to .67	A 1996 study cited on www.aamc.org

One important thing to remember is that neither you nor anyone else should use a test score to mean anything other than what they are intended to. Admissions tests do not measures intelligence (depending on who you talk to, even intelligence tests don't even measure intelligence particularly well). They do not tell you how successful you will be in school or life. They don't tell you how good a person you are, or what a great friend you are, or how creative or funny or talented you are.

Scaled vs. Raw Score

Guru Says...
Test scores are not fate. Always, always remember that.

When you take most admissions tests, you receive a raw point for each correct answer. In some cases, you may also lose a fraction of a point if you answer a question incorrectly (the SAT and PSAT do this, for example). Your raw scores are then converted using a standard scale to produce your scaled score. On a standard LSAT, there may be 101 questions, but the scaled score ranges from 120 to 180. On the SAT, there are 54 math questions, but the scaled math score ranges from 200 to 800. The ACT has 215 questions, but the final composite score ranges from 1 to 36.

From administration to administration, expect some variation in the raw-to-scaled score conversion. In other words, a raw score of 50 out of 54 on SAT math could give you a 720 on one SAT but a 740 on another. This variation is due to the fact that each conversion chart is unique to each test. No two test forms are exactly alike, so the conversion chart is adjusted to account for slight variations in difficulty, the distribution of test questions, and the performance of those students whose data was used to equate the test form.

Score Ranges

On tests with wide score ranges such as the PSAT, SAT, GRE, GMAT, and LSAT, the test makers recommend that your performance is best represented by a score range. Even the test makers don't believe their tests to be perfect. Studies have shown that the same person taking different versions of the same test will not get the exact same score every time. On the SAT, your score falls in a range about 30 to 40 points above and below your "true ability." According to the College Board, "To consider one score better than another, there must be a difference of 60 points between your critical reading and mathematics scores, 80 points between your critical reading and writing scores, and 80 points between your mathematics and writing scores." On the LSAT, your "score band" is plus or minus three points from your earned score. So a score of 160 would give you a score band of 157–163.

Percentile Rank

Standardized test results often include both the score itself plus a percentile score, which indicates how well you performed on the test in relation to other test takers. On the SAT, your percentile rank is measured by comparing your performance to that of the preceding year's graduating class. On the LSAT, your percentile rank is calculated based on the previous three years' worth of test takers. Obviously, the higher the percentile rank, the better, since it shows how "good" your score is compared to everyone else's. Percentile rank may change depending on whose scores yours is compared to. For example, your SAT percentile rank may vary depending on whether your scores are being compared to those of all test takers, only those in your state, or only those in your school or grade.

Be careful here, though—not all percentile ranks are comparable. The SAT Subject Tests are a good example of scores you can't compare to each other. A score of 700 out of 800 may sound impressive, but what it really means about what you know depends on which test you are taking as well as who you are. On the SAT Math Level 1 test, a 700 puts you in the 85th percentile, meaning you did better than 85 percent of other testers. Not bad. But on the SAT Math Level 2 test, a 700 is only 58th percentile—a far less impressive number on its face.

Guru Says..
Percentile ranks are comparative. If you compare your score with a different population, don't be surprised to see a different ranking.

Don't panic. Admissions folks looking at these scores know how fierce the competition is in SAT Math L2 and how much more difficult the L2 is than the L1, so they will know how to interpret your score and percentile rank. Similarly, if you score a 600 on the SAT Chinese test, that puts you in the 4th percentile, which looks tragic. However, if you are not a native speaker of Chinese, that score is actually pretty impressive, since the overwhelming majority of students who take this test are native speakers.

Test (Mis)use

The makers of standardized tests are usually pretty specific regarding what their tests are for and how scores should properly be used. Unfortunately, schools, colleges, and other institutions often use test scores in ways the makers didn't intend.

Test	Intended Use(s)	Common Misuse(s)
PSAT	To practice for the SAT To identify strengths and weaknesses in academic skills To enter National Merit Scholarship competition To receive information from colleges if you opt into the Student Search Service	To determine college admissions or athletic eligibility As part of high school transcript—scores should not be released to colleges without the student's or parent's explicit consent
SAT	To determine student readiness for college-level work When combined with HSGPA and other information, to predict first-year college grades As one of many factors to determine college admission, scholarship and athletic eligibility	As an indicator of student intelligence or capacity for future learning As the sole factor in making athletic eligibility, scholarship, or admissions decisions As strict cut-off scores in high-stakes decisions For admission into gifted and talented programs for middle school students To measure the quality of education provided by a school, district, or state

GRE	When combined with college GPA and other information, to predict success in graduate school	As a strict cut-off score used to deny admission
	As one of many factors determining graduate school admission and scholarship eligibility	As the sole factor in making scholarship or admissions decisions

You can't always control how others use your scores, but in those cases you can, it is worth knowing your rights and how tests are supposed to be used.

SUMMARY

- Students who are tested regularly actually learn more content and retain it longer than students who have not been tested.

- Admissions tests do not measures intelligence (depending on who you talk to, even intelligence tests don't even measure intelligence particularly well). They do not tell you how successful you will be in school or life. They don't tell you how good a person you are, or what a great friend you are, or how creative or funny or talented you are.

- Be careful about interpreting percentile rank. Pay attention to how your score is being compared.

2
Testing and Learning Differences

HIGHLIGHTS

- Multiple intelligence quiz
- Learning styles
- Learning disabilities
- Special testing accommodations

Tests exist to measure your abilities as well as what you have learned. Once upon a time, psychologists didn't really acknowledge that people learned in different ways. Educated gentlemen of a certain class looked around at their compatriots—also educated gentlemen of the same class—and from this rather homogeneous pool drew some flawed, overly simplistic assumptions about what intelligence was and what kind of knowledge was the most important.

Luckily, we've come a long way since those days, and we are better equipped to adapt learning, teaching, and testing to the many different ways our brains work. In this chapter, we'll take a little historical tour of testing, learn about learning styles and learning disabilities, and talk about testing and accommodations.

MULTIPLE INTELLIGENCES

Post World War I (1920s mostly) saw the real explosion of serious study of the nature of intelligence. The majority of those at the forefront of the study of intelligence believed intelligence to be a single attribute that was hereditary (i.e. in your genes, passed down from your parents and their parents) and immutable (that is, not changeable, and thus unaffected by education). A rare exception among the big heads who led the intelligence measurement movement of this era was Edward Thorndike, an American psychologist at Columbia University in New York. As Diane Ravitch notes in her book *Left Behind*, Thorndike actually "recognized multiple intelligences, such as abstract intelligence, social intelligence, and mechanical intelligence. However, he did not consider these different intelligences to be equal in importance (131)." No surprise there. The kind of intelligence that is reflected on IQ tests and many modern standardized tests is heavily rooted in verbal and mathematical skills, exactly the kind of abstract or logical-analytical intelligence that was considered the most important in those earlier days.

Obviously the fact that certain kinds of intelligence are considered more important than others is still true in a lot of ways—just one look at the SAT or GRE proves that—but nowadays the idea of multiple intelligences is far more accepted than it was in Thorndike's day. Why is this noteworthy? Because as the idea of different kinds of "smart" gains credence, so too does the idea that a school should recognize those differences in its students and adjust expectations regarding how best to test for specific kinds of abilities as well as how best to lead instruction. For our purposes, we also will take a look at the dif-

Quote Me
My mother drew a distinction between achievement and success. She said that achievement is the knowledge that you have studied and worked hard and done the best that is in you. Success is being praised by others, and that's nice, too, but not as important or satisfying. Always aim for achievement and forget about success.
—Helen Hayes (1900–1993)

ferent kinds of learning styles out there to help you determine whether you are studying and learning in ways that aren't limiting your ability to excel.

In today's world, the name Harold Gardner is probably the most well known in educational circles when it comes to the theory of multiple intelligences. A professor of psychology at Harvard University, Gardner is the author of *Frames of Mind: The Theory of Multiple Intelligence*, which was published in 1983. In this groundbreaking book, Gardner challenged the traditional belief in a single, unitary intelligence, positing instead seven intelligences (in his view, an intelligence is a "biopsychological potential"): verbal-linguistic, logical-mathematical, bodily-kinesthetic, visual-spatial, musical, interpersonal, and intrapersonal. Though Gardner's work was not originally targeted toward an educational audience, many in educational circles latched onto Gardner's theories, using them to construct and support efforts to vary instructional styles to better serve the wide range of student intelligences.

MULTIPLE THEORIES OF MULTIPLE INTELLIGENCE

Robert Sternberg at Yale University is the creator of the Triarchic Theory of Intelligence, according to which there are three main intelligences: analytical (academic, problem-solving ability—the finding of the single "correct" answer), creative (dealing with new situation or creating new ideas—finding multiple answers to open-ended problems), and practical (the ability to adapt, often referred to as "street smarts").

Verbal-linguistic intelligence involves sensitivity to spoken and written language, the ability to learn languages, and the capacity to use language to accomplish certain goals. This intelligence includes the ability to effectively use language to express oneself rhetorically or poetically; and language as a means to remember information. Writers, poets, lawyers and speakers are among those that Howard Gardner sees as having high linguistic intelligence.

Logical-mathematical intelligence consists of the capacity to analyze problems logically, carry out mathematical operations, and investigate issues scientifically. In Howard Gardner's words, in entails the ability to detect patterns, reason deductively and think logically. This intelligence is most often associated with scientific and mathematical thinking.

Bodily-kinesthetic intelligence entails the potential of using one's whole body or parts of the body to solve problems. It is the ability to use mental abilities to coordinate bodily movements. Howard Gardner sees mental and physical activity as related.

Visual-spatial intelligence involves the potential to recognize and use the patterns of wide space and more confined areas.

Musical intelligence involves skill in the performance, composition, and appreciation of musical patterns. It encompasses the capacity to recognize and compose musical pitches, tones, and rhythms. According to Howard Gardner musical intelligence runs in an almost structural parallel to linguistic intelligence.

Interpersonal intelligence is concerned with the capacity to understand the intentions, motivations, and desires of other people. It allows people to work effectively with others. Educators, salespeople, religious and political leaders, and counselors all need a well-developed interpersonal intelligence.

Intrapersonal intelligence entails the capacity to understand oneself, to appreciate one's feelings, fears, and motivations. In Howard Gardner's view it involves having an effective working model of ourselves and being able to use such information to regulate our lives.

Curious as to where your intelligences lie? Take a moment to complete this very simple questionnaire.

Multiple Intelligence Quiz

Directions: Circle the bullets that describe you. Count how many you circled for each category and place that number next to the category title at the top of each list.

Verbal-Linguistic ____

- I like reading.
- I hear words in my head before I write, read, or speak them.
- I like word games, such as word searches and crossword puzzles.
- English and social studies tend to be easier and more enjoyable for me than science and math.
- When I'm in a car or walking around, I tend to notice and read signs a lot.

- I often get positive feedback for things I write.
- I need to take notes to help remember and understand.
- It is easy for me to explain things to others.
- Foreign languages are not hard for me.
- I write for pleasure.

Logical-Mathematical _____

- I'm good at doing math in my head.
- Science and math tend to be easier and more enjoyable than English and social studies.
- I like brainteasers and games that involve logic and strategy.
- I look for structure, patterns, and sequences.
- I like it when things are quantified, measured, or categorized.
- I am neat and orderly.
- I get frustrated with disorganized people.
- Solving problems is easy for me.
- Things have to make sense to me or I am unhappy.
- I can't begin an assignment until all my questions are answered.

Visual-Spatial _____

- I can see clear images, even when my eyes are closed.
- I like puzzles and 3-D images.
- I have vivid dreams.
- I have a good sense of direction and can navigate well in new places.
- I draw or doodle often.
- I prefer geometry to algebra.
- I like books and magazines that have many pictures and illustrations.
- Rearranging a room or an area is fun for me.
- I like charts, tables, and graphs.
- I like watching music videos.

Bodily-Kinesthetic _____

- I like sports or other physical activities.
- I have a hard time sitting for long periods of time.
- I like working with my hands.
- I gesture a lot when talking.
- I like to touch or hold things when I'm learning.
- To learn new things, I need to practice them in addition to watching or reading about them.
- I like non-verbal communication like sign language and charades.
- Physical fitness is important to me.
- I like expressing myself through dance.
- I like arts and crafts.

Musical _____

- I know when something is off-key.
- I enjoy listening to music a lot.
- I play an instrument or want to play one.
- I often have a tune in my head during the day.
- I can usually repeat music after hearing it only a couple of times.
- When I am working, I often tap, whistle, hum, or sing.
- I find it easy to move to a beat.
- I prefer musicals to plays.
- I notice and focus on sounds around me.
- I remember things more easily when I put them in a rhyme or tune.

Interpersonal _____

- People come to me for advice.
- I like team sports more than individual ones.
- I like to solve my own problems with the help of others.
- I have several close friends.
- I like playing games with people as opposed to doing solitary hobbies.
- I like teaching.
- People consider me a leader.
- I am at ease in a big group or crowd.
- I am involved in group activities.
- I'd rather be at a party than home alone.

Intrapersonal _____

- I think about important life questions often.
- I enjoy activities that help me learn more about myself.
- I feel like my views distinguish me from others.
- I have a hobby that I do alone.
- I have specific and personal goals that I think about often.
- I have a pretty clear sense of my strengths and weaknesses.
- I would rather spend a vacation somewhere peaceful than somewhere with lots of people.
- I am an independent thinker.
- I write in a journal or diary.
- I am self-employed or wish to be someday.

Determining your style

Put the numbers from each blank in order from highest to lowest. The highest numbers represent your more dominant intelligence(s). Don't be surprised if you have circled lots of statement in many categories—no one has just *one* intelligence and no ability in any another. What you are likely to see instead are certain dominant intelligences and others that are less developed. Be sure to write down your responses somewhere; you will need to refer to them later in this book when we discuss study skills and preparing for tests.

LEARNING STYLES

Quote Me
You don't need fancy highbrow traditions or money to really learn. You just need people with the desire to better themselves.
—Adam and Bill, *Accepted*, 2006

Even though they are often conflated, according to Gardner, multiple intelligences are not the same as learning styles, so we want to be clear to make this distinction here. There are obvious similarities in how multiple intelligences and learning styles are defined and discussed, which is probably why some people mistakenly consider them to be interchangeable. Multiple intelligence theory is concerned with how people process different kinds of information, people's abilities and how those abilities manifest themselves. Learning styles more specifically concern how people learn best. Individual learners don't learn in only one way to the exclusion of all else; instead, people take in information in a combination of these ways, often favoring one more than the others.

There are literally dozens of models of learning styles, but many share three basic categories of learning: **auditory** (learning through listening), **visual** (learning through observation, demonstration, and non-verbal cues), and **kinesthetic** (learning through doing, touching, and interacting).

Auditory learners tend to learn best by listening to lectures and conversations and by taking part in discussions. These learners are more adept at interpreting what they hear by noting how speakers modulate their voices. They also tend to learn more effectively from hearing information than from reading it in printed form, and they often benefit from reading text aloud.

Visual learners tend to learn best by seeing a person's facial expressions and body language to fully understand what they are hearing. They often think in pictures and benefit when information is presented using diagrams, charts, illustrations, videos, and handouts. Visual learners often prefer to take detailed notes, which they need to fully absorb the information given in a lecture.

Kinesthetic learners tend to learn best using a hands-on approach, needing to touch or manipulate objects around them. They may find it hard to sit still for long periods of time.

Some models break out learning styles into as many as seven "perceptual styles": print, aural, interactive, visual, haptic (touch), kinesthetic, and olfactory (the MMPALT model does this). Others include emotional states or attitudes on their learning spectra. For example, the Felder-Silverman model uses dichotomous pairs to define learning styles: active/reflective, sensing/intuitive, visual/verbal, and sequential/global learners. Simple cognitive profiles may use just two bipolar descriptors—sensor/intuitive and thinker/feeler—which yield four combinations, or "quadrants." The Herrman model focuses on four ways of thinking: emotional, analytical, structural, or strategic. The list of models seems almost endless.

The important thing to understand is that there isn't just one correct learning style model, just as there is not just one best way to learn generally. These different models are useful in that they can help us understand more about how we process information, and we can make adjustments in our daily lives that can help us get more out of learning experiences and perform better on tests that measure our learning.

And just as there are dozens of learning styles models, there are also dozens of assessment instruments designed to determine one's strengths and weaknesses across learning styles. Some have snappy acronyms like ASSIST or PETALS, or impressive titles like "Herrman's Brain Dominance Instrument" or the "Multi-Modal Paired Associates Learning Test." These questionnaires (sometimes called "inventories") are pretty common, particularly in schools, so you've probably taken at least one of these at some point in your life.

If you want to help your child identify his or her learning styles, start with your child's school. Your child may have already been tested. If not, find out if the guidance office or special education department has assessment tools available. Don't spend money purchasing expensive assessment tools without finding out if the school can provide them to you first. If you have never been tested and are still a student, ask your guidance counselor (in high school) or your office of academic services (in college) if you can be tested.

Learning Styles Inventory

If you haven't taken one of these inventories in a while, here is a sample.

Directions: Respond to each question below by placing a check mark in the column that best describes you.

		Often	Sometimes	Rarely
1.	I can remember best about a subject by listening to a lecture that includes information, explanations and discussion.			
2.	I prefer to see information written on a chalkboard and supplemented by visual aids and assigned readings.			
3.	I like to write things down or to take notes for visual review.			
4.	I prefer to use posters, models, or actual practice and other activities in class.			
5.	I require explanations of diagrams, graphs, or visual directions.			
6.	I enjoy working with my hands or making things.			
7.	I am skillful with and enjoy developing and making graphs and charts.			
8.	I can tell if sounds match when presented with pairs of sounds.			
9.	I can remember best by writing things down several times.			
10.	I can easily understand and follow directions on a map.			
11.	I do best in academic subjects by listening to lectures and tapes.			
12.	I play with coins or keys in my pocket.			

13.	I learn to spell better by repeating words out loud than by writing the words on paper.			
14.	I can understand a news article better by reading about it in the newspaper than by listening to a report about it on the radio.			
15.	I chew gum, smoke, or snack while studying.			
16.	I think the best way to remember something is to picture it in your head.			
17.	I learn the spelling of words by "finger spelling" them.			
18.	I would rather listen to a good lecture or speech than read about the same material in a textbook.			
19.	I am good at working and solving jigsaw puzzles and mazes.			
20.	I grip objects in my hands during learning periods.			
21.	I prefer listening to the news on the radio rather than reading about it in the newspaper.			
22.	I prefer obtaining information about an interesting subject by reading about it.			
23.	I feel very comfortable touching others, hugging, handshaking, etc.			
24.	I follow oral directions better than written ones.			

SCORING

Place the point value on the line next to the corresponding item below. Add the points in each column to obtain the preference score under each heading.

OFTEN = 5 points   SOMETIMES = 3 points   SELDOM = 1 point

VISUAL		AUDITORY		TACTILE/ KINESTHETIC	
Question	Points	Question	Points	Question	Points
2	_____	1	_____	4	_____
3	_____	5	_____	6	_____
7	_____	8	_____	9	_____
10	_____	11	_____	12	_____
14	_____	13	_____	15	_____
16	_____	18	_____	17	_____
19	_____	21	_____	20	_____
22	_____	24	_____	23	_____
Visual Score	_____	Auditory Score	_____	Kinesthetic Score	_____

LEARNING DISABILITIES

Definitions

According to the Learning Disabilities Association of America,

> "Learning Disabilities (LD) are neurologically-based processing problems. These processing problems can interfere with learning basic skills such as reading, writing, or math. They can also interfere with higher level skills such as organization, time planning, and abstract reasoning. Generally speaking, people with learning disabilities are of average or above average intelligence. There often appears to be a gap between the individual's potential and actual achievement. This is why learning disabilities are referred to as 'hidden disabilities': the person looks perfectly 'normal' and seems to be a very bright and intelligent person, yet may be unable to demonstrate the skill level expected from someone of a similar age."
>
> (Source: www.ldaamerica.org)

That's a lot of verbiage! The important thing to understand about learning disabilities is that they are neurological problems that creates a gap between what a person can do and what he or she actually can demonstrate. This is the crucial point when it comes to testing, and the reason why testing accommodations exist: so that those with neurological processing issues can be tested under conditions that allow them to demonstrate what they really know.

Here is a partial list of learning disabilities that usually allow one to test with some sort of accommodation:

Disability	Area of difficulty	Symptoms include trouble with	Example
Dyslexia	Processing language	Reading, writing and spelling	Letters and words may be written or pronounced backwards
Dyscalculia	Math skills	Computation, remembering math facts, concepts of time, and money	Difficulty learning to count by 2's, 3's, 4's
Dysgraphia	Written expression	Handwriting, spelling, composition	Illegible handwriting, difficulty organizing ideas
Dyspraxia	Fine motor skills	Coordination and manual dexterity	Trouble with scissors, buttons, drawing
Information Processing Disorders			
Auditory Processing Disorder	Interpreting auditory information	Language development, reading	Difficulty anticipating how a speaker will end a sentence
Visual Processing Disorder	Interpreting visual information	Reading, writing, and math	Difficulty distinguishing letters like "h" and "n"
Other Related Disorders			
Attention Deficit Hyperactivity Disorder (AD/HD)	Concentration and focus	Over-activity, distractibility, and impulsivity	Can't sit still, loses interest quickly

(Source: National Center for Learning Disabilities)

Do I Have a Learning Disability?

According to the National Center for Learning Disabilities, the following may be indicators of a learning disability:

- Often spelling the same word differently in a single document.
- Reluctance to take on reading or writing tasks.
- Trouble with open-ended questions on tests.
- Weak memory skills.
- Difficulty in adapting skills from one setting to another.
- Slow work pace.
- Poor grasp of abstract concepts.
- Inattention to details or excessive focus on them.
- Frequent misreading of information.
- Trouble filling out applications or forms.
- Easily confused by instructions.
- Poor organizational skills.

FAMOUS DYSLEXICS

Sir Winston Churchill, British statesman

Orlando Bloom, actor

Anderson Cooper, journalist

Cher, singer and actress

Tom Cruise, actor

Patrick Dempsey, actor

Whoopi Goldberg, actress and comedienne

Anthony Hopkins, actor

Jay Leno, comedian

Ozzy Osbourne, rock musician

Joss Stone, singer

Keira Knightley, actress

Many people may experience some of these characteristics here and there in life, so noticing one or more in yourself or your child does not necessarily mean a learning disability exists. While teachers, parents, and others may inform the process of diagnosing a learning disability with their observations of the learner, the opinion of any of these people does not qualify as a diagnosis!

Testing Accommodations

Guru Says... To benefit from programs and legal protections for learning disabilities, you must undergo testing by a qualified professional.

Testing accommodations for those with learning disabilities vary tremendously from the classroom to standardized tests, so it is important to learn as much as you can about what accommodations are available and—most crucially—how you go about getting the accommodations you need.

In High School

There are two major laws that define the accommodations teens can get while in high school: Section 504 of the Vocational Rehabilitation Act of 1973 and the Individuals with Disabilities Education Act of 2004 (IDEA). Section 504 requires that all educational organizations receiving any kind of federal funding provide equal opportunity for and prevent discrimination against students with LD.

To determine whether a student is protected by Section 504, a team comprising the student, his or her parents, teachers, counselors, and special education experts evaluates the student's needs and develops a "504 Plan," which describes the reasonable accommodations to instruction and testing that the student needs to perform at the level of his or her peers.

If it is determined that the nature of a student's disability requires individualized instruction, then that student may be eligible to be served under the Individuals with Disabilities Education Act (IDEA). IDEA mandates that qualified students in grades K through 12 are entitled to "free and appropriate public education" in the least restrictive environment possible so that students both with and without disabilities have their needs met.

The accommodations an LD student receives are outlined in an Individualized Education Plan, or IEP. An IEP is a legal contract created by a team of parents and professionals that defines the school's responsibilities to the student, including what kind of testing accommodations the student receives.

On College Admissions Tests

Testing accommodations for college admissions tests have changed considerably over the past ten years. Once upon a time, the scores of students who took the GRE, GMAT, SAT, PSAT, or AP tests with accommodations were "flagged" so that admissions committees would know a given student's scores were the result of a "nonstandard administration" and be able to consider that fact in their decisions. In 1999, a federal lawsuit was brought against Educational Testing Services (ETS) by a student born with no hands. The suit claimed that marking accommodated tests this way violated the 1990 Americans With Disabilities Act. ETS lost the suit and stopped flagging scores on the GRE, GMAT, and other tests that at the time they owned. The College Board, which owns the PSAT, SAT, and AP's, followed suit by ending flagging on those tests as of October 1, 2003. ACT, Inc. did the same, ending flagging on its test in September 2003.

Since 1987, the number of students requesting SAT accommodations increased by more than 300 percent (Freedman 2003), leading many to believe that some students—particularly more affluent students—were trying to game the system by buying phony LD diagnoses so they could get extra time on the SAT. At the same time, however, the College Board raised the hurdle for accommodations by requiring not only LD evaluations from specialists but also that students receive accommodations for their schoolwork for at least 4 months before the SAT (Lewin 2003). This latter requirement made it nearly impossible for anyone buying an LD diagnosis just for the SAT to be granted accommodations, which many suspected (though couldn't prove definitively) was happening, particularly at certain schools. Since 2003, the percentage of students denied accommodations has risen to 25 percent (Olney 2007), even though the number of students diagnosed with LD continues to rise. Many other students get some accommodation, but not the exact one(s) they require.

So what does this all mean for students today? For starters, it means that having a 504 Plan or IEP does not guarantee that you will get the accommodations you request, or even any accommodation at all. If you are applying for 100 percent extended time or testing over multiple days, the 504 Plan or IEP is a required part of your request, but neither document guarantees your request is fulfilled.

Nowadays, to determine a test taker's eligibility for accommodations, the College Board and ACT look for evidence of functional impairment as measured in two ways:

1. Does the student's disability impair his or her daily life and daily academic performance?

2. How does this student perform in relation to the average person?

If a student is already performing above average, it is unlikely she will receive accommodations. However, if a student is performing below average, accommodations are more likely.

Requesting Accommodations

- Every major testing organization posts information for accommodated testing on its website. Download this information and read every word of it so that you understand what you need and what your deadlines are.

- Be a pro-active participant in compiling your request. Never just assume that your school is "taking care of everything" for you. Follow up with your counselor or whomever is working on your application to make sure that he or she is doing everything outlined in the directions. If a school staff member is new or lacks experience dealing with accommodated testing, mistakes can happen, and the last thing you want is to find out about mistakes or oversights in a rejection letter!

- Make sure your IEP is up to date. The College Board has been known to reject requests because a student's IEP is more than three years old. Also, if you change schools, your IEP does not follow you—you will need to get a new one at your new school. Make sure you have your new IEP in hand before requesting accommodations.

- Fall of your junior year is a good time to get this process started—definitely get the ball rolling before January 1 of your junior year. If there are any problems with your application, you want to be sure to give yourself time to appeal or pursue other options. The College Board, for example, must receive your request for SAT accommodations at least six weeks before your test date. If you appeal, at will take at least 30 days to get a response. If additional evaluations or documentation is needed to appeal, it will take time to get that together. It is not unheard of for extended appeals and counter-appeals to go on for a year.

Before You Know if You Have Accommodations

- Don't postpone preparing for the PSAT, SAT, ACT, APs or other tests until you get your accommodations.

- Don't assume you will get exactly what you ask for. Stories abound of students, even those with fairly restrictive disabilities such as dyslexia, being given less time than requested despite seemingly through documentation reaching back to elementary school.

If Your Request is Denied

- If your request is denied outright, or if you are only granted minimal accommodations when more significant ones are needed, you can appeal the decision, more than once if need be. Sometimes persistence pays off, especially if your request was denied because of missing documentation. Don't just give up.

- If you only have an IEP provided by a private evaluator, consider getting one from your school as well. An evaluation from public school specialists are generally seen as less likely to be manipulated by students or parents than are outside evaluations, which are more susceptible to pressure from the parents seeking to "buy" a diagnosis.

- If you have the resources to do so, consider hiring a lawyer. Look for one who specializes in disability rights.

- If you don't have time to appeal, or if your appeal is unsuccessful, take the test anyway under the conditions granted to you, if any. If as a result your scores are not competitive, then address the situation in your application. Many students with IEPs for their school work are given different accommodations from what they requested, or are rejected outright, leading to test scores that are lower than their GPAs would predict. Admissions committees will consider your explanation of the situation with the rest of your application.

- Look into taking a different test. Students denied SAT accommodations can sometimes get them on the ACT and vice versa, so it doesn't hurt to apply for accommodations to both tests as a back up.

- Look into applying to schools that don't require SAT or ACT scores. More than 700 schools no longer require admissions tests, and this list is growing all the time. Go to www.fairtest.org to see which schools are included, and what, if any, restrictions there may be; some schools do not require SAT or ACT scores, but only if your GPA is above a certain level.

In College

One of the most important differences between high school and college is that the protections and special accommodations provided to high school students by IDEA do not carry over into college. That means that you need to be proactive about reaching out for the help you need.

- Before you even apply, do your research: What resources and support services for LD students are available at different institutions? Check out The Princeton Review's *K & W Guide to Colleges for Students with Learning Disabilities*, published by Random House, to help compile your list of schools. If you go on college visits, definitely go to the LD student services office if there is one and meet the staff.

- Disability laws require colleges to provide *access* to basic support services for LD students, but those services are not going to come to you. To receive services, you need to self-identify that you have a learning disability, provide documentation, and contact the support services yourself.

- If you require resources beyond the scope of a college's basic services, you may need to pay additional fees for those resources.

On Graduate and Professional Admissions Tests

There are lots of similarities between college and graduate admissions exams when it comes to requesting admissions.

- Always apply earlier rather than later. You don't want to have to find out the day before the exam if you have accommodations or not!

- Expect the process to take a long time, longer if you need to appeal.

- Always read carefully all the information from the test makers regard how and when to apply.

- Follow all application directions exactly. Don't take any chances here—why give anyone a reason to deny your request?

- You can always appeal if you are not granted the specific accommodations you requested.

- Make sure your evaluation documentation is current. If you are older than 21, your documentation is current for five years, but if you are under 21, it is only current for three years.

- Materials must be received by a particular date, and if they are even one day late, you will probably be denied outright.

- Testing organizations will evaluate your application for how well it demonstrates you have a real functional impairment rather than just a disability.

TESTER TEST THYSELF

If you have been denied accommodations, or if you are just curious how well you could score with extra time, you can test yourself. Dr. Stephen Mouton, a clinical psychologist in Pasadena, California who has a great blog on learning disability testing, suggests taking a real practice test on your own. Set your timer for the standard length of a section and start the section. Then, when time is up, give yourself 50 percent more time and continue working the section in a different colored pencil. Do this on all sections of the test. Score your test and calculate your score at regular time and 50 percent more time. How much did you improve?

Having a disability and having an impairment not the same thing. If you have a learning disability but cannot demonstrate that your performance is substantially impaired because of it, or that your disability does not impact other areas of your life, your request for accommodations on many tests is less likely to be granted. For example, a number of lawsuits have been brought against LSAC—which administers the LSAT—and AAMC—which administers the MCAT—by students with a range of reported physical, neurological, and psychological disabilities. These students had been given accommodations on other tests, but were denied them for the LSAT and MCAT. In most cases, the verdict relied heavily on the plaintiff's ability or inability to adequately demonstrate functional impairments. Similar cases can be found in the GRE, GMAT, and other graduate testing realms.

Here are a few test-specific points of interest for test takers with learning disabilities.

LSAT: The LSAT differs from many any other tests in how scores are reported. According to the LSAC website, "Scores earned with additional test time are reported individually and will not be averaged with standard-time scores or other nonstandard-time scores. Percentile ranks of nonstandard-time scores are not available and will not be reported."

GRE, TOEFL, PRAXIS: All three of these tests are created by ETS, which also creates the PSAT, SAT, and AP. The GRE, TOEFL, and PRAXIS are governed by the same set of rules, which are outlined in detailed directions available at www.ets.org. Scores for non-standard testing are not flagged, except if an entire section of the test was omitted because of the disability. For example, a deaf student cannot take the Listening part of the TOEFL, so neither the Listening nor the total score is reported, and the report indicated that the testing was done under nonstandard conditions.

MCAT: Anecdotally, the MCAT is considered to have the most stringent accommodations requirements of all graduate tests. As other testing programs do, the AAMC uses the American with Disabilities Act as the basis of its judgments. But, if opinions are to be believed, the AAMC interprets the ADA more strictly than other testing program, denying accommodations to students who have had them through college and on other tests.

Websites

Learning Disabilities Association of America: www.ldaamerica.org

LDOnline, in association with the National Joint Committee on Learning Disabilities: www.ldonline.org

National Center for Learning Disabilities: www.ncld.org

Schwab Learning: www.schwablearning.org

Jed Said blog: www.appelrouthtutoring.com/jedsaid.php

ACT: www.act.org/aap/disab/index.html

Dr. Stephen Monton: www.learningdisabilitytesting.blogspot.com

AP, PSAT, SAT and SAT Subject Tests: www.collegeboard.com/ssd/student/index.html

GMAT: www.mba.com/mba/TaketheGMAT/RegisterfortheGMAT/GMAT-Appointments/TestTakerswithDisabilitiesin2006.htm

GRE: www.gre.org/disatest.html

ISEE: www.erbtest.com/parents/admissions/isee#testing-with-accommodations

LSAT: www.lsac.org/LSAC.asp?url=lsac/accommodated-testing.asp

MCAT: www.aamc.org/students/mcat/disabilities.htm

PRAXIS: www.ets.org/praxis/prxdsabl.html

SSAT: www.ssat.org

TOEFL: www.toefl.org/disbindx.html

SUMMARY

- The kind of intelligence that is reflected on IQ tests and many modern standardized tests is heavily rooted in verbal and mathematical skills.

- Seven intelligence types are generally accepted in the educational circles: verbal-linguistic, logical-mathematical, bodily-kinesthetic, visual-spatial, musical, interpersonal, and intrapersonal.

- There are literally dozens of models of learning styles, but many share three basic categories of learning: auditory, visual, and kinesthetic.

- People with learning disabilities are of average or above average intelligence, but there often appears to be a gap between the individual's potential and actual achievement, which is why testing accommodations exist: so that those with neurological processing issues can be tested under conditions that allows them to demonstrate what they really know.

3
Study Skills

HIGHLIGHTS

- Study preparation
- Time management
- Active reading
- Taking notes
- Plagiarism
- Group studying

While doing well on tests depends to a great extent on how finely tuned your test-taking abilities are, the greater share of doing well depends on everything you do and don't do before the test. Studying for tests can be separated into two spheres: study strategies and study skills. Strategies are behaviors that anyone can integrate into his or her routine with the proper motivation and support. Study strategies include:

- Planning and organizing
- Managing time
- Studying in a group or studying alone

Study skills are abilities that many, of not most of us, need to practice over time to master. These skills include:

- Skimming, scanning, and reading texts
- Note taking and review those notes
- Vocabulary learning

Study skills aren't always taught in a straightforward manner the way math or other academic content is; instead, it often seems as if our teachers and professors just assume students have learned how to study through some sort of mysterious process of osmosis. The older you get, the harder it may become to admit your weaknesses in this area, and your instructors may be less sympathetic. "It's not *my* job to teach them how to read—they should have learned that in high school!" are words that have passed the lips of more than one college professor.

Guru Says...
It is never too late to learn how to learn.

Always remember that study skills are just that: skills that you need to learn and practice. It is never too late to learn them, and it is always worth reaching out for help if you need it. Many students feel that certain subjects—or even school in general—just "isn't for them," often because they simply never learned how to learn.

Once your skills get stronger, learning becomes easier. Really.

Before we jump in, let's simplify our approach to study skills even further.

Effective studying for tests can be boiled down to three essential steps:

1. Get it.
2. Write it down.
3. Remember it.

Let's take a look at each of these steps in greater detail.

STEP 1: GET IT

Getting it is all about how to retrieve the information, concepts, and ideas from the readings and lectures that are so much a part of the learning experience. Once upon a time, educators envisioned the educational process kind of like this: the instructor was a pitcher full of refreshing, delicious knowledge, and the students were little empty cups, waiting to be filled. When a student failed to learn, the fault lay with the student—everyone else was filling up with knowledge, so why can't you? If you "got it," you did well and moved on, and if you failed to "get it," you did poorly and failed to continue on in your schooling.

We admit that this scenario may be a *tad* oversimplified, the basic central tenet is still true: You need to "get it" to do well. So how do you get it, and what exactly is the "it" we are trying to get? Read on!

Prepare to Succeed

Must-have supplies:

1. Your brain—don't leave home without it!
2. The motivation to succeed can come only from you. Get motivated, and ask for help if you need it. If you are a middle or high school student, remember that there are many people who can help you improve your study habits. Your parents can help, as can your friends. Your school may also have resources available to help. Colleges certainly have academic success, tutoring, and writing centers that can help you. All you need is the motivation to reach out to these resources.

3. Post-it or other sticky notes, which are a must-have for annotating texts in books that you can't (or don't want to) write in.

4. Writing instruments of your choice: pens or pencils that you love (we all have our favorites).

5. A place to take notes, either paper (a notebook or binder) or electronic (a laptop). Don't just write on whatever spare pieces of paper you can find that day. Loose-leaf paper is too easy to lose!

6. A dedicated place to organize assignments and deadlines, either paper (a datebook or other planner with a calendar) or electronic (PDA or other electronic organizer). Just as with notes, don't just write your assignment down on some random piece of paper, cocktail napkin, junk mail, or handouts. Keep all information about assignments in one place so you can't lose it.

7. A quiet place to work with limited distractions. Distractions include friends and family, phones, pets, TVs, the Internet (unless you are actually using it as part of your studying), and food.

8. An organizational plan to effectively manage your "time on task."

Time on Task

Time on task simply refers to the amount of time you devote to the task of learning, inside and outside of class. In class, time on task includes:

- Simply being in class. Missing classes automatically puts you at a disadvantage—this is lost time on task.
- Taking good notes from class lectures and discussions.
- Coming to class prepared, having read or finished the assignment for the day, and perhaps even having questions for the instructor.

Outside of class, time on task includes:

- Active, engaged studying, which involves much more than just looking over your notes or textbook.
- Having a dialogue with your textbook or other course readings, otherwise known as active reading.
- Connecting your notes from class with the course text as part of content review.

- Adding notes as you continue to study.

- Working with other students to discuss course content.

- Visiting your instructor during office hours or making use of academic support services.

Time Management

In today's world, it seems that there is never enough time to do everything we need to do. But have you ever met people who just seem to be able to accomplish twice as much as anyone else? News stories of these students abound nowadays: the high-school student who takes four AP classes, is a varsity athlete, writes for the school paper, represented Norway at the mock United Nations, volunteers at her local church, is writing a novel, and has a part-time job (but who for some reason worries about getting into the right college). Or the college student who has a full course load, works a full-time job, is raising a family, feeds the homeless, and still manages to have a social life. These students do not have exclusive access to a Harry-Potteresque time stoppage device (though that would be useful, wouldn't it?); what they do have is excellent time management skills and the motivation to succeed, which means working sometimes when you would prefer to be having fun.

Guru Says...
Students who spend more time on task do better academically than those who do not.

If you can't seem to figure out where your time goes, try to keep track of everything you do for a few days. Include everything from when you get up to when you go to sleep at night and how long you spent on each activity, including eating, traveling, working, studying, and using free time. Often we don't realize how much time we spend online answering email, IMing, blogging, or just reading. Are an accumulation of little things eating up a bunch of your time? Are you spending hours watching television or managing your Facebook page? If so, try setting yourself a stricter limit on how long you will spend on certain activities. You will amaze yourself with how much time you can find.

Making a Date With Studying

Here are few handy tips to help you manage your time better:

- Create slots in your schedule for dedicated study time. Think of studying like its own course, which has regular meeting times. If you have a lot going on in your life, study time often gets squeezed out unless you are strict with yourself about when you study.

- Consider using your phone, PDA, or other electronic organizer to set weekly study tasks to be completed and to send yourself reminders. If you don't have anyone else to nag you about studying, you can nag yourself through the magic of technology!

- Break your studying up into reasonable periods. Make sure you take a break when you need to. There is a certain point of diminishing returns when you are so tired that any studying you do has little to no actual effect.

- Just say no to cramming. Last-minute cramming doesn't work—studies have proven this. Your study schedule should not have 24 hours of studying squashed into the Thursday before a test. Instead, studying should be something you do continually over the course of the school year. If you study a little every week, by the time that test comes up, you won't *need* to cram for 24 hours because you will already know the material pretty well.

Prepare to Learn

Guru Says...
Regular studying will give you more bang for your buck when it comes to learning than cramming ever will.

So you're motivated to learn and know how much time you need to devote to learning. So how do you decide what to learn, and how to do you go about it? One of the most basic steps to learning is preparing properly, which entails more than just showing up in a classroom and staying awake. When your instructor gives you a reading assignment for a class, there is a very good reason why you should do it: Doing the assigned reading for a class will make it easier to take notes during class for three reasons. It will help you understand the lecture better, it will help you determine what information is the most important so you know what to write down in your notes, and you will be able to fully participate in class discussions.

Pre-Reading

If your assignment is from a textbook, make use of the structure of the text to get a brief overview of the contents.

- Start with the most basic review of any content you are given to read, which means review the chapter title, headings, and subheadings. Also read any introductory or summary material provided.

- Use the study guide or questions that are contained in the textbook to focus your reading on the most important aspects. If you can answer the questions that are contained there, you'll be ready for class.

- Take note of any highlighted words. Anything that is italicized or bolded in the text should be familiar to you by the time you are done, since it is likely those terms will be part of the next class lecture.

Skimming is a great way to get a handle on the salient points of any reading assignment, and it it is a quick read intended to produce an overall impression of the text rather than an in-depth active read. Skimming can't take the place of annotating, but it can at least get you mentally prepared for a more careful read.

How to Read for Understanding

How often have you had this happen to you? You are given a reading assignment, and you dutifully go home and read every page of the assignment and then go to class expecting to be able to participate comfortably. But when the discussion starts, you are totally lost; others are discussing ideas that you just didn't get out of the reading. What happened? You did the reading, so why did everyone else seem to get so much more out of it than you did?

If this has happened to you, you are not alone. Many students read assignments but don't seem to extract the information for the reading that they should. Just looking at words on a page is not reading; instead, this is "fake reading," a term coined by Cris Tovani in her excellent book *I Read It, but I Don't Get It*. To avoid fake reading, which represents a significant investment of your time with little or no actual payoff in knowledge gain, there are some specific techniques you can use to read in such a way that you retain more of what you read.

Why and How do we Read?

Think back to the last four or five things you have read (not including this sentence.) What did you read? A short story? A novel? A textbook? A newspaper? A recipe? Now, ask yourself a question: *Why* did I read? That may sound like a weird question, but think about it for a second. Now, here's an even stranger question, one you might not have asked yourself before: *How* did you read?

We read in different ways, depending on what we're reading. For example, when reading a newspaper article, we may skip the last few paragraphs of a story without missing out on too much detail, but we probably wouldn't want to skip too many lines in our science textbooks. Or what about the last book you read for pleasure? There are times, though, when we want to get the most from our reading. We're going to discuss a method of reading that maximizes our comprehension. We're going to learn how to read actively.

What is Active Reading?

Active reading is a way to involve yourself in the text you are working with. How many times have you found yourself halfway through a chapter in a textbook, only to realize you have no clue what you just read? That's a perfect example of passive fake reading: You have no connection with the text, which translates into zero comprehension. And that's not good.

How Do We Read Actively?

You Can Quote Me
"Reading without reflecting is like eating without digesting."
—Edmund Burke

Active reading requires the following steps:

1. Grab a pencil, then find the main idea and/or purpose.
2. Find textual markers.
3. Annotate, connect, and summarize.

Sample Text

Here is a short text that we can practice on.

> The fall of Constantinople in 1453 is generally
> considered to be the dividing line between the medieval
> and modern periods of history. But around that same time
> *Line* another event was taking place: the invention of printing,
> 5 or typography, as the art of printing with moveable types
> is more precisely termed. Though not heralded by clash of
> arms or ruin of empire, no other discovery has had such far-
> reaching influence upon the history of the civilized world.
> The art of printing with moveable types was preceded
> 10 by the production of single pictures printed from wood-
> blocks. It seems a natural development that text should
> be added to such woodcuts. These "blockbooks," which
> consist of pictures and text cut on the same wood-block,
> have usually been regarded as occupying a position midway
> 15 between the single picture and the book printed from
> moveable type, thus forming a link in the evolution of the
> invention.
> Since the contents of each individual page had to be
> engraved upon a block of wood, the making of a block-book
> 20 was a laborious process. While this method of reproduction
> was fairly convenient for the class of book for which it
> was used, it was inadequate for the cheap and speedy
> multiplication of those books which the revival of literature
> and learning was demanding. The immense superiority
> 25 of typography lay in the fact that, while the wood-blocks
> could be used only for the work for which they had been cut,
> the moveable type, composed of separate letters, could be
> used over and over again for any book, with corresponding
> economy in time and in material. It was an epoch-making
> 30 difference.

Step 1: Find the Purpose

The main idea of most reading passages will be either introduced at the beginning of the passage or summarized at the end, and sometimes both. While the main idea is the general theme of the passage, the purpose is more about the author: What is the author trying to do in the text? Is he providing information or trying to argue a particular point of view?

Is he presenting a unique viewpoint or summarizing other's views? Is the tone objective, or is the author providing a critique? In the passage above, a quick read of the first paragraph is enough to determine the main idea:

- How could you summarize this passage in one sentence? *The invention of moveable type (typography) changed the world.*

This is the author's main contention, and he will provide details in the rest of the text to show why it is true.

2. Find Textual Markers

As you read, use your pencil to indicate textual markers, which help determine the direction and tone of the text and well as any particular points that the author emphasizes. Textual markers also will contain important ideas.

Type of Marker	Meaning	Examples
Direction	Indicate if the author is continuing the same line of reasoning or countering it	and, because, so, therefore, in fact, for example, yet, despite, although, however, but
Tone	Indicate how the author feels about the subject	clearly, curiously, strangely, doubtfully, best, worst, overwhelmingly
Emphasis	Indicate the development or ordering of ideas	first, second, recently, next, then, before, after, once, previously, finally, lastly

3. Annotate, Connect, Summarize

Unfortunately, finding textual markers are not enough; we need to note other important features of the text and mark them with consistent symbols. Some ideas to consider are:

Symbol	**Meaning**
Underline	Key point or idea
+/– (plus or minus sign)	Positive or negative tone, idea, attribute
Circle ⬭	Key term or phrase, including textual markers
Numbers (1, 2, 3, etc.)	Tracking a sequence of ideas or list
Star ★	Marks a major point or argument

Then you want to jot down in the margins just a few words that either describe what a paragraph or section of text does or a very brief summary of the content. And when we say brief, we mean BRIEF—use as few words as possible to accurately represent the main ideas described in that paragraph. You don't need to re-write everything in the passage!

Let's try this with a short passage so you can get an idea of what this looks like.

The fall of Constantinople in 1453 is generally considered to be the dividing line between the medieval and modern periods of history. But around that same time another event was taking place: the invention of printing, or typography, as the art of printing with moveable types is more precisely termed. Though not heralded by clash of arms or ruin of empire, no other discovery has had such far-reaching influence upon the history of the civilized world. +★ ★

The art of printing with moveable types was preceded (1) by the production of single pictures printed from wood-blocks. It seems a natural development that text should be added to such woodcuts. These (2) "block-books," which consist of pictures and text cut on the same wood-block, have usually been regarded as occupying a position midway between the single picture and (3) the book printed from moveable type, thus forming a link in the evolution of the invention.

development of printing

Since the contents of each individual page had to be engraved upon a block of wood, the making of a block-book was a laborious process (–). While this method of reproduction was fairly convenient (+) for the class of book for which it

Typography
superior to
predecessors,
more efficient +

–

++

was used, <u>it was inadequate</u> for the cheap and speedy
multiplication of those books which the revival of literature
and learning was demanding. <u>The immense superiority of</u>
20 <u>typography</u> lay in the fact that while the wood-blocks could
be used only for the work for which they had been cut,
the <u>moveable type,</u> <u>composed of separate letters,</u> <u>could be</u>
<u>used over and over again for any book, with corresponding</u>
<u>economy in time and in material.</u> It was an epoch-making
25 difference (positive sign and star).

You may find it hard to annotate while you read. If so, read a paragraph at a
time, then go back and annotate. As your skills improve, increase your reading to two or three paragraphs at a time.

Breaking Down Test into Bite-Sized Pieces

The further along you get in your education, the longer and more complex
sentences and paragraphs seem to become. Very long sentences can be hard
to understand because there are so many ideas embedded in them. Never fear!
The best way to make sections of text more understandable is to break it into
smaller pieces. If you can understand the parts, you can put the parts back
together to understand the whole. Here is an example:

> *Court gossip and the story tellers of the common people*
> *alike love to play with such details as these, and to invent*
> *them, with or without malice prepense, especially when the*
> *early life of the royal personage was (as in this instance) a*
> *romantic one, and had been lived in a foreign land.*

Draw a vertical line at every major piece of punctuation or wherever it seems
a new idea is coming. The sentence above could be broken down this way:

> *Court gossip and the story tellers of the common people*
> *alike / love to play with such details as these, / and to*
> *invent them, / with or without malice prepense, / especially*
> *when the early life of the royal personage was / (as in this*
> *instance) a romantic one, / and had been lived in a foreign*
> *land.*

Now, translate each piece into your own words:

Original Text	Ideas in your Own Words
Court gossip and the story tellers of the common people alike	Everybody gossips
love to play with such details as these	Likes to share info
and to invent them	And make it up
with or without malice prepense	Regardless of intentions (*prepense* means "planned beforehand," but if you didn't know that, it would be enough to focus on "malice")
especially when the early life of the royal personage was	Especially when it's about public figures
(as in this instance) a romantic one	(For example) one with an active love life
and had been lived in a foreign land	And from somewhere else
Combined Summary: Everyone gossips about celebrity relationships.	

How to Read an Academic Article

In college and sometimes in high school, you may be asked to read an article from a news source or academic journal. Unlike textbook text, articles don't come with glossaries, study questions, or other helpful elements that can help guide you to the most important information. Many students read the article at home, only to find upon questioning in class that they didn't get the contents the way their instructor and other students seemed to.

When faced with pre-reading an academic article for class, begin by reading the article actively. As mentioned above, this means that you need to have a dialogue with the text—use a pencil to mark up the text; to take notes in the margins; and to highlight what you believe to be important passages, statistics, key terms, and concepts. How do you know what is important? Authors emphasize the important bits in a number of ways. The title is a good place to start, as are the subheadings that delineate different sections of the text. Trust us, if there is a subheading, it marks an important new concept or element the author is using to argue his point.

As with any kind of reading, always pay special attention to the first and last sentences of paragraphs (where new ideas are introduced, summarized, and

Guru Says...
If you get lost as you read, break the text—sentences, phrases, or paragraphs— into more understandable, bite-sized pieces that you can put into your own words. This takes time at first, but you will get better at reading as a result.

linked with other parts of the text) and to words that authors use to empha-size and organize their ideas, such as *first, second, last, because,* and *however,* just to name a few. Finally, highlight and define key terms and concepts as well as any words you don't know the meaning of. Once you do all these things, answer these questions about the article:

- What are the keys concepts and terms (and their definitions) men-tioned in the article?

- What is the author's primary question, problem, or issue that he is addressing? In other words, what is the main idea of the article?

- Articles are almost always written to convince the reader of some-thing; the author has an opinion or theory and provides support to argue his case. What is the author's main conclusion? In other words, what is he trying to convince you is true?

- What background information does the author provide to introduce the issue?

- What evidence does the author provide to support his conclusion or main argument?

- In what ways does the content of the article relate back to the main themes and concepts of the course?

LEARNING VOCABULARY

Learning vocab is like learning anything else—you will learn better if you actively approach the task. Many students, when asked how they learn vocab, answer, "I just look at the words, and I know them." While for a lucky few who actually have photographic memories, this may be true, for most stu-dents, just looking at words is not enough.

Here are a few pointers to start:

- Don't just ignore words you don't know that you come across in your readings. Stop and write them down so you can look them up, or at least take a moment if you can to see if you are able to infer the meaning of a word from the context.

- Always have a dictionary on hand, whether it be a good pocket dic-tionary, a web-based site such as www.dictionary.com, or a widget or other plug-in that can make looking words up a snap. Not near a computer? If you have a text-enabled cell phone, try Google SMS: Send a text message on your cell phone to the Google Personalized SMS service and get a dictionary definition texted back to you.

- Jot down the meaning of new words in the margins of your reading or on a sticky note near the spot the word appears. Having it there will make it easier to refer to later when you are reviewing for a paper or test.

- Keep a vocabulary journal, in which you write down all the new words you come across and want to learn. For each word, jot down a brief definition and some sort of mnemonic device that will help you remember the word's meaning. Your mnemonic could be a sentence in which the word it used, but it could be more fanciful as well. Draw a picture! Make up a little rhyme! Quote song lyrics! Anything that jogs your memory is a good thing, but it is best that you come up with the mnemonic yourself, especially if it is linked with your life, your friends, and anything else that is familiar. You can also include etymological information about the root meanings of the word, and any prefixes or suffixes that may be present. The origins of the word can often really make word meanings more memorable for you, and broadening your knowledge of word roots can make decoding new words easier. Trust us: The more words you know, the easier reading will be and the easier it will be to figure out the meanings of new, unknown words.

- If this kind of vocabulary study is too much for you to do, let technology bring vocabulary to you! Sign up for free Word of the Day service from www.dictionary.com. Try to find a reason to use new words every day.

- Give mobile learning a try. Thanks to the ever-more ubiquitous Internet and wireless devices with more and more capabilities, you can use your iPod, cell phone, or other mobile devices to learn vocabulary or to supplement other academic content learning. Check out the offerings from your cell phone service provider. Mobile learning is not so great for everything you may need to learn, but it is great for on-the-fly drilling and anything you might be tempted to create your own flashcards for.

STEP 2: WRITE IT DOWN

Taking Notes from Class Lectures

Notes should:

- Have a reason for existing—you never just write stuff down for the sake of writing.

- Help you organize information, so your notes themselves should by extension be organized. Develop a system and stick with it.

- Help you stay focused and understand the material better. Note taking is active!

- Help you save time, because they help you know where to focus your attention when reviewing for a test.

- Make it easy to review and remember course material, since they represent the course content as mediated and translated by your brain.

- Be easily understood by you even weeks after you took them, so they must be neat and make sense.

"Just listening" is not a note-taking technique. Unless you are some sort of savant who literally remembers everything he hears, just listening is a delusional fake-out that won't help you learn. Even auditory learners benefit from taking notes.

Let's start with the basics. First, sit where you can clearly see the teacher, the board, and any other visual aids. If your eyesight isn't great, sitting where you can see is particularly important. Keep away from anything or anyone that could pose a distraction.

Second, remember that **if it's on the board, it's important**. Good instructors write information on the board for a reason; of all they have to say, the stuff on the board constitutes the most important. I remember a possibly apocryphal but nevertheless instructive anecdote about a college professor who drew a diagram and supporting information in one corner of the chalkboard and left it there for an entire semester. He never mentioned or referred to it in class, but it was there every day. At the final exam, the diagram was gone, but there was a question about that diagram on the test. Students protested: "You didn't tell us that would be on the test!" The professor replied something to the effect of: "Anything on the board in important—you shouldn't need me to tell you that."

There are a few other **ways you can tell if what the instructor is saying is important**. Pay attention to:

Guru Says...
If it's on the board, write it down.

- Repetition of particular concepts or terms.
- How the instructor emphasizes certain information by changing the tone of his voice, using hand gestures, or simply spending more time discussing it.
- The same words that serve as textual markers in written texts: lists, trigger words indicating direction, words indicating judgments or opinions, concluding words, etc.
- Introductory and concluding remarks.

Third, try to **ask questions**. If there is something you don't understand in class, it is not going to make more sense days or weeks later just because you wrote it down. You don't have to ask brilliant, insightful questions. Your questions could be as simple as a request to have certain information repeated or for clarification of a certain point. Trust us: If you ask a question, there will be at least one other person who silently says to herself, "Thank goodness he asked that question! I was wondering the same thing."

If you are having problems determining what information in a lecture is the most important, go talk to your instructor and let him know that this is a problem for you and request that he provide some pointers on how to tell when he is reaching a main point. In some cases, you just need to learn the particular style of an instructor, but other times the instructor may not actually be lecturing in the clearest way possible. If you politely ask for more emphasis on key points, most instructors will do what they can to adjust their presentations.

Another benefit of asking questions in class is that the instructor will know who you are. Particularly in college lecture courses, which can hold hundreds of students, it is good to be memorable in a positive way to your instructor. Even in smaller classes, asking good questions on a regular basis can help you stand out and earn your participation grade. Some teachers request that you hold questions until the end of a lecture, so write them down as they come to you. Otherwise, you will likely forget them by the end.

GENERAL PRINCIPLES OF GOOD NOTE-TAKING

1. Keep all notes for a class in one place.

2. Label every page at the top corner with date, class/teacher (if class notes), title/author (if from reading), significant happenings of the day (memory jog).

3. Number the pages in the same place in all your notes.

4. Use space meaningfully on the page (organized so you know where to find what you're looking for).

5. Use abbreviations or your own kind of shorthand to write quickly.

6. Leave space for later additions such as elaborated examples.

7. Distinguish direct quotes, personal thoughts, questions you want answered either by having a "usual" place on the page or by style (all caps, underlines, fonts, etc.).

8. Use symbols to indicate important things such as teacher's clues in a lecture about what is important to study, definitions, and key ideas.

Next, **be sure to include in your notes the ideas that tie details together**. In other words, you should always make note of WHY you are writing something down. Details and concepts are equally important. The details are easy to copy down, but overarching concepts that tie all those details together are more challenging and more likely to be the key to correct answers come test time. Rather than rushing out just as the bell rings, take a moment at the end of class to sum up the important themes of the day while the information is still fresh in your mind.

And lastly, don't be afraid to respond emotionally to material, good or bad. Your emotional responses can help you remember things, but if you aren't careful, they could distract you from the lecture.

Specific Techniques

The Two-Column System

The organizing system most frequently recommended by universities and colleges is a two-column system such as the Cornell Double Column. It is a good overall framework for all note taking because many types of note-taking methods can be used within this system. The double columns leave you room to add information and to summarize the important points later.

Here's what to do:

- Write the date, class, teacher or author and a memory jog in the upper right-hand corner.

- Divide page into two halves so that the left-hand column is one-third of page, and the right-hand column is two-thirds of the page.

- Record notes during class in right-hand column.

- List key words, important facts, etc. in left-hand column when reviewing notes afterwards.

- Summarize at the bottom of each page.

	Date
	Class/Teacher
	Memory Jog
	Page 1

After class use this area to note	Record notes during class here
• Key ideas	
• Items your teacher mentioned that you'll see again	You can use webs, trees, charts, chains, sketches, outlines— anything!— as long as you are
• Any questions you have about the info	getting the main points and ideas down quickly
• Connections between theclass notes and other	

Leave space to summarize your page of notes here.

Outlines

A traditional outline—the kind with Roman numerals, capital letters, small Roman numerals, and lowercase letters—is good for planning essays so they have a logical order. They can also be useful for figuring out the structure of a chapter or another piece of reading, but it's too complicated for classroom notes. A simplified outline structure is much better for taking notes from a well-organized lecture. Just forget about all the complicated rules of upper and lower case I's and II's and A's, B's, and C's:

- Listen to the speaker (or survey the reading) so you understand the organizational structure.

- Write the major points farthest to the left and indent each more specific point or detail one level to the right.

- Use dashes and indenting to separate ideas instead of letters or Roman numerals. The end result will look just like a traditional outline, but without letters and numbers that indicate each group of ideas. You can use any other symbol to denote a new tier—just be consistent with what you use; try bullets, arrows, stars, dashes, or other simple symbols.

I. Main Topic of a paragraph or chapter section
    A. Subtopic 1
        1. Detail One
            • Sub-detail
                ◦ first detail of sub-detail
                    - Additional details
                    - Additional details
                ◦ second detail of sub-detail
            • Sub-detail
            • Sub-detail
        2. Detail Two
            • Sub-detail
                ◦ first detail
                ◦ second detail
                    - Additional details
                    - Additional details
            • Sub-detail
    B. Subtopic 2

Webs

Webs are useful for organizing ideas around a central concept. Make links to any ideas that are smaller parts of the whole, such as details, definitions, attributes, examples, or characteristics. The categories of ideas in the bubbles are all related to the topic in the middle, but no particular detail is any more important than the others at the same level. You can add detail links to each of the categories around the central concept. If you begin to create too many details of details of details, you may actually need to use a tree (which we will discuss in a bit).

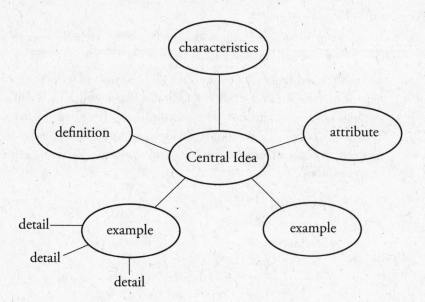

Try mapping this text:

Paul Auster is an author that doesn't allow himself to be pigeonholed in the "novelist" compartment. He certainly does write fiction; with nine novels under his belt so far, such as *Moon Palace, Leviathan, Mr. Vertigo,* and *The Book of Illusions,* he is a prolific writer. He began his writing career as a poet and translator (specializing in French). Then he began producing his successful series of novels. While assisting with the preparation of one of these novels, *The Music of Chance,* for the big screen, Auster rediscovered his love of film. He took to writing screenplays and directing films, turning out *Smoke, Blue in the Face,* and *Lulu on the Bridge.* Luckily, Auster has also turned out five volumes of biography and autobiography, just in case there are any other aspiring translator/novelist/poet/filmmaker/memoirists out there looking to follow in Paul Auster's footsteps.

Does your map look something like this?

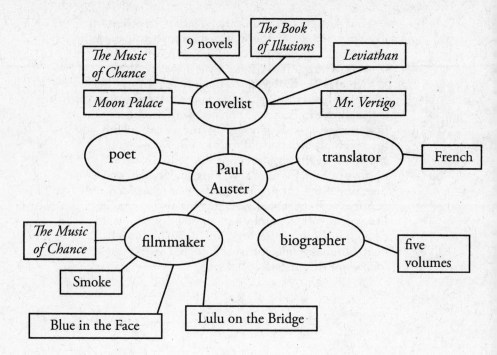

Trees

Trees are helpful in representing hierarchies: a series of ordered groupings of people or things within a system. Trees are great for representing things such as scientific classification, analysis, structure, attributes, and examples. It may remind you of a *family tree* in which all the descendents of a particular couple are listed: The children born to the couple and the children that were born to each generation after are shown so that the relationship of all the individuals in the family is clear.

For your schoolwork, trees are great for any hierarchical structure, such as historical lineage, political organizations, and scientific taxonomies.

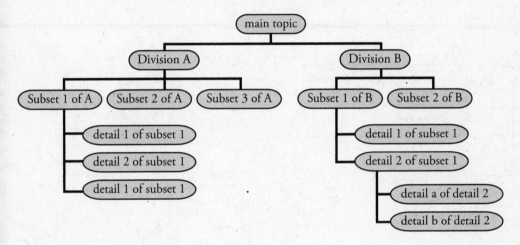

Chains

Chains are a very organized type of drawing that represents changes over time. You can use a chain to show the steps of a process, to illustrate a sequence of events, to organize events chronologically using a timeline, or to show cause and effect. Just adjust the complexity of your chain to fit the complexity of information.

Creative Writing Process

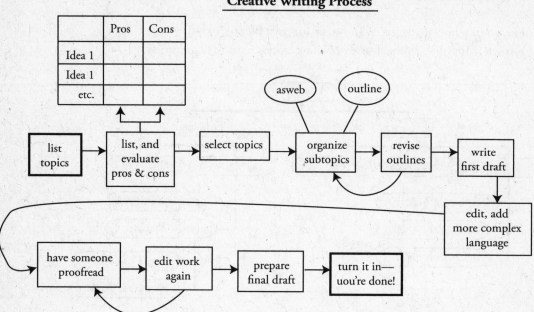

How to Choose

Not sure which type of notes to use? Don't limit yourself: Sometimes you want to vary the kind of notes you are taking depending on what the content is.

Graphic Type	Relationships of ideas appropriate to this type graphic	Examples		
		Humanities	Social Science	Physical/Life Science
Web (for a concept)	Definitions Attributes Examples	Characteristics of cubism in art	Attributes of the demand curve in economics	Attributes of sun spots in astronomy
Tree (for hierarchies)	Classification Analysis Structure Attributes Examples	Family tree of the Tudor Monarchy in England	Organization of the White House staff	Classes of isotopes in chemistry
Chart (for similar concepts)	Compare Contrast Attributes	Comparison of imagery in poems by Anne Sexton	Comparison of the Viet Nam war to the 1988 war in the Persian Gulf	Comparison of planets of the solar system
Chain (for changes over time)	Process Sequence Cause/Effect Chronology	Plot sequence of a novel	Stages of Piaget's theory of cognitive development	Process of cell division
Sketch (for visualizing a description)	Physical structures Descriptions of places Space relations Concrete objects Visual images	Description of the Elizabethan stage set in a drama	Description of a complex apparatus for studying eye movements in reading	The structure of the epidermis and dermis, the two layers of skin

(Source: Johnson (1990))

Experiment with different types of note-taking methods. Many students learn the outlining method of note-taking, which is a good start, but a single method doesn't always give you everything you need. Outlines are great for lists of information, but not so great when it comes to representing relationships between ideas. Also, as we learned in the Learning Styles chapter, different people process information in different ways, and different organizational schemes may work better for some people as well as some content.

Other Kinds of Notes: Discussions

Guru Says...
Experiment with different types of note-taking methods to determine which works best for your learning style and the content at hand.

Discussions are not notes-free zones. Many students neglect to take notes during discussion-based course sessions, but this is a mistake. You can modify your note-taking to get the most out of discussions. Consider a three-column format: one for the question posed, one for student responses, and one for follow-up commentary. It may take some practice for you to be able to write down notes and not get so distracted that you lose track of the conversation. If you have an auditory processing disability, consider recording discussions for later review. If you want to record a class this way, be sure to ask your instructor for permission to do so.

What if My Instructor Provides Notes?

Some college instructors do what they think is a favor for their students by putting lecture notes online or on reserve for students to review. While this is a well-intentioned gesture, *lecture notes provided by an instructor should not take the place of your own notes*. At most, they are a very useful supplement, since they can fill in gaps you missed, correct errors in your notes, and provide insight into what may eventually be tested. You will get much more out of writing your own notes, since doing so forces you to mentally process the material and to represent it in a way that makes sense to you.

Taking Notes from Readings

You Can Quote Me
Education is what survives when what has been learned has been forgotten.
—B. F. Skinner

In the long run, once you are done school and are out in the workplace, the details of the British Industrial Revolution or Plato's philosophy will be less important than the general skills of reading, analyzing, synthesizing, and summarizing texts. These latter skills will be far more useful—even necessary—in a professional setting, which is why it is so important that you learn the skills now.

Why Highlighters are Not a Magic Wand

You may have noticed that nowhere in this chapter do we talk about using highlighters when you read. There's a reason for this: Highlighters are one of the most misused study tools out there. **Highlighting text is not active reading**, nor is it dialoguing with the text, or even annotating. In most cases it is coloring, and not much else. Many students overuse their highlighters, marking up entire paragraphs, or even whole pages, with a solid block of neon pink or yellow.

The problem is that highlighting does not help you learn, nor does it help you read better (though it does give you something to do and can be quite pretty to look at). Rampant highlighter abuse indicates that **the reader is not spending enough time discerning between important content and unimportant detail**, and we can guarantee that a student who actively annotates with a pen or pencil will learn the content far better than one who simply highlights with absent-minded, wanton abandon.

This is not to say that highlighters should be banned like DDT; instead, highlighters should be used sparingly and smartly. Highlight things you need to find later, such as the most important, high-level ideas in a text. The annotations that you write down with a pen or pencil should far outnumber what you highlight.

Guru Says...
Control your highlighter addiction—use it only to highlight the most important ideas. Use handwritten annotations for everything else.

STEP 3: REMEMBER IT

Reviewing Notes

Don't forget to review what you have written. Just writing notes down does not mean you know the content. You should review notes regularly—read the notes from the previous class before the next class to remember what was discussed last time.

Don't wait until the day before your test to review your notes. Reviewing should ideally be something you do on a regular basis, since the notes you take in class are more like a first draft than a completed manuscript. You will want to keep working with your notes, honing them, adding to them, enhancing them with additional information as you keep learning.

The Five R's

Following the Five R's of note taking will make your notes make a lot more sense to you the next time you look at them. Using the Five R's also helps to solidify the knowledge you're supposed to be learning during the note-taking session, which allows you to spend less time trying to figure it all out on the night before a big test, for example. Using this system could very well make your high school and college career a whole lot easier.

Here's how the **Record**, **Reduce**, **Recite**, **Reflect**, and **Review** steps fit into what you need do to while you take notes as well as what you should be doing before and after your note-taking session.

BEFORE NOTE-TAKING

- **Clarify the kind of information you will need to note.** What do you need to find out during the class or from your reading? What questions do you want answered? Do you need specific information for a test or to complete an assignment?

- **Decide on a format to use for note-taking.** Starting with the double-column format is a great framework for the Five R's, and it will allow you to use any of the other systems within it. Choose techniques for recording your notes within the double columns, based on the subject or type of information, and on what methods you are most comfortable and productive using.

- **Give yourself some base knowledge to attach new ideas to.** Read material, such as the chapter of your textbook, before the class or lecture. Create a list of questions from the reading that you want answered in the lecture. When you are taking notes from your reading, don't just start copying all the words that are there. Before you even start reading, you should survey the text: Note the organization and structure, look at the section headings, observe how the information in one section leads into the next bit of information you're given. Write down any questions that occur to you during the survey that you want answered by the actual reading.

DURING NOTE-TAKING

Here's where we get to the first R—**RECORD**.

- Capture the main ideas—not every word! Use consistent abbreviations so you know later what you meant.

- Use words, pictures, graphs, concept maps, outlines—whatever it takes to get information down quickly and legibly.

- Organize as you go along.

- Leave blanks to fill in explanations later.

- Identify the main points and supporting points.

- Note key vocabulary, important facts, and formulas.

- Avoid direct quotes. When you do briefly quote someone, use quotation marks and identify the speaker or author.

- Clearly indicate connections of your own that did not come from the lecture or reading (i.e. what it reminds you of, links to other subjects).

- Ask questions when you need to clarify the information during class.

- Clearly indicate any questions about the material to ask later. This is helpful when interrupting a lecture is not possible or when you are taking notes from reading: Either further reading will answer your question or you can ask your teacher later.

AFTER NOTE-TAKING

The other Four R's happen after you finish taking notes.

REDUCE—After class use the left hand column to:

- Note key words.

- Summarize ideas from the right-hand column into phrases or labels.

- Record questions that have not yet been answered or that have arisen during review.

- Note links between the lecture and the textbook or any connections to other sources.

- Identify any information that the teacher gives hints about during the lecture, such as "this is important," or "you're going to need this/see this later," etc.

- Highlight, underline, and use symbols to indicate the most important information from the entire note-taking session.

RECITE—Spit out the information that you remember so far.

- Review from memory what you have learned in the **record** and **reduce** steps.

- Using the key words and questions you listed in the left column, talk through or illustrate definitions, concepts, etc.

- Create your own examples for the information.

REFLECT—Think about connections this new information has to what you already knew.

- How does this new info relate to what you knew before?

- Has what you learned changed how you feel about the topic?

- Does it remind you of, or relate to, any events in your personal life?

- What connections does the new information have to other subjects in school?

- How can you use this information in the future?

- Think about the note-taking process you used as well: Is there anything you would do differently next time you take notes? What is one thing you can do to be even more effective next time you take notes?

REVIEW—Solidify knowledge while it's still fresh.

- Summarize the page of notes at the bottom.

- If you have more than one page of notes, write a summary at the bottom of each page and summarize the entire lecture on a page at the front or back of the session's notes.

- Re-copy or reorganize notes in a way that makes sense in light of the big picture or the overall topic and for easier reference later.

- Identify questions you still have about the material and any ideas that need clarification.

Studying in Groups

Working in groups to study can be incredibly fruitful, but only if done the right way. Working in groups helps us learn if we have problems with procrastinating and need the support and motivation of others to keep us on track. Groups also force us to more actively delve into the material, which is one of the keys to effective learning. In a group, you can discuss the material, hear new viewpoints you otherwise may not have come up with on your own, and develop your own opinions more thoroughly since you will be put on the spot to explain your own ideas. However, there are downsides to working in groups: you may get distracted or have some members who aren't doing the work, a.k.a. the freeloader syndrome.

To avoid some of the problems, here are a few pointers:

- **Find a distraction-free place** to work that still allows you to have discussions without disturbing others. Many libraries have special rooms you can reserve for this purpose. Avoid primarily social areas such as cafes and coffee shops. If you are studying at home, stay away from TVs and stereos.

- **Always have an agenda for your study session.** This can be as simple as a list of general questions, a study guide provided by your teacher, or an outline for an upcoming test. An agenda will provide structure to follow and a goal to reach. That way, you have a finite point you need to reach before you can go have fun.

- **Each member of the group should take a turn as the group's leader.** This person will be responsible for developing the agenda, leading the discussion, and generally keeping the rest of the group on track.

- **Each member should also be responsible for "presenting" to the rest of the group at some point.** This serves two purposes. First, making everyone prepare at least once eliminates the freeloader syndrome. Second, learning doesn't get much more active than when you are the "expert" who is instructing others. By the time you explain something to someone, you probably know it pretty well.

A Word on Plagiarism

Plagiarism means presenting others' ideas, theories, or words as your own, without clearly acknowledging the source of that information. Many students are unclear as to what exactly constitutes plagiarism, since *everything* they seem to learn was someone else's idea first. To avoid plagiarism when writing papers or take-home essays, always give credit whenever you use:

- Another person's idea, opinion, or interpretation of facts
- Any information that is not common knowledge
- Quotations of another person's actual spoken or written words
- Paraphrase of another person's spoken or written words

Guru Says...
If you take someone else's ideas, even if you change a few words here and there, and neglect to cite your source, that's plagiarism.

If you find yourself copying *anything* word for word, or mostly word for word, from the Internet, your textbook, or any other source and don't specifically mention the source, that's plagiarism.

Avoiding plagiarism is easy if you follow a few rules:

- When you take notes, always include information about the source material including page number. If you decide to take down a direct quote word for word, copy it down accurately, make sure it is in quotation marks, and cite the source work and page number.

- Try to paraphrase whenever possible in your notes—you should always be trying to boil down longer texts into something more brief and put them in your own words. Still include info about the source in your notes, though, so you know which ideas are yours and which are someone else's.

- Read the source text, then set it aside. Unless you are quoting directly from it, you don't want it in front of you as you write. You want your ideas to come out of your head and your note.

- If you aren't sure if you should include a reference to an outside source, always *include it anyway*. You are unlikely to be penalized for over-citing, but you will certainly be penalized for not properly citing source material.

ON A PERSONAL NOTE...

Everyone learns and takes notes differently.

Taking notes using as many senses and associations as possible builds paths back to the memory of that knowledge. It's like the difference between a bridge across a river made of one rickety board and one made of five boards connected together. Which bridge is more likely to allow for a return trip? Obviously, it's the one that has connected planks. Successful note-taking is about making connections among the ideas that are being presented and connecting these new ideas to things you know from other classes or your own personal interests. Organizing the ideas and connections on the page will organize these ideas in your memory too, allowing you to bridge back to the knowledge later, when you need it.

Depending on your preferred learning style, certain practices may yield better results for you. Here are a few suggestions for each major learning style:

Visual	Auditory
• Take lecture notes.	• Study in groups and talk things out.
• Underline, highlight, or circle printed material.	• Get a mini tape recorder.
• Borrow others' notes to compare to your own.	• Record lectures, tutoring and study group sessions, etc. (makes a permanent verbal record of material).
• Draw pictures in notes to illustrate concepts.	• Read texts out loud (into recorder).
• Use a variety of colors—in pens, pencils, markers, highlighters, paper, etc. for different categories or concepts.	• Listen to lecture/text tapes while driving, walking, working out, etc.
• Write it out!	• Dictate papers, to be typed later.
• Use outlines, pictures, graphs, charts, and diagrams.	• Read questions aloud.
• Draw out ideas.	• Use word association.
• Make sure you can take any visual materials away with you—from class, tutoring and study group sessions, etc., so you can go back and look at them.	• Work out problems aloud.

Tactile	Kinesthetic
• Trace letters of words with finger (to memorize spelling, for example). • Use finger as a guide while reading material. • Take, and type out or rewrite, class notes. • Be a hands-on participant—in science or computer labs, for example—don't just watch someone else do it. • Use models—of the human brain, DNA, etc. • Write out everything. • Draw charts or diagrams of relationships.	• Use musical rhythms as patterns for memorization. • Associated different movements or gestures for different ideas. • Study or brainstorm while walking or working out. • Incorporate building or putting things together into studying. • Organize ideas by rearranging sentences that have been cut out. • Do role-plays and skits. • Make letters, numbers, or shapes with body for memorization.

In the end, though, the goal is the same regardless of your learning style: to understand the material you are given to learn, to create accurate notes that will enable you to access that material over time, and to remember the information so you can apply it in a testing or other environment.

SUMMARY

- Studying involves both study strategies, which can be implemented right away, and study skills, which take more time to practice and master.

- Time on task is a big part of academic success: More time on task means more and better learning for you.

- Time management involves reserving time in your schedule to study and holding firm on that commitment to yourself. Reach out for help if you need it.

- Come to class prepared to learn: Do all pre-reading assignments so that you have a basis for learning in the classroom.

- Take good notes from lectures and course readings.

- When reading, read actively and annotate as you go.

- Don't forget to review your notes regularly.

360-Degree Preparation

HIGHLIGHTS

- Testing resources
- Getting a tutor

TESTING RESOURCES: STANDARDIZED TESTS

Depending on the standardized test you are planning to take, there may be very few to literally hundreds of resources at your disposal, but they are not all created equal, and the quality of those resources can make a big difference on how ready you are on test day.

PREP FOR STATE & GRADUATION TESTS

This chapter deals mainly with the major standardized tests for high school, college, graduate, and professional programs. For information and test prep resources for a specific state's test, start by contacting your school or going to the website for your state's Board of Education. Nearly every state posts information and sample questions on its website that can get you started.

What Kinds of Information and Resources are out There?

The basic way to break down test preparation material is into two groups: resources created by the test makers themselves and resources created by everyone else. In those two groups, there is a sliding scale when it comes to the level of support resources can provide—everything from totally self-directed study to one-on-one tutorials. Depending on the level of personal motivation, the time frame, the needs, and (unfortunately) the financial resources available, nearly every person can find resources that fit his or her needs.

Sample Tests

If you are going to study for a standardized test, you simply must take practice tests before you go into the real thing. There is too much at stake for you not to. This should be everyone's first step when it comes to developing a study plan so that you:

- Have a benchmark score against which you can gauge your progress.
- Know how much work you need to do in order to reach your goal score.

- Can get a sense of how you may need adjust your approach to the test (did you run out of time, get confused by the directions, make a lot of careless errors, etc.).

Sample tests made by the test makers themselves are the best to use, bar none. Test preparation companies and writers of various books may provide sample tests that are modeled on the real thing, but there are lots of things that can go wrong when outsiders try to mimic real tests.

1. "Real" practice tests provide the most realistic experience and accurate forecast of how you will perform on a real test. Many test makers do not release the algorithms used to calculate scaled scores, so any test prep company that lacks access to that information can provide an approximate score at best.

2. Items that appear on real tests have gone through a significant amount of validity testing and other quality checks. When done properly, validating test items is an expensive process requiring large data sets that only the largest prep companies have the resources to fund.

3. The content of real tests has uniform standards for the difficulty of items, the proportion of questions testing particular concepts, and the distribution of items by difficulty and content. There is also a distinct style for phrasing questions, right answers, and wrong answers that real test items generally adhere to.

Practice tests from companies other than the test makers themselves often lack the subtle details that may seem trivial, but actually can affect your test taking experience in ways you may not even be aware of. However, some companies' tests are better than others, so if you can't get real tests or want additional practice material, there are some resources out there that can still be of use to you.

Depending on the test, the real tests you can obtain may also come with explanations, which are nearly always a valuable added bonus! (Worst-case scenario, there are explanations that are so badly written as to be useless.) As most good test takers know, you learn more from your mistakes than from your successes, and carefully reading detailed, well-written explanations to test items makes you much more likely to get a better grasp on the content and to avoid certain mistakes in the future. Here is a list of the major standardized tests and the practice test resources available from their makers as of this writing. (Note that numbers of tests and prices are subject to change.)

Test	ACT
Practice Tests Available?	Yes and no
Where?	Four previously released tests are available for purchase from ACT: two can only be purchased by high schools or colleges, and two are only available to test prep companies. Call ACT Customer Service at (319) 337-1429 to request an order form. The Real ACT Prep Guide contains three full-length tests. The Preparing for the ACT annual bulletin also includes one full test.
How much?	The tests available to high schools come in packages of 25 tests for $25. The Real ACT Prep Guide retails for $24.95. The test is the Preparing for the ACT booklet is free—you can get it from your school or download it from the www.actstudent.org website.
Explanations included?	The booklets do not, but The Real ACT Prep Guide does.
Test	PSAT
Practice Tests Available?	Yes
Where?	PSAT/NMSQT Official Student Guide, published annually and available from your school's guidance office, contains one (1) complete test. In addition, at least six (6) released tests from previous several years are available from the College Board's online store: store.collegeboard.com
How much?	The Official Guide is free. Previously released tests are $3.00 each (bulk discounts are available as well)

Explanations included?	No explanations are included in the practice test booklets themselves, but you can access explanations for real PSATs that you have taken online in the PSAT section of the College Board website.
Test	SAT
Practice Tests Available?	Yes
Where?	The Official SAT Practice Test, published annually in the SAT Preparation Booklet, is available from your school's guidance office. This test is also available online at www.collegeboard.com in the SAT area. Also, The Official SAT Study Guide, published by the College Board, contains eight (8) practice tests.
How much?	The SAT Preparation booklet is free. The Official SAT Study Guide is $19.95 (cover price), though many booksellers offer it for less.
Explanations included?	Explanations to questions in the SAT Preparation booklet are available online on the College Board website. No explanations are included in the Official SAT Study Guide book, but you can access full explanations with purchase of the College Board's SAT Online Course. Book owners get a $10 discount on the Course.
Test	SSAT
Practice Tests Available?	Yes
Where?	Four (4) complete tests—two lower and two upper level—in Preparing and Applying for Independent School Admission and the SSAT, published by SSAT and available only through their website: www.ssat.org
How much?	$25
Explanations included?	Yes, explanations are included in the book

Test	ISEE
Practice Tests Available?	Sort of
Where?	One half-length tests each for the Middle and Upper Lever ISEE are available in What To Expect on the ISEE, published by ERB and available only through their website: www.erb.org. For the Lower Level test, only sample questions are provided.
How much?	$15
Explanations included?	No explanations for the practice tests, but they are provided for the sample questions.
Test	SAT Subject Tests (all)
Practice Tests Available?	Yes
Where?	The Official Study Guide for All SAT Subject Tests contains twenty (20) practice tests across all 16 subjects.
How much?	$18.95 cover price, but many booksellers offer it for less
Explanations included?	No
Test	SAT Subject Tests in History
Practice Tests Available?	Yes
Where?	The Official SAT Subject Tests in U.S. and World History Study Guide contains two (2) U.S. and two (2) World History tests. Note: The U.S. and World History tests from the All SAT Subject Tests book above are included in this book, too.
How much?	$18.95 cover price, but many booksellers offer it for less
Explanations included?	Yes, full explanations for all test questions are included in the book.
Test	SAT Subject Tests in Mathematics
Practice Tests Available?	Yes
Where?	The Official SAT Subject Tests in Mathematics Study Guide contains two (2) Level 1 and two (2) Level 2 tests.

How much?	$18.95 cover price, but many booksellers offer it for less
Explanations included?	Yes, full explanations for all test questions are included in the book.
Test	Advanced Placement (AP)
Practice Tests Available?	Yes
Where?	The College Board sells one complete released AP exam from most subjects through its website: store.collegeboard.com. Free-response questions and sample essays from the previous several years of all AP tests are available for download from the AP area of the College Board website.
How much?	Complete released tests are $25 each. The free-response questions and sample essays are free.
Explanations included?	Yes, full explanations for both multiple-choice and free-response questions are included in each exam booklet. In addition, all essay samples on the free online materials include scores and comments from the reader.
Test	GRE General Test
Practice Tests Available?	Sort of
Where?	GRE: Practicing to Take the General Test, published by ETS, contains seven (7) full-length paper-based tests. However, the GRE is a computer-based test, so the experience is a bit different in reality. A sample paper-based practice test is also available for download from Educational Testing Services in the GRE area of their website: www.ets.org. Lastly, two (2) computer-based sample tests are available for download from the ETS website, along with the PowerPrep® software needed to run them.

How much?	$21 is the cover price for Practicing to Take the General Test, but many booksellers offer it for less. The sample paper-based test is free, as are the PowerPrep® software and online practice tests.
Explanations included?	No
Test	GRE Subject Tests
Practice Tests Available?	Yes
Where?	One (1) sample test is available for download from the ETS website for the following subject tests: Biochemistry, Cell and Molecular Biology; Biology; Chemistry; Computer Science; Literature in English; Mathematics; Physics; and Psychology.
How much?	Free
Explanations included?	No
Test	GMAT
Practice Tests Available?	Sort of
Where?	The Official Guide for GMAT Review, GMAT Quantitative, and GMAT Verbal books provide hundreds of sample questions and the GMAT Review has a diagnostic test, but doesn't mimic a real test experience. Since the GMAT is a computer-based test, the paper practice materials can only provide so much preparation. Retired older paper tests can be downloaded from the GMAT website: www.mba.com. There are three sets, each of which contains three (3) tests. Lastly, two (2) computer-based sample tests are available for download from the GMAT website, along with the GMATPrep® software needed to run it: www.mba.com
How much?	GMAT Review retails for $36.95, and GMAT Quantitative and GMAT Verbal retail for $16.95 each. Retired paper tests cost $25 for each set of three. GMATPrep® is free, as are the tests that come with it.

Explanations included?	The Official Guides include full explanations, but the paper tests and computer-based tests do not.
Test	LSAT
Practice Tests Available?	Yes
Where?	The June 2007 LSAT is available for download on the LSAT website: www.lsac.org. This test is the first to include a new comparative reading comprehension passage. The Official LSAT SuperPrep is published by and available for purchase from LSAC on its website: www.lsac.org. SuperPrep contains three released tests. Three (3) collections of released LSATs, each containing 10 tests, are also available, as are individual tests from previous administrations of the test.
How much?	The June 2007 test is a free download. The Official LSAT SuperPrep retails for $19.95, as do the 10-test collections of released LSATs. Individual test booklets are $8.00 each.
Explanations included?	The Official LSAT SuperPrep is the only resource that contains full explanations. All other tests come only with an answer key and score conversion chart.
Test	MCAT
Practice Tests Available?	Yes
Where?	At least eight (8) full-length online practice tests are available to access through the MCAT website: www.aamc.org
How much?	$35 buys you a full year's access to each test
Explanations included?	Yes

Test	TOEFL
Practice Tests Available?	Yes and no
Where?	Official Guide to the New TOEFL® iBT with CD-ROM, published by ETS, provides sample questions for the TOEFL. In addition, TOEFL Practice Online allows you to order complete tests or just certain sections of the tests from the ETS website.
How much?	The Official Guide is $34.95. For online practice, you can purchase complete tests, either scored or unscored. ($34.95 for scored, $19.95 for unscored). You can also buy just sections of tests, either scored ($24.95) or unscored ($5.95).
Explanations included?	No, but in the scored versions of Speaking tests, performance feedback is provided.
Test	PRAXIS
Practice Tests Available?	Yes
Where?	Practice tests in a range of subject areas are available for download from the ETS website: www.ets.org
How much?	$12.00-$13.95 depending on the test type
Explanations included?	No

What you won't always get with materials from the test makers, however, are full-length tests. When administered for real, tests such as the SAT and LSAT include an equating or experimental section that does not count toward your score. That means that when you take a practice test on your own, your testing experience will be 30 to 35 minutes shorter than the real thing. It may not seem like much, but in building your mental endurance for test day, those missing minutes may cost you.

Self-Study Resources: Books

If you are a person who is really self-motivated and organized, there are many self-study guides out there that you can buy or get from your local or school library. Keep a few things in mind as you choose a guide:

- Start with guides provided by the test maker, since you can at least be sure the practice questions contained are accurate and representative of what you will see.

- Supplement resources created by test makers with guides from other test prep experts. Test makers do not always provide comprehensive self-study resources, and they are not going to divulge all of their secrets. Test prep companies and other interested parties can provide lots of different approaches to tests that the test makers don't agree with or aren't aware of BUT that might work great for you.

- Pay attention to your needs and the audience a given guide is targeting. If you are already scoring well, but are looking for a perfect or near-perfect score, you may not want to slog through a general guide targeting a wide, lower-scoring audience. Instead, find a guide specially created for high-scoring test takers. Similarly, if you are in need of more basic skill building, make sure any guide you buy is comprehensive and thorough.

- Camp out at your local bookstore and go for a test drive. Some guides are serious, some irreverent, some linear, some scatter-shot. You need to find the one that speaks in a language that makes sense to you, and you won't know which is right until you read it.

- Look for useful added tools and bonus resources. Many books have online components, DVDs, or other fancy enhancements. Not all are useful, amounting to nothing more than shiny marketing tricks to get you to buy. But others have substantive additional resources, so pay attention to what you are really getting when you buy to make sure you aren't spending more money for no reason.

Self-Study Resources: Online From The Test Makers

For many test takers, passively reading a study guide is not enough; many students need to hear someone explain the content or at least actively interact with the content in order to process it. If so, there are a range of multimedia-rich options available. When it comes to online tests such as the GRE, GMAT, MCAT, and the TOEFL iBT, it is important for test takers to be comfortable working in an online environment, so online preparation is

Guru Says...
Format matters. Practice online tests whenever possible, and when it comes to tests administered on paper, stick to paper practice tests.

particularly useful when it comes to these test types. For those test types that are administered only in paper form, online lessons that help you master the content can be extremely valuable tools, but online tests are far less useful.

Here is a list of the online resources available from the test makers. Keep in mind that other online courses may be of better quality and more affordable; definitely look into all options before you buy (see page 99 for some pointers on how to choose online test prep).

Test	Online Prep Available	Cost
ACT	ACT Online Prep from ACT	$19.95 for a year
SAT/PSAT	The Official SAT Online Course from the College Board	$69.95 for four months
AP	APCD CD-ROMs from the College Board, available for Calculus, English Literature, European History, and U.S. History	$49
	AP Exam Review, a comprehensive course from Apex Learning, offers online programs for AP Math, Science, English, Social Studies, and Languages**	Contact Apex for program pricing: www.apexlearning.com or (800) 453-1454
GRE	GRE PowerPrep Software	Free
GMAT	GMATPrep Software	Free

** While this program is not created by the College Board, it is a suggested resource on the College Board website and its curriculum is aligned to AP specifications.

From Test Prep Companies & Other Providers

Online test preparation courses are expensive to create, and as a result they are mainly offered by large test preparation and publishing companies with the requisite financial resources at their disposal, though there are some notable exceptions. When it comes to choosing an online preparation program, keep a few things in mind:

- More expensive doesn't necessarily mean better quality. Take advantage of any free services before you spend serious money on a more costly option.

- Make sure your browser, computer, and Internet connection are up-to-date prior to enrolling in online programs. Older browsers and slow Internet connections can result in sluggish performance or errors in the way information is displayed on the screen. In addition, be aware that filters and popup blocking software may need to be disabled in order to use a commercial test prep service.

- Before purchasing, contact the service by phone to confirm who is running it and that it will be possible to receive a refund if you cannot successfully log in. Also, during this call, ask the customer service representative about the site's privacy policy and whether a student's private information will be shared with companies and advertisers.

- Don't purchase services that won't be used. Once the mandatory testing period is over, students' use of the services quickly diminishes. Unless you are self-motivated or can follow a schedule established prior to the test you are preparing for, online test prep may not be the best option.

(Source: www.ConsumerWebWatch.org)

SAT Alert!

If you are prepping for the SAT, the review of 10 online SAT preparation courses conducted by *Consumer Report*'s WebWatch is a must read. Go to their website to download the report: www.consumerwebwatch.org. Do a search for "SAT prep" and click on the link that appears.

Classes and Tutors

The next step up from do-it-yourself, self-directed test prep is taking a class specially created to prep for a specific test. Arguments abound as to whether classes actually help students and whether—with so many free and low-cost test prep options available—they are necessary at all. Let's step back a moment and consider both sides.

Will a Class or Tutor Raise Your Score?

Despite the claims of many a large, test prep company that significant score improvements are possible on standardized tests, there are a number of studies available that say quite the opposite. Score improvement studies on the SAT are probably the most common. Test prep companies claim 200 point improvements (or more) on the SAT, while statistical studies claim that "coaching" for the SAT only raise scores an average of 20 points. A pretty big difference, right? Well, there are a few reasons for this discrepancy.

First, there is the problem of who is conducting these "studies" of score improvements. Test prep companies rarely, if ever, subject their score improvements to the kind of outside scrutiny their critics demand, so you kind of have to take their word for the improvements they claim their students see. Which students are included? How are they selected? Are their improvements measured from real SAT to real SAT? These are crucial questions to ask, since the answers to these questions can seriously impact the validity of the data. On the other hand, ETS (the Educational Testing Services, which creates the SAT) and the College Board (which owns the test) are hardly objective parties either; the standard "coaching doesn't work" opinion originates with the test makers studying their own tests using internal data they don't share with others, which makes their research about as suspect as test prep companies'. One of test makers' primary assumptions about the tests they create is that those tests accurately measure something meaningful about the test takers' skills, knowledge, and abilities. To admit that targeted test preparation can significantly alter scores weakens that assumption and undermines the test's validity. Therefore, just as a test prep company has a vested interest in studies that support their improvement claims, the test makers have a vested interest in studies that support the contention that preparation has little or no effect on scores, so it pays to maintain a skeptical stance toward claims at both extremes.

Second, and perhaps more importantly, there is the problem of scope. When discussing score improvements, test prep companies are not interested in the average improvement of *any* student who did *any* old prep; instead, they might be only looking at and citing the improvements seen by those students who took their courses and completed all of the requirements of those courses. Similarly, any tutor, whether independent or corporate, will point to individual students she has worked with as proof that students' scores can go up. But large statistical studies typically look at a much larger population of students, which includes those who did any kind of prep at all: read a book (the whole thing or only a few pages), took a class (completing all requirements, some, or none at all), hired a tutor (for 100 hours, or 50 or one), bought an online program (completing the whole thing, or barely any), or even those who may have claimed to "prepare" but in fact did nothing. When you combine the improvements of all students who reported doing any prep and average that improvement across the entire population, it is no wonder that the conclusion usually reached is that test prep has little effect on raising scores.

As a test taker, you aren't really that interested in the average improvements of thousands, even millions, of students—you should only be interested in the score improvement that you are capable of and what you need to do to reach that goal. In the end, every student is different. Some will see huge gains, while others already working near or at the edge of their abilities will see little, if any, improvement. Some will put in hours of preparation and see only small improvements, while others may need to master just a few key concepts to see large improvements. Much depends on you. How much work are you willing to put into your preparation? Are you being given good advice? Do you already have the knowledge and skills that you need to do well, or are their things you need to learn and practice before you can see improvement? Focus on *your* goals, *your* skills, and *your* needs when it comes to deciding which, what kind of, and how much test prep is best for you, since in the end, only your improvement matters!

Do I Really Need a Course or Tutor?

As you focus on your needs for doing better on tests, you need to be honest with yourself about how much preparation you can successfully complete on your own. While it is possible for anyone to go to the library, check out a test-prep book for free, and study on his own, this scenario will simply not work for everyone. Many, many people lack the self-motivation or time-management skills to create their study plans and to stick to them. Not everyone can read a book and figure out everything on his own, and many need someone to explain new content or difficult concepts. And not everyone can accurately self-diagnose his own issues and find effective, efficient solutions to overcoming academic shortcomings. Instead, many of us need someone to advise us, to teach us what we don't know, to lay out a structured study plan and to make us stick to it, to act as cheerleader when we are feeling frustrated, and generally to hold us accountable for putting in the necessary effort. Ever notice how much easier it is to hit the gym at 7:00 A.M. or go for that run in 40-degree weather when you have a friend counting on you to be there? Or can you imagine how much more you would exercise if you had a personal trainer telling you what to do? The same applies to preparing for tests; you don't need to do it alone, and sometimes you just need someone to help you along the way.

So while some people really don't need a course or a tutor to get great test scores, many do. You—perhaps with the assistance of a parent, teacher, or counselor—are the only one who can really answer the question, "Do I really need a course or tutor to improve my test scores?"

How to Choose a Course or Tutor

If you decide the answer to the abovementioned question in the affirmative, i.e., "Yes, I really need a course or tutor!" be smart about choosing the right program for you.

- **General philosophy and atmosphere**: A good fit is important when it comes to effective test prep. If you are a serious student, you may not respond well to a course that takes a more free-wheeling, casual approach to preparation. Or you may find that a particular course's general approach to the test is too rigid—or not structured enough—to give you what you need. If you can, get a taste of what a course is like. Contact a test prep provider and ask whether you can observe a course. Many test prep companies provide a free teaser or orientation session specially designed to introduce newcomers to their services. At these sessions, you can often meet teachers and get an introduction to what the course is like. Visit the provider's website and read their company philosophy, and also check to see if there are other resources such as videos of actual instruction to help you get a feel for what the course may be like.

- **Scoring level**: Knowing roughly how well you are scoring on a test is important, since scoring level is an important variable to consider as you choose a course or tutor. If you are already scoring well above the median, you will probably not enjoy a course that is targeted for lower-scoring students; you'll get bored and frustrated that you aren't getting what you need to improve. On the other hand, if you are scoring at or below the median, a course that moves quickly, glosses over the basics, and focuses only on harder concepts is likely to make you feel as if you are wasting your time. Find out if students are pre-tested and put into classes that are grouped by ability so that other students in your class are scoring at about the same level you are. Courses that do so are more likely to pace instruction at the right level for you and generally yield a more comfortable learning environment. In the tutoring world, some tutors are better at adapting instruction to the needs of high- or low-scoring students than others, so request a tutor who is experienced and has proven results with students at your level.

- **Scheduling**: Finding time to study for tests can be a challenge when the rest of your life is so busy: school, homework, sports, a job, family, a social life, extracurricular activities, volunteer work, day-to-day errands, and household chores...whew! Finding a course that fits your busy schedule can be a challenge, so look carefully at the options available. Courses come in many shapes and sizes: meeting once a week, twice a week, weekends only, every day during holiday breaks. There are crash courses (short, intensive prep right before a test), extended courses (long-term prep), and intensive courses, to name a few more. But if a course doesn't fit your schedule, consider a tutor who can meet on your schedule. While tutors typically cost more than courses, the flexibility a tutor provides is, for many test takers, an absolute necessity.

- **Special needs**: Most companies are pretty flexible when it comes to serving special needs students. If you require any kind of special accommodation due to a physical limitation or documented learning disability, make sure that the test prep provider you choose will provide instruction adapted to your needs. And if you want a course but need special assistance, it is absolutely worth asking whether you can get tutoring for the same rate as the course, or at least if you can get a discount on tutoring. Also, be sure to ask if the teacher or tutor has experience working with students with your special needs. Lastly, if you feel more comfortable working with a tutor of a particular gender, don't be afraid to ask for a tutor or instructor with the particular characteristics you need. The perfect person may not always be available, but you will never know unless you ask.

- **Quality of instruction**: Test prep companies may employ tens, hundreds, even thousands of teachers whose levels of experience, teaching abilities, and content knowledge vary considerably. When you sign up for a course or tutoring, it is more likely than not that a teacher will be randomly assigned, meaning you could get a seasoned veteran or a teacher teaching his first class. Before you sign the dotted line on the enrollment form, be sure to ask about who will be teaching the course. If you want a more experienced teacher, ask for one. When it comes to tutoring, you often have to pay more for the most experienced tutors when you go to a test prep company. However, it doesn't mean that the lower-cost tutors can't provide a great learning experience or don't have years of experience. Again, just be sure to ask for what you want; doing so will make it that much more likely you will get the instruction you want.

- **Guarantees and refund policies**. Be sure you read the fine print in the enrollment agreement before signing up for any course so that you know what your responsibilities are and what conditions there are to any guarantee or refund policy provided by the test preparation company. Is there a requirement that you complete all assigned work? Must you take the test on a given test date, or can you postpone taking the test and still have the guarantee hold? Is there a time limit for the guarantee? Under what, if any, conditions are you due a refund? How is score improvement measured? Make sure to ask these questions if the answers to them aren't in the enrollment agreement.

LIST OF TEST PREP COMPANIES

Here is a list of some of the major, minor, and new players in the test prep industry and some information about the instructional services they provide. Obviously this list is always changing, and there are many small providers out there as well, so this is not a complete list. Consider it simply a good place to start your research!

TUTORING FOR STATE TESTS

If you are interested in tutoring for state achievement or graduation tests, definitely ask companies you are researching if they can provide tutors for a specific test. While they may not advertise it, many companies do have qualified staff who can help students with state exams. Also, find out if your school provides free tutoring for state tests through supplemental educational services (part of NCLB) or other funding sources.

The Berkeley Review (www.berkeley-review.com)

MCAT courses, available only in California.

Blueprint (www.blueprintprep.com)

LSAT courses and tutoring only. Available in New York, Texas, and California only.

Double800.com (www.double800.com)

SAT and PSAT courses and tutoring in Arizona; Austin, Texas; and Long Island, New York only.

Eureka One-on-One Review (www.eurekareview.com)

Tutoring only for ACT, PSAT, SAT, SAT Subject tests, and ISEE. Available in California only.

Examkrackers (www.examkrackers.com)

MCAT courses in 13 states and Washington, D.C. LSAT courses in Boston, New York, Philadelphia, and Washington, D.C. only.

Falcon Physician Reviews (www.falconreviews.com)

Courses (classroom and online) for MCAT and USMLE. Course available in Dallas, Texas only.

Get Prepped (www.getprepped.com)

LSAT courses and tutoring only. Available in more than 30 states and Washington, D.C.

Ivy Bound (www.ivybound.net)

ACT, AP, PSAT, SAT, SAT Subject tests, and LSAT classes and tutoring in more than a dozen locations in the United States.

Ivy West (www.test-prep.ivywest.com)

High school admissions tests, AP, PSAT, SAT, SAT Subject tests tutoring. California only.

Kaplan (www.kaptest.com)

Courses (classroom and online) and tutoring for high school, college, graduate, and professional school admissions tests and a number of other entrance and certification exams. Active in the United States, Canada, and international locations.

Manhattan GMAT (www.manhattangmat.com)

GMAT courses and tutoring only. New York area, Philadelphia, Chicago, Boston, Washington, D.C., Los Angeles area, and San Francisco area only.

Peterson's (www.petersons.com)

Online courses for ACT, SAT, and PSAT only.

Prep101 (www.prep101.com)

Undergraduate course test help, MCAT, and LSAT courses only. Available only in Canada.

The Princeton Review (www.princetonreview.com)

Courses (classroom and online) and tutoring for high school, college, graduate, and professional school admissions tests. Active in the United States, Canada, and international locations.

Power Score (www.powerscore.com)

GRE, GMAT, LSAT, and SAT courses and tutoring. LSAT also available as online (virtual) course. Courses available in more than 30 states and Canada.

Revolution Prep (www.revolutionprep.com)

SAT courses and tutoring only. Available in multiple locations on the east and west coasts.

Sherwood Test Prep (www.sherwoodtest.com)

ACT, SAT, GRE, GMAT, CBEST, and LSAT courses. Available only in California, Idaho, Oregon, Nevada, and Washington.

Summit Educational Group (www.mytutor.com)

ACT, SSAT, ISEE, PSAT, SAT, and MCAS courses and tutoring. Available only in Massachusetts.

Sylvan Learning (www.tutoring.sylvanlearning.com)

K-12 state tests, SAT, and ACT tutoring. Nationwide.

TestMasters (www.testmasters180.com)

LSAT, GRE, GMAT, and SAT courses and tutoring. Nationwide.

Veritas (www.veritasprep.com)

GMAT courses, tutoring, and online preparation. Available in more than 25 states and more than a dozen international sites.

Online-Only Products

www.800score.com

Provides online GRE and GMAT preparation and practice. GMAT course $39.95 for one year of access. GRE course $24.95 for one year of access.

www.number2.com

Provides free ACT, GRE, and SAT preparation.

SUMMARY

- Successfully preparing for tests is a combination of good note-taking and study skills, effective time management, a good attitude, and test-taking savvy. Whether you are preparing for a pop quiz in geometry or a standardized admissions or achievement test, there are a common set of effective practices that can help.

- There is a sliding scale when it comes to the level of support resources can provide—everything from totally self-directed study to one-on-one tutorials.

- If you are going to study for a standardized test, you simply must take practice tests before you go into the real thing.

- Many of us need someone to advise us, to teach us what we don't know, to lay out a structured study plan and make us stick to it, to act as cheerleader when we are feeling frustrated, and generally to hold us accountable for putting in the necessary effort.

5

Tackling the Test:
Tips for Any Kind of Question

HIGHLIGHTS

- Types of questions
- Quick strategies
- Efficient reading
- Vocab hints
- Strategies for exam methods

Here at The Princeton Review, we have five simple rules to live by when it comes to taking tests:

1. **RTFQ**. Any question with words in it should be read carefully—there is nothing worse than giving the wrong answer because you didn't **R**ead **T**he **F**ull **Q**uestion and answered the wrong question. Similarly, read directions carefully. If you are preparing for a standardized test, you should never need to read the directions when you take the real test—have them memorized before you ever step foot in the test site! You'll save time.

2. **Don't make stuff up**. If you don't have the slightest idea what the answer is on a free-response question, don't waste the grader's time (or your own) by writing a bunch of empty, pointless stuff as an answer. On multiple-choice standardized tests, watch out that you don't make inferences where they don't exist or create an alternate, bizarro universe in your mind where your answer (rather than the actual right answer) is correct.

3. When given answers to choose from, **use POE** (Process of Elimination). We may not know the answer, but we often know what definitely *isn't* the answer. Also, rather than looking for reasons you should pick an answer, you should always be looking for reasons to *eliminate* it. This naturally puts you in a more critical frame of mind and less likely to fall into traps.

4. **Keep your pencil moving**. You are not married to (or even going steady with) any one question. Don't let one question suck up all of your time. Learn to pay attention to how much time you are spending on a question so you can do what you can and move on.

5. **There is no crying in test prep**. Freaking out doesn't help your score on any test, so you need to stay calm and keep your wits about you.

Beyond these five basic premises is much more specific advice for a range of question types. Let's take a tour through the many varieties of questions, effective approaches to those questions, and some insight into how to avoid traps that test writers create.

MULTIPLE CHOICE

Multiple-choice questions are by far the most common type on standardized tests. While there are some general rules for how to approach these questions, there are also some more test-specific pointers worth knowing. However, not every multiple-choice question is the same, so keep that in mind as you read this section. Many teachers have their own quirks and habits, resulting in questions that will not fall into the same patterns as those written by standardized test developers. And even if you know the content cold, a bad multiple-choice question (or a sloppy approach to the question) can still trip you up, keeping you from demonstrating what you know.

Here are a few basic principles when it comes to multiple-choice questions:

1. **The answer is in there somewhere.** The nice thing about multiple-choice questions is that somewhere inside there is a correct answer, waiting for you to find it. Imagine yourself a well-read archeologist—you know your content, sure, but there is definitely an element of technique at work as you brush away the detritus to dig out the good stuff in a test question.

2. **Beware common trap answers.** A distracter answer choice is a wrong answer that tempts you to choose it anyway. Test writers insert distracter answers to make a question more difficult. To create a distracter, a test writer considers the common errors a test taker might make in a certain situation and crafts a choice that will be appealing for anyone making those mistakes. Often the test writers will include numbers that appear in the question, assuming that a student who is unsure of how to solve the question may be drawn to such "familiar" numbers. In questions dealing with time, don't be surprised to see numbers such as 30 and 60, which are common "clock" numbers. Other answers may simply be there to fill gaps between correct answers and other traps, so that no single answer sticks out as much smaller or larger than the others. In short, little is completely random when it comes to the source of wrong answers. Pay attention to any patterns like these you notice in answer choices. The better you are at spotting them, the less likely you will be to pick one.

3. **Don't go into the answer choices unprepared.** Always know what you are looking for when you dive into the answer choices.

If you don't know what you are looking for, look to see if there is any answer you can definitely eliminate. If you have no idea what you are looking for, it may be a good question to skip, since it means you likely don't understand the question.

4.   **Note the difficulty of the question if it's predictable.** On certain standardized tests, questions are presented in order of difficulty from easier to harder. If this is the case, you should approach these questions differently. Easy questions have easy answers, so what seems right probably is right. Medium questions are where you may start to see more trap, or "distracter," answers, so you want to be more careful when reading the question and choosing your answer. Hard questions have hard-to-find answers, so if you solve a hard math question in your head in 5 seconds, or one answer is generally screaming, *"PICK ME! PICK ME!"* your spider sense should most definitely be tingling, since you are almost certainly looking at a wrong answer. If the order of difficulty is random, you simply need to be on your guard at all times to avoid picking a trap answer or making a careless mistake.

5.   **Don't over-think.** Many students, particularly higher-scoring students and perfectionists, cause themselves problems when they over-think questions. Studies have shown that when high-scoring students are given more time on multiple-choice tests, their scores can sometimes go down because they are talking themselves into all kinds of crazy things. If you are overly suspicious of answers you've chosen and go back to change them, you are more likely to choose a wrong answer. Other students are so critical that they think *all* the answers are wrong and can't find just one that seems to work. If any of this sounds familiar, stop the madness. Only change an answer if you have a concrete reason to do so, such as a sudden realization that you miscalculated or misread the question. If you think all the answers are incorrect, pull back and start again, focusing on the what makes an answer wrong on the particular test you are taking. The credited answer may not pass your personal litmus test, but that is not what the test is about.

Multiple-Choice Math

Math is one of the easiest places to start using the multiple-choice format to your benefit. The nice thing about math is that the answers are concrete and rule-bound, not a matter of opinion. But math problems can still trip you up in a number of ways. Understanding trap answers is a big part of testwiseness so it is worth your time as you are studying to pay attention to wrong answers, even when you get a question right. Prep guides for standardized tests can clue you in to most if not all common distracters, but you may be on your own determining the nature of distracters on course tests that your instructors write. Once you master the common standardized traps, you will be better equipped to start analyzing your instructors' tests.

Beware the partial answer.

For any math question whose solution involves more than step, a very common distracter is the partial answer. Let's take a look at several examples from different test types. Note that all the questions appearing in this chapter have been closely modeled on real test questions, so trust us: We aren't making this stuff up!

Here is an SAT question:

12. If x is directly proportional to y^2 and $x = \dfrac{1}{2}$ when $y = \dfrac{1}{3}$, what is the positive value of y when $x = 2$?

    (A) $\dfrac{1}{6}$

    (B) $\dfrac{2}{3}$

    (C) $\dfrac{4}{9}$

    (D) 2

    (E) 3

Guru Says...
When doing practice questions or reviewing any test you have taken, pay attention to wrong answers, even if you got the question right. What patterns can you identify?

The first thing to do is note the difficulty of this question. A #12 on the SAT is probably a question of medium difficulty. That means we should definitely be on the lookout for traps! Let's go ahead and work out the solution to this question to see what the trap here is. Since this is a proportion question, our set-up looks something like this: $\dfrac{x}{y^2} = \dfrac{x}{y^2}$. Now, plug in the values given in the problem, making sure to square the y value: $\dfrac{\frac{1}{2}}{\frac{1}{9}} = \dfrac{2}{2}$. Next, cross-multiply: $\dfrac{1}{2}y^2 = \dfrac{2}{9}$. Isolate the variable by multiplying both sides by 2: $y^2 = \dfrac{4}{9}$.

Now take a look at the answer choices—notice anything? Answer (C) should pop out at you. Congratulations! You found the trap answer. Go back to the question and re-read it: We are supposed to be trying to solve for y, not y^2. The correct answer is (B) $\dfrac{2}{3}$, which you get from calculating the square root of $\dfrac{4}{9}$. The only reason why $\dfrac{4}{9}$ is in the answer choices is to catch students who are moving too quickly. Don't let this happen to you! This kind of trap is very common, appearing all over the PSAT, SAT Subject, AP Calculus, CLEP and GRE tests, which is no wonder: All these tests are created by the same company, Educational Testing Services (ETS).

Here is another example, this time from the ACT:

7. A trapezoid is shown below with the given dimensions in inches. What is the area, in square inches, of the trapezoid?

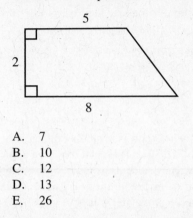

A. 7
B. 10
C. 12
D. 13
E. 26

Here we need to work a little with the figure. There is no geometric formula for "area of a trapezoid," so we need to draw a vertical line and create two figures for which there *are* formulas: a triangle and a rectangle.

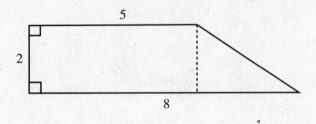

Once we draw the line and label all parts of the figure, the dimensions of the rectangle are 5 by 2, meaning the area of that part of the figure is 10. Now take a look at the answer choices—notice anything? Answer B 10 should pop out at you. Ha! The partial answer strikes again!

The correct answer is D 13, which you get from adding the area of the rectangle, 10, with the area of the triangle, 3. While this is not a very hard question, it's still easy to choose the wrong answer.

Guru Says...
Before you put down your final answer, re-read the question to make sure you have worked it all the way through.

Answer the right question.

Though math problems, you would think, exist to test your math skills, math word problems also test something else: your reading skills. The difference between a right and a wrong answer can hinge on just one little word, so always read the question carefully. Underline any key terms so you don't miss them. If a problem requires a lot of calculations, it is easy to forget while you are working what the actual question you are answering is, so re-read the question before you put down your final answer.

Here is an example from ACT:

8. The graph below shows the number of students absent from school on the first 4 days of a 5-day week. How many students would need to be absent from school on Friday for the 5-day week's mean to equal the mean of the first 4 days?

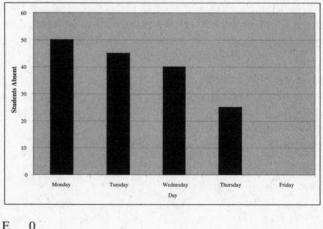

F. 0
G. 32
H. 40
J. 60
K. 160

This problem is solved by first finding the mean number of absent students for the first 4 days: 50 + 45 + 40 + 25 = 160. Hey! 160! I see that in the answers! Yes, you do, but it is a partial answer. Read the question again: How many students would need to be absent from school on Friday for the 5-day week's mean to equal the mean of the first 4 days?

If you misread or misunderstand the question, other answers will start to look even better. Answer F. would look good if you think, "Well, I want the mean to remain the same, so I shouldn't have any students absent Friday." But that's not what the question asks. If 160 absences are recorded over a 5-day period, we divide 160 by 5 to get a mean of 32. But wait! That's in the answers too!

OK, I'm lost. What was I looking for again?

You see our point: On complicated word problems with lots of steps, there are lots of places to lose track of what you are looking for and to misunderstand the question. The correct answer is H: If the 4-day mean is 40 with a total of 160 absences, we want to keep the mean the same over a 5-day period. To make that happen, we multiply the mean 40 by 5 days, giving us 200 absences total for the week. Since 200 − 160 = 40, that's the number we need on Friday to keep the mean the same. Tricky, but made even trickier by distracter answers that are either part of your calculations or that look good if you aren't answering the right question.

Let's look at a GMAT sample as well:

4. Jayne's cell phone plan provide 200 minutes of free calling per month for $30. For any minutes used in excess of 200, she must pay an additional $0.15 per minute. What additional cost does Jayne incur if she uses 245 minutes in one **month?**

(A) $36.75
(B) $30.00
(C) $24.75
(D) $15.00
(E) $6.75

The answer is (E): 45 extra minutes times $0.15 per minute is $6.75. That much is easy. But again, notice what other answers await you if you don't read carefully and answer the wrong question. (A) is what you get if you multiply the total number of minutes used (245) by $0.15, which is the most likely answer to tempt you if you calculated her *total* bill rather than just the *additional* charge the question actually asks for. (B) is her monthly payment for the first 200 minutes. (C) is what you get if you subtracted the extra fee of $6.75 from her monthly payment. All valid results of various calculations—just not the one that we need to correctly answer the questions.

Hint:
Before marking your final answer, re-read the question: be sure you are answering the question that is asked!

Use the right numbers.

When dealing with charts and graphs, make sure that you read the problem and question carefully and use the correct numbers. If you aren't careful when reading charts, there will absolutely be a trap answer awaiting you.

Here is an example from the ACT:

4. A jewelry maker sells her products online and in a small store. Her total sales consist of total revenues from both online and in-store sales. The table below shows online revenue and total revenue for a three-month period.

Online Revenue			
Month	Number of Orders	Total Sales	Average price per item
June	30	$540	$18
July	37	$703	$19
August	42	$714	$17
Total Revenue			
Month	Number of Orders	Total Sales	Average price per item
June	95	$1,805	$19
July	104	$2,184	$21
August	113	$2,034	$18

In June, what was the total dollar amount of total revenue that was in-store sales?

F. $1,150
G. $1,265
H. $1,320
J. $1,481
K. $1,644

Now the first thing you should probably note about this problem is how much extra information is provided that you don't need to answer the question. Way too much information is a signal that you want to be careful wading through the chart, using the correct values and ignoring the rest.

The question is very simple, but you need to infer from the information given that you subtract the online revenues from June ($540) from the total revenues for that month ($1,805) to get the in-store revenue: $1,805 − $540 = $1,265, or answer G. But the wrong answers are interesting: Answer J. is what you get if you use numbers from July rather than June ($2,184 – $703 = $1,481), and answer H. results from doing the same with the August numbers ($2,034 – $714 = $1,320). Answer K. comes from subtracting June online revenues from July total revenues ($2,184 – $540 = $1,644). So here, trap answers are the results of correct calculations using the wrong numbers from the chart.

Let's take a look at another example, this time from GRE:

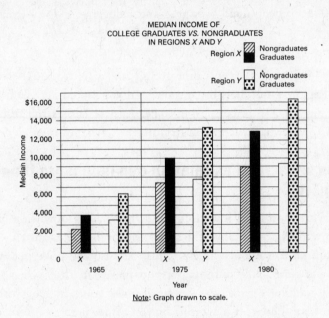

MEDIAN INCOME OF
COLLEGE GRADUATES *VS.* NONGRADUATES
IN REGIONS *X* AND *Y*

Region *X* — Nongraduates / Graduates
Region *Y* — Nongraduates / Graduates

Year

Note: Graph drawn to scale.

10. In 1975, the median income of nongraduates in Region X was approximately what fraction of the median income for graduates in Region X ?

(A) $\dfrac{3}{5}$

(B) $\dfrac{5}{8}$

(C) $\dfrac{3}{4}$

(D) $\dfrac{10}{13}$

(E) $\dfrac{4}{5}$

Notice again that the chart you are given is cramped and has a lot of extra information it, as we expect. Carefully choose the right information: we need data from 1975 (the middle set of bars) in Region *X*. Nongraduates are represented by the striped bar, and graduates by the solid one. Great, we have the right ones. The nongrad bar is around the $7,500 mark, and the grad bar is at $10,000. So put nongrad over grad and reduce: $\frac{7500}{10000} = \frac{3}{4}$, making (C) our answer.

Guru Says...
When using information from charts or graphs to solve a problem, be sure to use the right numbers.

Where did the other answers come from? You would get (A) if you used the 1975 Region *Y* numbers by mistake, and you would get (B) if you used the 1965 Region *X* numbers by mistake. Answer (D) is the result if you compare 1975 graduate income in Region *X* with that of Region *Y*.

Common sense and estimation can help more than you think.

Calculators are wondrous inventions, but they have a downside; if we rely on them too much, our brains stop working as well as they should. But your brain should *always* be on! Therefore, just because you poke madly at your calculator and a particular number pops up, make sure that is the answer you are actually looking for, of course, but also ask yourself: Does this answer make sense here? Did I push a wrong button somewhere?

Here is a sample question from the GMAT that illustrates this concept well:

> 11. If 12 is 20 percent of 30 percent of a certain number, what is the number?
>
> (A) 6
> (B) 20
> (C) 50
> (D) 72
> (E) 200

To solve this problem, you need to divide 12 by 0.2 and then divide the result by 0.3, which gives you (E) 200. But what if by mistake you *multiplied* instead of dividing here? You would get $12 \times 0.2 \times 0.3 = 0.72$. And hey, 72 is in the answers (maybe you figure you just made a decimal error but did the math right otherwise), so it looks very tempting if you are moving too quickly. But stop for a minute and consider what the question is asking. You know that 30 percent of a number is smaller than the number. Take 20 of that and you get an even smaller number. So, if 12 is 20 percent of 30 percent of a mystery number, that mystery number is *much* larger than 12. You realize that 72 is just not big enough for it to make sense as an answer here.

Common sense can not only help you catch yourself in errors like the one above, but it can also help you eliminate answers before you even do the problem, which saves time and can help you guess more effectively. Here is an SAT problem that shows how this works:

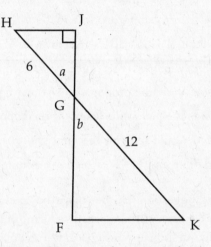

Note: Figure not drawn to scale.

18. In the figure above, $\overline{HJ}$ and $\overline{FK}$ are each perpendicular to $\overline{FJ}$. If $a = b$, the length of $\overline{HG}$ is 6, and the length of $\overline{GK}$ is 12, what is the length of $\overline{FJ}$?

(A) $4\sqrt{2}$ (approximately 5.66)

(B) $9\sqrt{2}$ (approximately 12.73)

(C) $12\sqrt{2}$ (approximately 16.97)

(D) $16\sqrt{2}$ (approximately 22.63)

(E) $18\sqrt{2}$ (approximately 25.46)

Even if geometry makes you want to run screaming from the room, stop to consider one very simple rule that you've known since grade school: The hypotenuse is the longest side of a right triangle. The sum of the hypotenuses of these two triangles is 18, so we know for a fact that the length of $\overline{FJ}$ cannot be greater than 18. Why? Because $\overline{FJ}$ is simply the sum of two other sides of these triangles, each shorter than its corresponding hypotenuse.

Now take a look at the answers. (D) and (E) can be eliminated for sure because they are bigger than 18. If you were to stop here and guess, you would have a one in three chance of guessing correctly. But we can improve those odds even more. (C) is probably too close to 18 to be the answer, and (A) seems too small, making (B) looks like a great answer. Are we right? Yes! If you have time to calculate, you'll see why: Since $a = b$, both triangles are isosceles right triangles. If you know the proportions of these figures, you know that the length of each side is equal to the length of the hypotenuse over $\sqrt{2}$ (the Pythagorean theorem would tell you the same thing). Therefore, $\overline{JG} = \dfrac{6}{\sqrt{2}}$ and $FG = \dfrac{12}{\sqrt{2}}$, and their sum is $\dfrac{18}{\sqrt{2}}$, which is the same as $9\sqrt{2}$.

Guru Says...
Use common sense and estimation to catch errors and guess more effectively.

Obviously, not every question can be solved by estimation only, and you should calculate rather than estimate when you can. But this is a #18, which on the SAT is a hard question appearing near the end of a section. If you were running out of time, using estimation to eliminate answers so you can guess is an ideal way to pick up an extra point (which in this case you would have gotten).

Write stuff down.

When solving wordy, multi-step problems containing variables, the last thing you want to do is try to keep track of all the math in your head. Many word problems aren't hard because they test difficult or obscure concepts—they are hard because they are complicated and require good organizational skills. If you write out your work, clearly labeling all the values in the problem, you are much less likely to make careless errors.

There are other benefits to writing stuff down as well. If you have time to review your work before the end of a section, you may be able to catch errors before it is too late to change your answer. If you start a problem, then get stuck and have to come back to it, you can just pick up where you left off, saving valuable time. Lastly, when you review your test later, you can trace your thought process and see just where you went wrong. Here is a GMAT problem that shows the value of good, organized work:

10. At a certain bookstore, $\frac{1}{6}$ of books sold in one day were biographies and $\frac{1}{4}$ of the remaining books sold were cookbooks. If y of the books sold were cookbooks, how many were biographies?

(A) $\frac{5}{12}y$

(B) $\frac{4}{6}y$

(C) $\frac{4}{5}y$

(D) $\frac{5}{6}y$

(E) $4y$

Working this problem algebraically is fraught with peril—let's plug in instead! When doing problems with multiple fractions like this one, start with a number that is a multiple of the denominators (the bottom number) of both fractions. Here 24 would work well. So, let's say that 24 is the total number of books sold this day. We are told that $\frac{1}{6}$ of the books sold are biographies, so $24 \times \frac{1}{6} = 4$ biographies were sold. Then we are told that $\frac{1}{4}$ of the remaining books... wait, how many remain? $24 - 4 = 20$ remain. If $\frac{1}{4}$ of 20 are cookbooks, that's $20 \times \frac{1}{4} = 5$.

So:

- 24 total books sold
- $24 \times \dfrac{1}{6} = 4$ biographies
- $24 - 4 = 20$ remain
- $20 \times \dfrac{1}{4} = 5$ are cookbooks

The problem says y is the number of cookbooks, so $y = 5$. The question asks how many were biographies, so the answer we are looking for is 4. Plug $y = 5$ into each answer choice and—voilá!—answer (C) works. This problem is a breeze when you organize your work and write everything down.

Use the answer choices to your advantage.

Guru Says...
It's your test, so mark it up! Write out math solutions carefully and label values in multi-step word problems. This is the best way to avoid careless errors.

Another nice thing about multiple-choice math tests is that you don't have to show your work. It doesn't matter *how* you get the right answer, as long as you find it. Even on tough questions, you can exploit the multiple-choice format to find right answers. The test makers don't intend for you to do this, of course, because it means that the test question actually tests something other than what they want, but tough luck for them: If they don't want you doing this, they need to design better questions!

15. At the first store Dan visits, he spends $6. At the second store, he spends one-third of his remaining money, and at the third store, he spends $9. If Dan has $15 left after visiting the third store, how much money did he have before he made his purchase at the first store?

    (A) $24
    (B) $30
    (C) $36
    (D) $42
    (E) $48

Now, you could tackle this question algebraically, but why bother? You can get 100 percent accuracy by working with the answer choices. Start with (C)—could $36 work? If you work through the question using $36 as your starting point, you end up with $11 at the end, so (C) is not the answer. Since you need to end up with more than $11, you can eliminate (A) and (B) as well. Now you only have two answers that could be right! Try (D): $42 – 6 = 36 – 12 = 24 – 9 = 15$. Yes! Even if you had tried (E) next, you would at most have to work through the question twice to get the answer. And you *know you got it right*, so it's a guaranteed point. How cool is that?

Whenever you work through the answers, start with (C). If the answers are listed in order from largest to smallest, you'll often know which to eliminate as we did above if (C) isn't the answer.

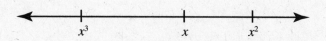

10. If x, x^2, and x^3 lie on a number line in the order shown above, which of the following could be the value of x ?

    (A) –2

    (B) $-\dfrac{1}{2}$

    (C) $\dfrac{1}{2}$

    (D) 1

    (E) 2

This is a easier example of how answer choices can work for you. The answers are all possible values of x. Great! Start with (C)—does this answer follow the rules described in the problem?

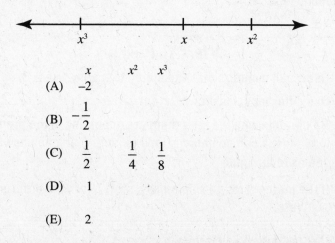

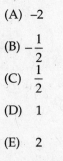

	x	x^2	x^3
(A)	–2		
(B)	$-\dfrac{1}{2}$		
(C)	$\dfrac{1}{2}$	$\dfrac{1}{4}$	$\dfrac{1}{8}$
(D)	1		
(E)	2		

(C) doesn't work, so you can eliminate it. But it isn't clear whether we need a bigger or smaller number. So for each value of x, calculate the values of x^2 and x^3 and then check to see if they correspond to the order of values on the figure:

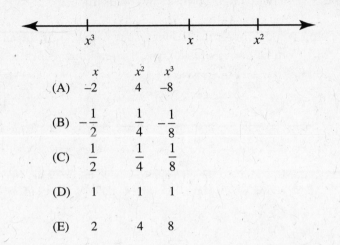

	x	x^2	x^3
(A)	-2	4	-8
(B)	$-\dfrac{1}{2}$	$\dfrac{1}{4}$	$-\dfrac{1}{8}$
(C)	$\dfrac{1}{2}$	$\dfrac{1}{4}$	$\dfrac{1}{8}$
(D)	1	1	1
(E)	2	4	8

It's pretty clear that (D) and (E) can be eliminated, so let's look more closely at (A) and (B). In (A), the value of x^3 is smallest, followed by x, then x^2 is the largest: $-8 < -2 < 4$, or $x^3 < x < x^2$. Does this match our figure? Yes.

Plug in when you see variables.

Questions with variables or unknown quantities are often testing your knowledge of the properties of numbers, your reasoning ability, or your ability to manipulate equations. But just because the questions are intended to test certain abilities, it doesn't mean you have to solve them that way. Many question containing variables become much easier if you plug in real values and then use arithmetic to solve.

WHAT TO PLUG IN

- Use small numbers that make the math easy, like 2, 3, or 4.

- Use different values for different variables.

- Be careful using 0, 1, and numbers appearing in the problem—these can sometimes lead to more than one answer that seems to be right.

- If the math starts getting messy, start over with different numbers.

---

17. If $\dfrac{3y^3}{2z}$, what happens to the value of x when both y and z are doubled?

(A) x is halved
(B) x is doubled
(C) x is tripled
(D) x is multiplied by 4
(E) x is multiplied by 8

Doing this problem algebraically is a nightmare. An easier way to solve it is to plug in some values for x, y, and z and then see what happens to the values. Start by assigning values to y and z. Use small numbers that are distinct from each other and that will give you a whole number for x when you solve. Let's try $y = 2$ and $z = 4$:

$$= \frac{3\left(2^3\right)}{2(4)} = \frac{24}{8} = 3$$

So, when $y = 2$ and $z = 4$, $x = 3$. Now, the problem tells us to double the value of both y and z. That means y now equals 4 and z equals 8. Plug those numbers back into the original equation and solve again for x:

$$= \frac{3\left(4^3\right)}{2(8)} = \frac{192}{16} = 12$$

The value of x is now 12, which is four times as big as 3, making (D) the answer. How easy is that?

Guru Says...
Turn tough algebra problems into doable math problems by plugging in values for variables whenever possible.

OTHER KINDS OF MATH

Quantitative Comparison

Quantitative comparison math questions appear on the ISEE and the GRE. They used to be on the PSAT and SAT as well, but were removed in the updates to those tests in 2004 and 2005, respectively, because they were deemed too easily "coached." Lucky for you then, if you are taking the ISEE or GRE! This question type is definitely crackable with a little math and a little test savvy.

This question has a distinctive structure. You are given two columns, labeled A and B, and sometimes also given some information to work with. You are given four answer choices:

> (A) means that the quantity in column A is
> always greater.
> (B) means that the quantity in column B is
> always greater.
> (C) means the quantities are always equal.
> (D) means the relationship cannot be
> determined from the information given.

There are a few key tips for acing these questions.

- If there are only numbers in the problem, there can only be one solution, so the answer cannot be (D).

- Do only as much work as you need to. The point to these questions is to *compare* the quantities, so once you get enough information to do that, stop calculating and put down your answer.

- If there are variables in the question, Plug In a value or values, calculate, then eliminate any answers you can. Then *Plug In again* with a different set of numbers. Keep Plugging In until you have only one answer remaining.

Let's do just a few so you can get a feel for this question type.

Column A	Column B
$\frac{3}{4} + \frac{3}{4}$	$\left(\frac{3}{4}\right)^2$

Column A equals $\frac{6}{4}$, and column B equals $\frac{9}{16}$. (A) is clearly the answer, since $\frac{6}{4}$ is greater than 1, while $\frac{9}{16}$ is less than 1. Notice how we didn't have to convert the quantities to decimals, or convert the fractions so that they had a common denominator. No reason to do extra steps when we don't need to!

Now let's see a more difficult question with unknown quantities. Since we don't have any answer choices, jot down ABCD on your test or scratch paper so you have something to cross out as we eliminate answers.

Column A	Column B
The perimeter of a rectangle with area 16	The perimeter of a rectangle with area 25

If we assume that the figures described above are squares (which are rectangles, after all), then Column A is 16 and Column B is 20. From our answer choices we can eliminate (A) and (C), leaving us with only (B) and (D). Since with our first numbers we got (B) to work, can we use different numbers so that Column B is *not* the greater quantity?

Sure. Instead of a square with sides of 4 for Column A, what if the rectangle instead had a length of 16 and a width of 1? The area would still be 16, but now the perimeter would be 34, making (A) the answer. We can now eliminate (B) and choose (D) with confidence.

Data Sufficiency

Data sufficiency is a problem type unique to the GMAT. This problem type contains a question followed by two statements, numbered (1) and (2). You need not solve the problem; rather you must decide whether the information given is sufficient to solve the problem. The answer choices are always the same:

> (A) if statement (1) ALONE is sufficient to answer the question but statement (2) alone is not sufficient;
>
> (B) if statement (2) ALONE is sufficient to answer the question but statement (1) alone is not sufficient;
>
> (C) if the two statements TAKEN TOGETHER are sufficient to answer the question, but NEITHER statement ALONE is sufficient;

Guru Says...
On quantitative comparison questions, if there are variables or unknown quantities in the question, Plug In different values and eliminate down to the answer.

(D) if EACH statement ALONE is sufficient to answer the question;

(E) if the two statements TAKEN TOGETHER are still NOT sufficient to answer the question.

Even more than on a multiple-choice or quantitative comparison question, on a data sufficiency question, you need to use the process of elimination to work your way down to a correct answer. Let's take a look at several examples that illustrate why this is so.

1. What is the ratio of a to b ?

   (1) The ratio of $3a$ to $0.25b$ is 4 to 3.
   (2) b is 1 more than 4 times a

Start with statement (1). If the ratio of $3a$ to $0.25b$ is 4 to 3, you can set up a proportion and manipulate the equation until you find the value of $-$:

$$\frac{3}{0.25} = \frac{4}{3}$$
$$9 =$$
$$- = \frac{1}{9}$$

This tells us that (1) alone is sufficient to solve the problem, so of the possible answers ABCDE, eliminate (B), (C), and (E). Now let's take a look at (2). If b is 1 more than 4 times a, that means that $b = 4a + 1$. If $a = 1$, then $b = 5$, so $- = \frac{1}{5}$. But is that the only value for $-$ we can come up with? If $a = 2$, then $b = 9$, so $- = \frac{1}{9}$, a different ratio. That means that statement (2) is not sufficient to answer the question, so we eliminate answer (D) and choose (A).

Let's try another question.

2. The prices of two items, a shirt and a dress, are reduced. Which item was reduced by larger dollar amount?

   (1) The price of the shirt was reduced by 20%.
   (2) The price of the dress was reduced by 30%.

Start with statement (1). Can we calculate the dollar amount by which the shirt was reduced? Not without the original price—all we are given is the percent by which it is reduced, which is useless without a real price. That means that statement (1) is not sufficient, so of possible answers ABCDE, we eliminate (A) and (D). A quick look at statement (2) shows that we have the same problem with it as we did with (1), so neither is sufficient, even when taken together. Therefore we eliminate (B) and (C) and choose (E).

Solving multiple-choice math problems is part content knowledge, part organizational skill, part reading, and part test savvy. Knowing what traps may be awaiting you can make you much less likely to fall for them!

Guru Says...
When solving data sufficiency problems, use POE every time, all the time.

MULTIPLE-CHOICE VERBAL

True/False

True/false questions are more likely to appear on course tests than on standardized tests, but there are still powerful benefits to understanding how these work. All of the tips below are applicable not only to T/F tests, but also to determining the correctness of many a multiple-choice answer choice on reading, literature, and social sciences tests.

Always read carefully.

The tiniest word can make the difference between a right and wrong answer on this kind of question, so read carefully and be sure you understand all parts of a statement when judging it true or not.

> *Manifest Destiny provided the sole justification for the expansionist Democratic administration of James K. Polk that came to power in 1845 and which brought California into the American empire after the Mexican War of 1846–1848.*

Wow, that's quite a lengthy statement, which would be true except for one little word: sole. Exchange *sole* for *one* and you have a true statement. But it's that one tiny word that ruins the whole thing!

Quotable Quotes
It has long been an axiom of mine that the little things are infinitely the most important.
—Sherlock Holmes

Be careful when faced with extreme or absolute language.

Words that describe "all or nothing" situations are dangerous on T/F tests; depending on the content, statements containing words such as *none, nothing, no one, never, always, only, everyone,* or *all* are much more likely to be false than true. Compare two statements:

> *Everybody loves Raymond*—As long as there is one person on the planet who doesn't love Raymond, this cannot be true. This statement is too absolute to be supportable.

> *Some people love Raymond*—As long as there is one person on the planet who loves Raymond, this must be true. Because this statement is less absolute, it is easier to prove as true.

Similarly, watch out for superlative terms. Again, if you see a statement like this—*The Vietnam War was the most divisive event of the 20th century*—consider how hard it is to prove true. Most divisive? How do you measure divisiveness? Compared to what?

However, especially in more rule-bound fields such as math and science, absolute language can still be true, so don't discount all answers that contain this kind of phrasing. For example, these statements are definitely true:

> *All prime numbers are positive.*
> *All nuclei have a positive charge.*

Partially true means all false.

A statement is only true if all parts of it are true. The longer the statement, the more likely it is that one, small part is wrong, so you will need to evaluate all the parts of the statement fully. When you see words such as *because, since, so, on account of,* or other words that denote cause and effect, beware. For example, consider this statement:

> *A prime number is only divisible by 1 and itself, so 1 is a prime number.*

While the first half of this statement is true, the second half isn't. That makes it all false.

> *The Federalists lost influence as a result of the XYZ Affair, which stirred up intense anti-French sentiment among the American populace.*

In this case, it is true that the XYZ Affair led to a rise in anti-French sentiment, but it actually made the Federalists more popular, not less. So here the first half is false, and the second half is true, but that still equals an answer of false.

Guessing isn't so bad.

With a 50-50 chance of getting it right, it makes sense to guess on a T/F question if you are really at sea and have no idea what the answer is.

Matching Questions

- Note if there is a one-to-one correspondence between the two columns of terms or statements. If there is, cross off each term from one column as you match it with one from the other.

- When finding a match for one item, read through all the possible answers, even if you think you found the answer. You never know if there may be an even better match further down the list.

- When you get down to the last few items, make sure you like the answers you put down. If you end up with items that don't go together, that's your cue that you may have matched incorrectly on earlier items. This is a great way to catch errors.

Verbal Analogy

Analogies appear on the SSAT and the GRE. On an analogy, your job is to figure out what the relationship is between the two words given in the question stem, and then find the pair of words in the answer choices that shares the same relationship. Here is a sample question:

5.   FELONY : MISDEMEANOR ::

(A)   criminal : judiciary
(B)   degenerate : corruption
(C)   provocation : debate
(D)   iniquity : peccadillo
(E)   prevarication : truth

Step 1: Make a Sentence.

The best way to start an analogy question is to try to make a sentence using the stem words. You don't need a long, fancy sentence—just make it simple and precise, starting with one word and ending with the other.

Let's assume that both FELONY and MISDEMEANOR fall into the "words you know" category. A good sentence would be "A FELONY is a more serious MISDEMEANOR." Now, plug each pair of words in the answer choices into the basic sentence "A _____ is a more serious _____."

(A)   Is a CRIMINAL a more serious JUDICIARY? No. A criminal may go in front of the judiciary. This is a trap—just because the words here and in the stem are legal terms doesn't mean they share the same relationship.

(B)   Is a DEGENERATE a more serious CORRUPTION? No. A degenerate is prone to corruption.

(C)   Is a PROVOCATION a more serious DEBATE? No. These words don't really have a relationship.

(D) Is a INIQUITY a more serious
    PECCADILLO? Sure. A peccadillo
    is a small sin, but iniquity means a
    serious transgression or sin, so this
    works. Keep it.

(E) Is a PREVARICATION a more serious
    TRUTH? No. A prevarication lacks
    truth.

Therefore, our answer is (D). Notice what we did when we know the meaning of the stem words:

1. Make a sentence.

2. Go through the answer choices, eliminating pairs that don't fit the sentence.

3. Go through ALL the answers—sometimes there may be more than one pair that seems to work. If more than one works, you may need to tweak your sentence, making it more specific.

4. Usually you want to use the words in the order they appear, but sometimes you may need to switch the order. If you do, though, make sure you also switch the order of the answers

Step 2: Work Backward.

The process demonstrated above works great when you know both words in the stem pair, but what do you do when you don't know one or both of the words? If this happens, go straight to the answer choices and make a sentence out of each pair of words, then work backward: Plug the stem words into each sentence from the answers and eliminate the pairs that don't work. Let's try it!

6. TRUDGE : WALK ::

   (A) bar : legalize
   (B) shunt : avoid
   (C) heave : lift
   (D) skip : jump
   (E) accost : approach

Let's assume that we are having trouble making a sentence with TRUDGE and WALK, so let's go to the answers and see if there is anything there we can work with. Skim the words in the answers—what parts of speech are we dealing with? Looks like two verbs, so make sure your sentence reflects this.

(A) To bar means to block or rule out, and legalize means to allow, so our sentence would look something like, "To BAR means to no longer LEGALIZE something." Does TRUDGE mean to no longer WALK something? No. Let's find something better.

(B) To SHUNT is to move aside in order to AVOID something. Does TRUDGE mean to move aside in order to WALK something? No. Eliminate and keep going.

(C) To HEAVE is to LIFT with great effort. Does TRUDGE mean to WALK with great effort? Sure! Let's keep this one, but check the others to be sure this is the only pair that could work.

(D) To SKIP is to JUMP lightly over something. Does TRUDGE mean to WALK lightly over something? No, it means the opposite.

(E) To ACCOST is to APPROACH aggressively. Does TRUDGE mean to WALK aggressively? Not really.

Therefore, (C) is the best answer.

Analogy Distracters

Distracter answers on analogies assume you don't understand what an analogy is, and so include pairs of words that seem connected thematically but that don't share the right kind of relationship. For example, a word pair such as SALT : PEPPER could never be a correct answer, but they do "sound" good together, don't they? Similarly, POLITICAL : ANARCHY could also never be a correct answer, since these words don't share the kind of definitional relationship we need. However, this choice may sound appealing because "political anarchy" is just a phrase you may have heard many times.

Last gasp? Eliminate answers with no relationship.

If you are struggling to make sentences out of stem words or answer choices, you can still eliminate some choices. We may not know much, but we know that the correct answer to an analogy question is a pair of words with a distinct relationship. So if any pairs in the answers lack any kind of relationship, they cannot be the correct answer.

Just to show how this can help, let's take a look at five answer choices with no stem words at all.

(A) precipitous : mountain
(B) judicious : system
(C) dispersive : discharge
(D) strident : sound
(E) epidemic : disease

What can we get rid of just on the basis of relationship?

(A) Are *precipitous* and *mountain* related? No. *Precipitous* means "like a precipice," or extremely steep. Is a mountain necessarily precipitous? No. Eliminate this choice; it's a distracter.

(B) Are *judicious* and *system* related? No. *Judicious* means "having good judgment," and it's a quality of a person, not a system. Eliminate this choice.

(C) Is there a relationship between *dispersive* and *discharge*? No. *Dispersive* just means "tending to disperse." Is a discharge necessarily dispersive? Nope. Cross out this choice.

(D) Is there a relationship between *strident* and *sound*? Perhaps you're not sure what the dictionary definition of *strident* is, so keep this choice. If you know that *strident* means "shrill," then you do have a good relationship: *Strident* means a harsh, unpleasant *sound*.

(E) Is **there** a relationship between
epidemic and *disease*? Sure. A disease
can be described as epidemic if it
spreads to a lot of people. There's
definitely a relationship, so this
answer stays.

So look at that—just by eliminating pairs of words that weren't related in the way a correct answer requires, we were able to eliminate down to two answers, so we have a 50-50 chance of getting this question right.

Synonyms

Synonym questions appear on the ISEE and SSAT tests. You already know what a synonym is—this kind of question is the most straightforward and probably needs the least amount of introduction. You'll be given a single word—we'll call that the **stem word**—and five possible answers, and you **need** to find the word in the answers that comes closest in meeting to the stem word. But even with synonym questions, there is a bit of strategy involved. Here's a sample:

1. EXTRADITE
    (A) adopt
    (B) deliver
    (C) overflow
    (D) conceal
    (E) accuse

In short, the most effective way to solve a synonym question goes like this:

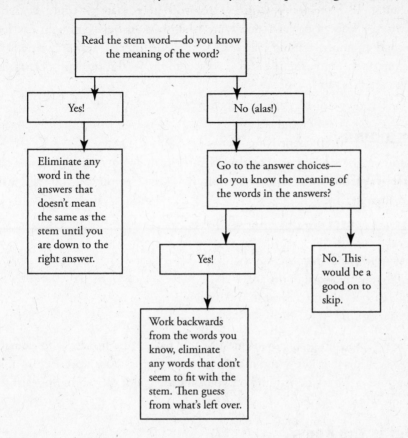

Let's assume for the moment that you don't know what *extradite* means. What do you do? First, it's important to start with simple things, such as what part of speech this is. Both the stem and the answers will always be the same part of speech.

In the answers we see all verbs, so we know that *extradite* is a verb. What else do we know? That the word contains either the prefix *ex-* or *extra-*, both of which mean "out of" or "away from," so let's get rid of any answers that don't contain a similar meaning. *Adopt* means "to take on or assume," which is the opposite of what we need—eliminate it. (D) and (E) don't mean "away from" either, so that leaves us with (B) and (C). This would be a good time to guess since you have a 50-50 chance of getting it right. But is there more you can do?

Think about the context in which you have heard the word for hints to its meaning. If you remember hearing this word in relation to people accused of a crime being sent back home to face trial, then answer (C) might not look so good anymore, leaving you with (B) *deliver*. Indeed, *extradite* means "to give up or deliver (a fugitive, for example) to the legal jurisdiction of another government or authority."

Antonyms

Antonym questions appear on the GRE. As with any question type, there are better ways to approach these questions that can help you save time and avoid trap answers.

> 2. PRAGMATIC
>
>   (A) dictatorial
>   (B) frivolous
>   (C) idealistic
>   (D) earnest
>   (E) unsophisticated

When approaching antonym questions, it pays to be honest with yourself: How well do you know the meaning of the words? Your approach to these questions will vary depending on your knowledge of the words appearing in the question.

Words You Know

Let's say that you took one look at question 2 above and knew the stem word PRAGMATIC. Great! But look out: You don't want to jump into the answer choices too quickly and choose the first answer that looks right. Avoid careless errors by following this basic approach:

Step 1: Cover the answers—don't let them distract you.

Step 2: Jot down your own simple opposite for the stem word.

Step 3: Uncover the answers and use the process of elimination to get rid of any word that has nothing in common with your own answer.

Step 4: If you can't eliminate down to a single answer, try making opposites of each remaining answer choice, then compare those to the stem word.

Let's try this with the example above. If we know the meaning of PRAG-MATIC, we know it mean something like "realistic," so our opposite word would be "unrealistic."

(A) Does *dictatorial* mean unrealistic? No,
it means bossy, so eliminate it.
(B) Does *frivolous* means unrealistic?
Maybe — let's keep it for now.
(C) Does *idealistic* mean unrealistic? Sure
— let's keep this one, too.
(D) Does *earnest* mean unrealistic? No, it
means serious, so eliminate it.
(E) Does *unsophisticated* mean unrealistic?
No, so eliminate it.

Now we are down to two. If you don't know the specific definitions of either word, you can at least guess and have a 50-50 chance of getting it right. But if you know that *frivolous* means "silly" or "trivial," you can get rid of it and choose (C) *idealistic*, which can mean "unrealistic or impractical."

Words You Kind of Know

So what do you do if you don't know a stem word well enough to be able to jot down your own opposite? If you've seen it before and know it well enough to use it in a sentence but can't provide a dictionary definition, you "kind of" know it. That's enough to get started. If you can at least determine if the word has a positive or negative connotation, jot down a positive (+) or negative (–) sign next to the stem, then go through the answer choices and label each answer this way.

Let's look at another example:

3. PERFIDY

(A) imperfection
(B) fealty
(C) humility
(D) nonchalance
(E) respect

Let's assume that you can't define PERFIDY, but know it enough to know it has a negative meaning. So you jot down a (–) next to it, then label the answers:

3. PERFIDY (–)

    (A) imperfection (–)
    (B) fealty (+)
    (C) humility (+)
    (D) nonchalance (–)
    (E) disrespect (–)

At this point we can eliminate (A), (D), and (E)—we are looking for a word with a positive meaning. Now go through the remaining answers and jot down an opposite for each.

    (B) betrayal
    (C) arrogance

At this point, if you know that PERFIDY means "treachery," then (B) will jump out at you. If not, then at least you are down to two answers, which gives you a much better chance of guessing correctly than you had when you started.

Let's try another:

4. FELL

    (A) purposeless
    (B) fruitful
    (C) inadequate
    (D) gentle
    (E) deceptive

Note a new things here. First, note the parts of speech in the answers—they are all adjectives. Therefore, we are looking for an antonym for FELL, which here is an adjective. Second, you may have seen this word in the phrase, "one fell swoop." If so, this can help you more than you may realize!

Assuming you don't know the meaning of FELL to even label it (+) or (–), let's go to the answer choices and come up with an opposite for each answer:

    (A) purposeful
    (B) barren or unproductive
    (C) adequate
    (D) fierce or violent
    (E) honest or true

Now, let's plug each into the phrase "one fell swoop" to see if it could work.

(A) Does "in one *purposeful* swoop" make sense? Sure—hold onto it.

(B) Does "in one *unproductive* swoop" make sense? Not really—eliminate.

(C) Does "in one *adequate* swoop" make sense? Not really—eliminate.

(D) Does "in one *violent* swoop" make sense? Sure—keep it.

(E) Does "in one *honest* swoop" make sense? Not really—eliminate.

Now we are left with two answers (A) and (D), giving us a 50-50 chance of guessing correctly. If you remember other phrases such as "to fell a tree," (D) looks better. "To fell" means to cut or knock down, and FELL as an adjective means "destructive or lethal," so (A) makes less sense. Choose (D) and get it right!

Guru Says...
Use word association to help you define words and to eliminate answers on antonym questions.

Words You Don't Know

Lastly, we inevitably come to words that you have never seen before. If you literally have never seen any of the words and cannot guess any of their meanings via roots or determine positive/negative meanings (in other words, you can't do anything), then that question is a good candidate to skip. But if you use **any** of the tools discussed here, eliminate what you can, then guess.

Sentence Completions

Sentence completions appear on the ISEE, PSAT, SAT, and GRE. Your job is to find the missing word or words based on context, so they are part reading test and part vocabulary test. Luckily, each sentence completion contains one or more clues that will tell you what goes in the blank or blanks. All you have to do is find the clues, and you've cracked the question.

1. **Cover the answer choices**. Test writers insert words into the answer choices that may tempt you because they "sound good" or are related to the concepts discussed in the sentence. To avoid falling for traps, don't even look at the answer choices until you know exactly what you are looking for. Cover them up with your hand or a piece of paper if you need to.

2. **Find and underline the clue(s).** Every sentence contains some information—we'll call it the clue—that makes one answer the best choice. Without the clue(s), you won't know what you are looking for. If you have trouble finding the clue, ask yourself: What is the blank talking about, and what else does the sentence say about this subject? This will usually put you on the right track.

3. **Look for trigger words**—revealing words or expressions that give you important clues about the meanings of sentences—and circle them. The most common "negative" trigger words are *but, though,* and *although.* These are words that indicated contrasting ideas. The most common "positive" triggers are *and* and *because.* These are words that maintain the direction of the sentence.

4. **Fill in the blank(s) with your own word(s).** You don't have to have the perfect word—as long as the meaning is generally correct, it will help you eliminate answer choices.

5. **Use POE** to eliminate answers that don't agree with yours until you find the right answer. However, never eliminate a choice unless you are sure of its meaning.

Let's do a few so you can get a feel for how this works!

> 5. It is widely accepted for colleges to have honor codes in place to discourage cheating; the specific features of these codes, however, are often quite -------.
>
>   (A) dangerous
>   (B) controversial
>   (C) anticipated
>   (D) restrained
>   (E) humble

OK, let's go hunting for some clues and triggers. Notice a few things right away. The semicolon is important, as is the word *however,* which indicates contrast. Semicolons and colons are often used to link together two statements that are closely related. By themselves, they serve as "positive" triggers. If you see one, look on the other side of it for your clue! But the word *however* indicates contrast. The combination of these triggers means if it is *widely accepted* to have honor codes, the features of those codes are...something opposite of *widely accepted.*

Therefore, the missing word means something like "not widely accepted." Great! Now let's use POE:

(A) Does *dangerous* mean "not widely accepted"? No.

(B) Does *controversial* mean "not widely accepted"? Yes—keep this one, but check the other answers just to be sure.

(C) Does *anticipated* mean "not widely accepted"? No.

(D) Does *restrained* mean "not widely accepted"? No.

(E) Does *humble* mean "not widely accepted"? No.

The answer is (E). Well done! See how much easier it is to find the correct answer if you know what you are looking for?

SENTENCE COMPLETIONS IN REAL LIFE

On standardized tests, test writers always make sure that there are no other cues that may help you find an answer, such as the use of *a* or *an* before a blank, which would tell you whether the right answer begins with a vowel or a consonant. However, on school tests, your teacher (wittingly or unwittingly) may leave this as a clue. Similarly, your teachers may be inconsistent with the part of speech (putting nouns in the answers when only an adjective could be correct) or number (putting singular answers when only a plural could be correct) of answers.

What To Do If You See Two Blanks

Attack two-blank sentence completions by focusing on one blank at a time—start with whichever blank you feel you have the most information about. Use the same techniques you would use on one-blank questions. If you can eliminate either word in an answer choice, you can cross out the entire choice (this harkens back to our "partly right is all wrong" principle again). If the clue for one of the blanks is the other blank, use the trigger word to determine the relationship between the blanks. Let's try one.

6. While many people enjoy observing rituals and customs not ------- their culture, they ------- participating in them.

   (A) sanctioned by . . encourage
   (B) endemic to . . eschew
   (C) upheld in . . condone
   (D) central to . . relish
   (E) accustomed to . . avoid

Let's start with the second blank, which is often a good place to start because you often have more information about it than about the first blank. Here, our clues are *people enjoy observing* and our trigger is *while*, which denotes contrast. So while they enjoy watching, they...*don't enjoy* participating. Thus our answer for the second blank is *don't enjoy*. What can we eliminate, just by focusing on the second word in each pair?

   (A) sanctioned by . . encourage
       Does this mean *don't enjoy*? No—
       eliminate the entire answer choice.
   (B) endemic to . . eschew
       Does this mean *don't enjoy*? Kind of—it
       means "avoid," so keep it.
   (C) upheld in . . condone
       Does this mean *don't enjoy*? No—
       eliminate the entire answer choice.
   (D) central to . . relish
       Does this mean *don't enjoy*? No—
       eliminate the entire answer choice.
   (E) accustomed to . . avoid
       Does this mean *don't enjoy*? Yes, so keep
       it.

Look at that—just by working through one blank, we have eliminated 3 of 5 possible answers! Now let's go back to the first blank. Given the meaning of the sentence as a whole, a good word for this first blank would be *part of*.

   (B) endemic to . . eschew
   (E) accustomed to . . avoid

Between (B) endemic to and (E) accustomed to, only (B) works. If you weren't sure what *endemic to* means, you certainly know that *accustomed to* does <u>not</u> mean *part of*, so you can choose (B) with confidence. See how much easier it is to see the answer when you use POE?

What To Do If You Can't Come Up With Your Own Word For The Blank

If you have a general sense of whether you need a word with a positive or negative connotation, that can be enough to start eliminating answers.

> 7. Ruggiero's vitriolic attack was the climax of the ---
> ---- heaped on Alden's paintings, which today seem
> amazingly ------- .
>
> (A) criticism . . unpopular
> (B) ridicule . . inoffensive
> (C) praise . . amateurish
> (D) indifference . . scandalous
> (E) acclaim . . credible

A *vitriolic* attack is something bad (and so is simply an *attack,* if you don't know what *vitriolic* means). The climax of a vitriolic attack must also be bad, and therefore the first blank must be a word with a negative meaning.

> (A) criticism . . unpopular
> (B) ridicule . . inoffensive
> (C) praise . . amateurish
> (D) indifference . . scandalous
> (E) acclaim . . credible

Already we can eliminate (C) and (E), since *praise* and *acclaim* are positive words. We can get rid of (D) as well, since *indifference* is sort of neutral—we need a negative word here, not a wishy-washy word like *indifference.* That leaves us with only (A) and (B).

Now look at the second blank. The first part of the sentence says that Ruggiero thought the paintings were very bad; today, *amazingly,* they seem—what? Bad?

No! The word in the second blank has to be a *positive* word.

> (A) criticism . . unpopular
> (B) ridicule . . inoffensive

(A) is definitely not a positive word, so choose (B) and get it right. And you didn't even have to use any big 50-cent vocabulary words to ace this one.

What To Do When You are Clueless

Sometimes you will come across a two-blank sentence completion which doesn't seem to contain any useful clues that would enable you to come up with your own word for either blank.

> 8. Most of Roger's friends think his life is unbelievably
> -------, but in fact he spends most of his time pursuing
> ------- activities.
>
> (A) fruitful . . productive
> (B) wasteful . . useless
> (C) scintillating . . mundane
> (D) varied . . sportive
> (E) callow . . simple

The trigger word in this sentence is *but*. We gather from the sentence that most of Roger's friends think his life is one way, but in fact it is another. We cannot tell if his friends think his life is great and busy while it's really lousy and slow, or vice versa. However, we do know that our blanks are opposites: The first is positive while the second is negative *or* the first is negative while the second is positive.

Knowing this is enough to get us to close to, if not find, the right answer. Let's look at each answer choice, keeping in mind that we need a pair of words that are opposites:

> (A) *Fruitful* is positive; *productive* is positive.
>   Eliminate this choice.
> (B) *Wasteful* is negative; *useless* is negative.
>   Cross it off.
> (C) *Scintillating* is positive; *mundane* is
>   negative. Keep it.
> (D) *Varied* is positive; *sportive* is positive.
>   Cross it off.
> (E) *Callow* is negative; *simple* is neutral. A
>   possibility, but not great.

The answer is (C): Roger's life may look *scintillating*, but he spends most of his time on *mundane* activities.

Not every technique described here will lead you to the correct answer *every* time, but they can help you avoid traps and eliminate at least some answers so you have a better chance of guessing correctly.

PASSAGE-BASED READING

Reading on a standardized test is a fundamentally different task from the reading you do in class, for homework, or for fun. The big difference here is the need for *speed*: If you are given a time limit, you can't take all the time in the world to read, re-read, annotate, have a snack, check your e-mail, take a nap, then read again. You're not even reading for comprehension most of the time. In fact, doing well on the reading sections of standardized tests is dependent mainly on two skills: reading efficiently and answering questions correctly.

How to Read Efficiently

If you remember anything from this section, remember this: You NEVER need to read every word of a passage to answer all the questions correctly, and on some questions, you almost don't need the passage at all. The trick is to read as little as possible in order to answer the questions. In this way, reading on standardized tests is more like hunting for buried treasure. Think about it: If you knew there was a big chest full of gold buried on a desert island somewhere, would you dig up the entire island hoping to come upon it, or only dig where there was a big "X" on the map? The latter option is a lot less work, and you get to move on to other things (such as spending all that gold!) that much faster.

Preview Questions

Previewing the questions before you tackle the passage is a great way to gain some efficiency. Read just the question stems of all the questions, underlining key words as you go. Once you've done that, you probably have some idea of what the passage is about, and you now have a list of words to look out for as you skim the passage. Spend no more than 30 to 45 seconds previewing the questions.

Learn to Skim

Many students read the entire passage before they begin to attack the questions, an inefficient use of time. Instead, the most you should do is *skim* the passage. The difference between skimming and reading for comprehension is a matter of varying your focus and depth of reading. Reading for comprehension involves reading every word and detail and weighing every sentence as equally important. However, not every sentence is equally important in a testing context: Some contain the answers to questions and some don't, so you waste time reading for comprehension.

Skimming involves getting an overall general idea of what the passage is about, focusing only on those parts of the passage that you need to. In most passages, the first one or two sentences of each paragraph provide enough information to know what the paragraph is about. When you skim, read the first few sentences carefully, but skim over the remaining details, making note only of trigger words that denote lists of ideas, contrasts, or other key shifts in meaning. Again, it doesn't matter at this stage that you understand, for instance, what two groups of scientists are arguing about—it is only important that you know they are arguing about something at all.

Read Only What You Need to

Many students dislike skimming because they don't feel they know enough to be able to answer the questions with any confidence. Those students are missing a crucial point: Skimming is not enough to answer questions in most cases, so you shouldn't feel confident yet! That confidence will come from reading certain parts of the passage very carefully once you begin attacking the questions. If a question asks about lines 25–27, go to around line 20 and start reading carefully. If a question asks about the third paragraph, then read that carefully. Just read what you need to.

Work From Specific to General

When reading only what you need to, it pays to start with the specific questions which ask about only certain parts of the passage first. Once you finish all the specific questions, the general questions will be a LOT easier to answer, since after all that reading you will have a much better idea of what the whole thing is about than you did after your skim.

Fiction Works Differently

The points made above are relevant the majority of the time, especially when dealing with factual passages. However, fiction passages may require a different approach. In a fictional passage, there are usually the characters, their thoughts and emotions, and the relationships between characters at the core of the text. Trying to answer questions without understanding all these things may be fruitless—you just need to know more about the whole story to answer questions correctly. Therefore, fiction passages may be the one place where you find yourself doing more reading than you otherwise would. That's fine—as long as the time invested in reading results in lots of right answers, it was time well spent.

Useful Approaches

Dual passages = sentence completions.

Treat questions that ask about more than one passage like you would a two-blank sentence completion: eliminate answers based JUST on what the first passage says, then based just on the content of the second passage. Be on the lookout for half right, half wrong answers—they are a common trap on this kind of question.

Use chronology if you can.

On the PSAT and SAT as well as some other tests, the specific questions—those that only ask about a small part of the passage—are presented in the order in which the answers can be found in the passage. This can help you save time because it can help you to find information in the passage more quickly. For example, let's assume that the answer to question #12 was found in lines 30–35 of a certain passage and the answer to question #14 was found in lines 48–52. If question #13 is a specific question, you can be fairly sure that the answer can be found somewhere between lines 35 and 48 of the passage. Not a huge time savings, but every little bit can help!

Be flexible.

Sometimes previewing the questions can help you more efficiently skim the passage. Sometimes you can start right in on the questions without reading the passage. Still other times you may need to skim the passage before you can really answer the questions. Because of this variation, there isn't really one "perfect" way to approach passage-based reading questions. Instead, you should learn to utilize all of these approaches so that you can use whichever works best for you depending on your strengths and weaknesses and the passage you have in front of you at any given time.

Lots of practice and experimentation will help you find the right approach at the right time. Vary your approach and track your results. Is there a particular approach on certain passages that yields better results? If so, adjust your approach accordingly. Don't guess at this: Experiment, track your results, and make adjustments to your approach based on solid evidence.

Focus on accuracy rather than speed.

It may seem counterintuitive to tell you not to worry about speed on a timed test, but it's true: If you work so fast that you miss most of the questions, then there is little benefit to working quickly. Speed alone doesn't get you right answers, accuracy does, so do what you need to in order to get as many questions correct as possible.

Start by working sample passages without timing yourself. If given unlimited time, how accurate are you? Once you've determined that, do a section timed and then calculate your accuracy. If it drops significantly, you will probably benefit from slowing down and doing fewer questions (if you are a slow reader, this is almost a given). After you have slowed yourself down, start pushing yourself little by little to work faster while keeping your accuracy near the baseline you created untimed.

Use Process of Elimination.

When it comes to reading questions, it is much harder to come up with the exact answer on your own and a lot easier to get sucked in by distracter answer choices. Know what you are looking for when you go to the answers, and look for reason to eliminate all answers but one. Approaching answers looking for reasons to get rid of them will help you avoid trap answers.

Traps to Avoid on Reading

Speaking of trap answers, reading questions certainly have their share! Here are some of the most common across nearly all test types.

Quote Me
There is nothing more deceptive than an obvious fact.
—Sherlock Holmes

The Mangler, a.k.a. Deceptive Language

One of the most popular traps involves language which appears somewhere in the passage, which makes it seem very attractive. This answer copies words or phrases from the passage but simultaneously distorts the meaning, mangling the message. This kind of deceptive language is particularly attractive to students who read the entire passage carefully before they attack the questions because they recognize the words in the wrong answers. If you rely on your memory instead of returning to the passage to find the answer, these answers can be too attractive to pass up. Too bad they are wrong.

The Flip

This kind of answer seems sooo close to what you want, but always falls short in the end. The Flip uses information from the passage as a template and then turns the information around to mean something different from that which the author intends. For example, if the passage says that "the author agrees with X but disagrees with Y," a Flip answer may instead say, "the author disagrees with X but agrees with Y." Other Flips may substitute one name from the passage for another, or mix up different points of view, or confuse the order of ideas or events.

The Seducer

Seducers make statements that seem so appropriate, so sane, so sensible, but in reality aren't mentioned anywhere in the passage or else don't answer the question posed.

The Irrelevant Truth

Similarly, Irrelevant Truths trap students by including a statement that seems to fully and genuinely repeat one of the author's messages. This statement is true, and something the author said, but it doesn't answer the question posed.

The Absolute

The Absolute is a trap that goes just a little farther than it should. Absolutes are problematic because they are disputable, and the correct answer must make a statement that is indisputable. Absolutes include words such as *always, must, everybody, all, complete,* and *never.*

The Extreme

If we know anything about the writers of standardized tests, we know that they will not include any information in a passage or a correct answer that anyone could possibly be offended by. When writers are given the task to write questions, they must avoid an often lengthy list of "taboo" subjects, including (but not limited to): sex, drugs, alcohol, any specific religious belief or holiday, ethnic or gender stereotypes, or anything that only certain classes of people might be familiar with. Test writers even avoid Extremes of opinion or emotion.

In general:

- Test writers are politically correct, so avoid answers that say anything bad about any group of people.

- Test writers are respectful of authors and subjects, so avoid choices that cast the authors or the subject of the passage in a negative light.

- Authors are neither overly negative nor positive in their views, so avoid answers that describe authors as expressing extremely negative or positive emotions.

- Authors are never disinterested in their subject matter, so avoid answer that suggest this. Why would they write about something they have no interest in?

In short, test writers are usually pretty middle of the road, so avoid answers that aren't. The one place where this rule may not apply all the time is with fiction passages, in which characters may feel extremes of emotion. But with pretty much any other kind of passage, extremes are unlikely to be the right answer.

Notes on Special Question Types
Vocabulary in Context (VIC)

The key word to note in these questions is *context*. We don't care about other meanings of this word—we want to know how it is used here. Treat these like sentence completions: Use the context of the sentence to come up with the meaning of the word, then go to the answer choices. To avoid trap answers, watch out for other meanings of a word. For example, the first thing you may think of when you see the word *tangent* may be the trigonometric function. However, *tangent* can also mean "irrelevant," "touching but not intersecting," or "a sudden digression." So if *tangent* is the subject of a VIC question, you can count on one or more of the alternate definitions to be present in the answer choices. Never answer these questions without going back to the passage and determining the use of the word in question in the context of the passage.

EXCEPT/NOT

These questions are so easy to get wrong because the correct answer is the thing that **doesn't** work or **doesn't** answer the question or that **isn't** mentioned in the passage. This is a counterintuitive kind of task, and many test takers get these questions wrong because they grab the first thing that does work.

Play it smart: Be sure to consider every answer choice and label each as T/F or Y/N or present/not present or whatever you need depending on what the questions is asking. Only after you have labeled every answer should you choose an answer, specifically the one that isn't like the others (see, Sesame Street is useful in the real world!). Doing so will keep you from jumping on the wrong answer prematurely.

Roman Numeral (I/II/III)

Questions in the I/II/III format are time-consuming, so they are best left for last or skipped altogether if you are running out of time. If you decide to do them, work efficiently using POE. If you determine that statement I is not true, eliminate any answer that includes I. Do the same for the other statements until you are left with only one answer.

ANALYTICAL REASONING (LOGIC GAMES)

Analytical reasoning questions appear on the LSAT. The folks who write the test call these "Analytical Reasoning" questions, but really they are just puzzles, so we call them "Games." You are presented with the basic format and structure of the game in the setup, an initial paragraph that also provides the elements; you will be asked to determine the relationships between these elements. Following the setup will be a number of conditions, or clues, which put restrictions on how the elements can be manipulated and sometimes give you valuable information about the overall structure of the game as well. Finally, you will have a number of questions, each of which may introduce new restrictions or even occasionally change one of the original clues. Each question is independent of the others, although work completed for one question may help in eliminating answer choices on another question.

Games test how well you can organize information, understand spatial relationships, and make deductions from those relationships when presented with limitations on the arrangements allowed by the rules. They also reward you for being able to extract this information efficiently.

Games: General Strategies

Following is a list of general strategies that you should use when you are working the games section. Make sure you take these strategies to heart.

Slow and steady wins the race.

More than any other type of question on the LSAT, games questions require a methodical approach. Trying to rush through the section to make sure you'll finish every question will not help your score. You will achieve the highest level of accuracy by using an approach that increases efficiency—not necessarily pace—without sacrificing your ability to be effective. If you find you can't finish a games section in the allotted time, don't fret—very few test takers can. Through consistent practice, you will be able to move more quickly through the section without having to work so fast that you start to make careless errors.

Survey the field.

Remember, every correct answer on the LSAT is worth an equal amount. Since time is of the essence on games, spend your time on easier questions. Remember, the LSAT games and the questions attached to them are not arranged in order of difficulty. Therefore, you should always try to estimate the difficulty of a game before you work it; if it looks difficult, move on. We'll spend time later outlining what characteristics make a game more or less attractive.

Just do something.

Keep working, keep moving forward, and don't ever just stare at a game in search of divine inspiration. The only way to deal with a difficult game is to work through it, not think through it.

Transfer your answers after each game.

As soon as you've finished working on all the questions on a particular game, transfer those answers to your answer sheet. This method has a number of advantages: It is the most efficient, it helps prevent careless errors, and it gives your brain a much needed change of task before you dive into the next game. When there are five minutes remaining in the section, fill in answers for all the remaining questions. Then you can go back and work on the remaining questions you have time for, changing the bubbles one at a time as you go.

Take short breaks.

After you've completed each game, take a short break. Not a nap, just ten seconds to take three deep breaths and ready yourself for the next game. Transfer your answers from that game, and then start the next game. You've cleared your mind, and you're ready to push on.

Games: Specific Strategies

The directions for the games section misleadingly state that "it may be useful to draw a rough diagram" when working the section. That's like saying it may be useful to train before running your first marathon.

Make it visual.

Games are a visual exercise. Games test your ability to determine how various elements can be arranged in space. Therefore, words don't help you; images do. Your goal will be to translate all the words that you are given in the setup and the clues, and sometimes in the questions themselves, into visual symbols. Once you've done this, you won't need to (or want to) refer to that confusing verbal mess again.

The LSAT writers are banking on the fact that most test takers will try to organize all this information in their heads in their rush to finish. That's a recipe for disaster. Accuracy is crucial on this section, and the only way to ensure accuracy is to work with the information on the page by translating it and drawing it out.

Be consistent.

There are various ways you can symbolize and diagram the information that is presented to you in a game. We're going to show you what we've found to be the best and most efficient way to diagram and symbolize. Whatever method you choose, be consistent with your symbols and your diagram. When the pressure is on, you don't want to misinterpret a symbol you've drawn.

Be careful.

You should be confident and aggressive on games, but there is a fine line between aggressiveness and carelessness; don't put yourself on the wrong side of it. This is the only section of the LSAT in which you can be sure an answer is right. Do the work required to take advantage of that.

Be flexible.

The four games that you will see on the real LSAT may look slightly different from the games you have practiced on. Once you understand how games work and can recognize the basic structures the test writers use to build them, you can see how consistent they really are. Just stay calm and take a step back to evaluate the information. The details will change, but the basic ingredients won't. Focus on the big picture. Focus on the similarities to other games you've already done. And get to work.

Games: A Step-by-Step Process

You will follow this process for every game that you do. Learn these steps, practice them rigorously, apply them consistently, and you'll improve your score. Sound good? Then let's get to it!

Step 1: Diagram and inventory.

Your first step will be to determine the appropriate diagram for the game by evaluating both the setup and the clues. You will be given enough information to understand the basic structure of the game. Your diagram is the fixed gameboard onto which you will place the game pieces—your elements. You will want to make an inventory of the elements next to the diagram, so that you'll have everything in one place and will be able to keep track of it easily. Don't rush through this step, because this is the core of your process. People often want to start scribbling a diagram as soon as something pops out at them from the setup. Take the time to evaluate both the setup and the clues, and you'll be well equipped for the rest of the process.

Step 2: Symbolize and double-check the clues.

After you've drawn your diagram, symbolize the clues listed below the setup. Once again, we'll convert the written clues into visual symbols. The clues should be symbolized in a way that is consistent with the diagram you have set up. The goal is to transform the clues into pieces that will fit into your diagram visually. Remember the three C's: Keep your symbols clear, concise, and consistent.

Never forget how important it is to symbolize everything correctly. Invest the few seconds it will take to be sure that your symbols match the information given in the clues. Be sure to go back over the information presented in the setup as well because some games may have longer, more complicated setups than others. A foolproof way to accomplish this is to work against the grain: Articulate what each of your symbols means and then carry that back up to the clues you were given. When you find a match, check off that clue. Once you're sure everything is all accounted for, you're finished. It's that simple.

Step 3: Look for links and size up the game.

Now that you're sure you've got everything properly symbolized, it's time to make sure that you've made any deductions that you can from the information that was given. Look for overlap between the clues and the diagram and among the clues that share elements, and see if there's anything else that you know for sure. It isn't enough to suspect that something has to be true; a deduction is something you're certain of. Does putting two clues together give you a third piece of definite information? Add your deductions to the information you already have. You'll notice that many deductions give you concrete limitations about where elements are restricted—where they can't go—rather than where they must go. While you're looking for these deductions, you'll find that you're also learning how the game is going to work. Keep your eyes open for anything that seems as if it will have a particularly large impact on the outcome of the game. The most restricted places and the most restrictive clues tend to have the most impact when you start working the questions. The more you know about how the game will work, the more efficient you'll be at working through the questions.

Step 4: Assess the question.

Not all games questions are on the same level of difficulty. We'll show you which types of questions to attack first and why. As a rule, you should always look for specific questions that further limit the initial conditions of the game and provide you with more information. Once you've done these specific questions, you'll be better able to work general or complex questions on a second pass through the game. You should also make a point of either circling or underlining what each question asks you for. This will help you to determine the best approach to the question and the type of answer you'll need.

Step 5: Act.

Each question task requires its own strategy. Making sure that you use the proper strategy means saving time on a given question without sacrificing accuracy. Plus, by approaching the questions in an efficient order, you'll find that the work you've done on earlier questions will often help you to find the right answer on a later question.

Step 6: Use process of elimination.

Different questions require POE to different degrees. Sometimes you'll be able to go straight to the right answer from your deductions, but often you'll need to work questions by finding the four wrong answers. As a last resort, you may need to test answer choices one at a time to find the right one.

GRAMMAR

Fill in the Blank and Cloze Passages

Cloze passages are reading passages which contain systematically deleted words. They are frequently used to test foreign language learning, grammar, and vocabulary. It is always important, though, to know exactly what is being tested when facing a Cloze passage. Sometimes the passage is testing your knowledge of grammar at the sentence level, so the focus is usually on verb forms, idioms, pronoun case, and other smaller-scale issues. Some parts of the passage, though, may be testing discourse level concepts, such as the logical flow of ideas, pronouns, vocabulary, and chronology of events. Knowing what is being tested can help you focus your attention on the right parts of the passage.

1. Read the entire passage first to get a sense of what is going on. While doing this, pay attention to how the paragraphs relate to one another.

2. Focus on one particular type of item, such as verbs, first. This can keep you from getting confused or missing important pieces of information.

3. Before putting down an answer, always know what is needed. Do you need a pronoun, a verb, a transitional phrase? Use the context surrounding the blank to figure this out.

4. Be sure to read the whole passage through when you have finished. Does the completed text make sense as a whole?

Improving Sentences

Improving Sentences questions appear on the SAT, PSAT, and GMAT tests. These questions give you a sentence, part or all of which is underlined. The underlined part may or may not contain a grammatical error. Here is a sample:

1. Rescuers managed to pull out a 15-year-old <u>from the backseat, whose legs were injured,</u> while emergency workers extracted the driver and front passenger.

   (A) from the backseat, whose legs were injured,
   (B) whose legs were injured from the backseat,
   (C) the legs of whom were injured, from the backseat
   (D) from the backseat, the legs of which were injured
   (E) from the backseat, his legs were injured

There are some important things you need to know about improving sentences questions:

- Answer choice (A) is a reprint of the underlined section. Therefore, if you decide that the sentence contains no error, choose answer choice (A).

- Approximately 20 percent of all improving sentences questions are correct as written, so don't be afraid to pick choice (A).

- If you decide the underlined portion of the sentence contains an error, eliminate choice (A). Also, eliminate any other choice that contains that same error.

- If you are unsure whether the sentence contains an error, look to your answer choices for a clue as to what may be the issue.

- KISS: Keep It Short and Sweet. Concise answers are nearly always preferable to wordier ones.

Error IDs

Error ID questions (officially called "Identifying Sentence Errors") are unique to the SAT and PSAT. They consist of a sentence in which four words or phrases are underlined and labeled A through D. Answer E always indicates that there is "No Error." Here is a sample:

2. Taylor's <u>shoes, swathed</u> in a stylish coating of mauve
        A

    suede and olive patent leather, <u>is</u> the <u>envy of</u> all
                                      B   C

    fashion-forward <u>students in</u> the senior class. <u>No error</u>
                         D   E

Some important thing to know about this question type:

- There is never more than one error per sentence.

- If there is an error, it's always underlined.

- Approximately 20 percent of all error ID questions are correct written, so don't be afraid to pick choice (E).

- Error IDs are short, and you should usually be able to eliminate least one answer choice, so guess on all error ID questions.

In theory, both Improving Sentences and Error ID questions only test a finite list of grammatical concepts, so if you know and can recognize when those rules are broken, you'll probably do well on these. However, it still pays to be on the lookout for the traps that the test maker lays out for you. Error ID distracters are a little different from other distracters in that there is only one distracter answer: (E) No error. ETS loves to put examples of common, everyday speech that is grammatically wrong into questions. Because they sound so natural, certain errors are just hard to see, so here are a few ways to help unearth them.

Trim the fat.

Often an Error ID will contain extraneous phrases that distract from the meat of the sentence and cause you to miss an error. The sample question above is a great example of this concept. Note how far apart the question writer has placed the subject of the sentence—*Taylor's shoes*—from the verb—*is*. Wait, "Taylor's shoes... is?" That's not right! Of course—this is the error; the verb should be *are*, not *is*. But notice how much harder it is to see that error with that enormous phrase *"swathed in a stylish coating of mauve suede and olive patent leather"* stuck between the crucial elements.

How can you avoid getting waylaid by distracting phrases? Trim the fat. As you work through a sentence, cross off anything that is not essential to the sentence: prepositional phrases, phrases offset by commas, etc. Crossing out the distracting phrases puts the important parts of a sentence, such as the subject and verb, together and prevents you from missing these errors.

Don't trust your ear.

Certain types of errors are fertile ground for trap answers. These errors are so common in everyday speech that we have grown accustomed to hearing them and simply don't recognize them as errors when we see them on a test.

3. Any student <u>who</u> wants to be on the student
            A

    newspaper staff should <u>come to</u> the meeting at 4
                    B

    o'clock and bring an example <u>of their writing</u> for the
                                   C

    editorial team <u>to review</u>. <u>No error</u>.
                  D   E

The sentence above is one that wouldn't raise any eyebrows if it were announced over the address system at any school in the nation, but lurking inside is a pronoun error: *any student* is singular, but *their* is plural. It sounds natural, but using *their* in this context is just plain wrong on a standardized test.

The first example about rescuing a 15-year-old has the same problem. Though common sense tells you that it is the 15-year-old whose legs were injured, the actual syntax of the question says it is the *backseat* of the car whose legs are injured. Here it doesn't matter that you understand what the sentence is getting at—it's just not what it says.

Expect the obscure.

These are some obscure rules out there that you may not even know but you can be darned sure will be tested here.

5. Rachel Ray's nearly ubiquitous presence in magazines, on television, and on the Internet has made her the target of a rather vicious critical backlash.

    (A) Rachel Ray's nearly ubiquitous presence in magazines, on television, and on the Internet has made her the target of a rather vicious critical backlash.

    (B) Rachel Ray's nearly ubiquitous presence in magazines, on television, and on the Internet have made her the target of a rather vicious critical backlash.

    (C) Rachel Ray's presence, nearly ubiquitous, in magazines, on television, and also on the Internet making her the target of a rather vicious critical backlash.

    (D) Rachel Ray has become the target of a strong and rather vicious critical backlash because of her nearly ubiquitous presence in magazines, on television, and on the Internet.

    (E) Rachel Ray's nearly ubiquitous presence in magazines, on television, and on the Internet, she has become the target of a rather vicious critical backlash.

You may think this sentence is correct (you even trimmed the fat to be sure!), but if you thought the answer was (A), you'd get it wrong. A pronoun by definition takes the place of a noun. In this sentence, it seems that *her* refers to Rachel Ray, but "Rachel Ray" does not appear in this sentence as a noun. Instead, *Rachel Ray's* appears in this sentence. Unfortunately for you, *Rachel Ray's* is acting as an adjective here, not a noun, so *her* is actually incorrect. Only answer (D) avoids this error and avoids introducing others.

There are many other tricks to these questions which we won't go into, but you get the idea. It's not just about knowing the rules being tested, but it's also about applying those rules systematically and avoiding the traps that the test writers leave for you.

OPEN-ENDED QUESTIONS

Free Response

Tests such as the AP and the PRAXIS series, and probably many tests you take in at school or college, contains free-response questions. In math and the sciences, this entails showing all the steps of your solution to a problem, and sometimes justifying your solution by citing the specific rules or principles that underlie it.

When answering free-response questions:

- Read the questions carefully before beginning. If you are given a choice as to which you answer, start with the one(s) you feel most prepared to answer.

- Be sure to answer all parts of the question. If the parts of the question have labels such as Part I or Part A, label your responses using the same headings.

- Include all steps to your solution—don't leave anything out.

- Present your solution in a neat and organized manner so that it is easy for the grader to follow. If you make a mistake, cross it out instead of erasing it.

- Write in complete sentences where applicable.

- If there is a scoring rubric or set of guidelines, read it carefully so you have a better idea how your score is to be calculated.

Essay

Writing essays for standardized tests has one thing going for it: If nothing else, standardized essays are predictable, and there is a lot you can do to improve your score by understanding what you are supposed to do (and actually doing it). However, many of the tips below will work well for nearly any essay you may write, since in the end, "good" writing has certain characteristics in nearly any context.

Answer the question posed, and address all parts of the question. This seems like a no-brainer, but it is worth stating loud and clear. Each standardized essay test has its own format and requirements. Write the proper essay for the proper test, and don't leave anything out. ETS doesn't care what kind of essay your 4th period English Composition teacher gave you an A on last week. ACT could give a hoot about the story you wrote for your local newspaper that won accolades or even the SAT essay you wrote last weekend. AP graders will not look kindly on your essay if you ignore half of the task at hand, even if the part you *did* do is spectacular. Follow the directions and give the test makers what they ask for (and no one will get hurt!).

Think, *then* write. Clear, logical organization requires planning—the perfect essay is not going to come flowing out of your head like water from a crystal clear mountain stream. Take some time to brainstorm ideas and plan out your essay. This will keep you from writing yourself into a corner, or ending up somewhere you didn't intend to.

There is one more reason why thinking before writing is important. Simply put, your first, knee-jerk reaction to the essay topic may not be the best one for you to write on. Remember: Your goal is to have an opinion, yes, and to back it up with specific, relevant examples. Your gut reaction, though, may be based less on logic and more on emotion or belief. Therefore, it pays to take a moment to contemplate both sides of the argument before coming down on one side or the other—which will you be able to support better with concrete, specific examples?

Clear, logical organization is always important. Always. A good essay knows where it starts, where it is going, and how to get there. There are no random jumps from idea to idea. Each idea follows logically from the one before it and leads clearly to the next. The reader never has to ask, "Why is this writer talking about armadillos all of a sudden?" or "The entire essay railed against censorship, so why is the conclusion talking about the benefits of censorship?" Therefore, sketching out an outline of your essay from beginning to end is crucial, so always make time for it. Once you have created an outline, stick to it. Changing gears in the middle of your essay is a recipe for confusion.

Use transition words to show the grader where you are going. When continuing an idea, use words such as "furthermore," "also," and "in addition." When changing the flow of thought, use words such as "however" and "yet." Transition words make your essay easier to understand by clarifying your intentions. Better yet, they indicate to the graders that you know how to make a coherent, persuasive argument.

Use structural indicators to organize your paragraphs. Another way to clarify your intentions is to organize your essay around structural indicators. For example, if you are making a number of related points, number them ("First…Second…And last…"). If you are writing a compare/contrast essay, use the indicators "on the one hand" and "on the other hand."

Define your terms, summarize books, and describe historical and current events that you use for evidence. Don't assume that the person grading your essay has read *Catcher in the Rye*, or knows what happened during the XYZ affair, or even what happened in the news this week. In fact, assume the examples you provide are totally new to the reader. Provide just enough detail so that this person understands why the example illustrates your point but avoid getting caught up in too many details that you don't need.

What "you think" is not evidence—what you think *requires* evidence to back it up. Many students make the mistake of believing that their opinions are all the evidence they need to support their point of view. While many of us are taught in this era of political correctness that "all viewpoints are valid," this is simply irrelevant when it comes to writing essays. No matter what you call it—your point of view, world view, viewpoint, opinion, or personal belief—it's just not evidence in the world of standardized essay writing. Concrete, specific evidence from literature, history, current events, or your personal experience is essential to supporting your opinion or beliefs.

Specific, apt examples are a must, but you still need to do more. Unfortunately, providing specific examples is not enough to get a top score. The writers of top essays also knows how to *develop their examples*, which is test-maker secret code for "clearly explaining why the evidence supports the thesis."

First, describe your evidence in enough detail so that the reader isn't forced to fill in gaps on her own, but not get so caught up in the telling of the story that you provide too many details that aren't important (College Board calls this "lack of focus"). Second, clearly explain WHAT the example means and WHY it proves your point. It is this last part—the "why this example supports my thesis" part—that many students leave out, only to wonder later why they didn't get the top score.

Facts are nice, but facts plus analysis is better. Similarly, when writing a content-heavy essay, such as an AP History essay, it is not enough to provide a laundry list of facts and nothing else. You need to provide analysis of the facts and explain why they support your thesis.

Keep sentences as simple as possible. Don't worry about trying to sound fancy or smart. Long sentences get convoluted very quickly and will give your graders a headache, putting them in a bad mood.

Throw in a few big words. But don't overdo it, because it will look like you are showing off. Remember that good writing does not have to be complicated; some great ideas can be stated simply. NEVER use a word if you are unsure of its meaning or proper usage. A malapropism might give your graders a good laugh, but it will not earn you any points, and it will probably cost you.

Write clearly and neatly. As long as we are discussing your graders' moods, here is an easy way to put them in good ones. Graders look at a lot of chicken scratch; it strains their eyes and makes them grumpy. Neatly written essays make them happy. When you cross out, do it neatly. If you are making any major edits—if you want to insert a paragraph in the middle of your essay, for example—make sure you indicate these changes clearly.

Longer essays are better than shorter essays (usually). The connection between score and essay length is a complicated one. On the one hand, it makes sense that in order to fully address an issue and be as thorough as possible, you need to write enough words to express all you have to day. A too-short essay may be faulted because it simply needs more—more detail, more analysis, more description, more argumentation—to effectively and thoroughly address the task. However, disjointedly rambling on and repeating the same ideas over and over for two pages will not earn you a top score. Similarly, a very gifted writer may be able to present a complete, coherent argument in a very concise manner. Test makers address the issue of length when they train essay graders, explicitly instructing readers not to reward or penalize an essay solely on the basis of length. In short, writing more shouldn't always lead to a higher score, since in the end, the quality of the writing matters more.

That's the theory at any rate. In reality, studies have shown that on standardized essay tests such as the SAT, longer essays tend to receive higher scores. Dr. Les Perelman, a professor at MIT who runs the undergraduate writing program there, analyzed the sample SAT essays published by the College Board and discovered a very strong correlation between length and score. In essence, he concluded that longer essays received higher scores. The College Board actually admitted that longer essays tended to get higher scores, but claims the correlation is not as strong as Dr. Perelman contends and that his study was not based on a representative sample of essays. Regardless of the degree to which Dr. Perelman's conclusions are true, play it safe: When faced with the decision to write more or finish early and stare out the window for the remaining time, write more.

Understand Essay Scoring Guidelines

Standardized essays for the most part are scored "holistically." What this means is that the reader goes through your essay and gets an overall impression. That impression is translated into a single number, whether that be a zero to 9 for AP or 1 to 6 for SAT and ACT, which is your essay's score. There is no checklist of points, such as two points for style, two points for grammar, one point for vocabulary, and one point for writing a through conclusion. Nothing like that.

What does a top-scoring essay need to have? If you don't know, imagine how hard it will be for you to write one! The scoring guidelines for any standardized essay are a good place to start when preparing for a specific test, since they can tell you what criteria the graders will be looking for in general. From a quick glance at the ACT scoring guidelines, for example, it is easy to see that you need to have a thesis, address possible counterarguments to your thesis, maintain focus on the issue at hand, logically organize your ideas, and express your ideas in clear, correct English.

Understanding the scoring guidelines *really* happens, though, when you pair the guidelines themselves with concrete examples and grader comments, which are available from the test makers for most of the major tests that include essays. If you don't review these examples and comments, you will just have the list of abstract descriptions from the guidelines that is very hard to translate into an actual essay.

General Analysis/Argument Essays

Tests such as the SAT, ACT, GRE, and GMAT include general essay tasks that provide a topic and ask you to argue for one side or the other. There is no wrong answer to these questions, only badly organized, badly supported responses. Nearly every grading rubric for general essay-writing tasks include the following criteria:

- **Organization**: How well is the essay organized? How logically are the ideas within the essay presented?

- **Argumentation**: How clear is the writer's point of view presented? How well does the writer support his or her ideas with support or examples? If the task is to analyze an argument, how well does the writer recognize the parts of and explain flaws in the argument presented?

- **Language**: How well does the writer adhere to the rules of standard written English and generally use the language? Is sentence structure apt and varied, and is vocabulary broad and well chosen?

Typically, essays that receive top-half scores do so because they fulfill most or all of the requirements of the task. On the other hand, essays that receive bottom-half scores do so because they are lacking one or more crucial elements of the task.

Variation exists, of course. The ACT, for example, adds at least one criterion to this list. Part of the ACT essay task is to "address the complexity of the issue at hand," which basically means that you address both sides of the issue.

So for example, let's say you sit for the ACT and get a prompt that asks you whether students should be allowed to have cell phones at school. You need to come down clearly on one side or the other, but spend at least a paragraph on what someone on the other side of the issue believes.

Content-Specific Essays

AP essays and those you write for school or college courses are places where content knowledge, not just organization and expression, is important. The nice thing about AP exams is that the essay questions, grading guidelines, and sample essays are available for you to study from. The purpose of studying examples from previous exams is not that these exact questions will appear again, but rather so that you can better internalize the scoring guidelines and get a much better sense of what a top-scoring essay must have.

If you are in the market for AP study materials, the College Board website is the place to start. However, you need to log in as an "Educator" rather than as a "Student" to get your hands on the really useful stuff. The student AP area does provide the free-response and essay questions from previous exams, but only the Educators area also provides the scoring guidelines, examples of student responses, and comments to those responses.

The Educators' area of the College Board website that deals with AP—called "AP Central"—will ask you to create an account. Don't be afraid to do this. You don't have to prove you are a teacher or professor—just follow the directions and create an account, which will then allow you into AP Central. Once there, click on "The Exams" on the left-hand navigation page, then "Exam Questions." This will take you to a page that links to materials for every AP exam offered.

Whenever you are asked to write essays for a class in school or college, be sure you understand what your instructor is expecting from you and how your essay will be scored. The more organized instructors will have a rubric or guidelines that they can hand out and discuss with the class, but many instructors (particularly at the college level) are not quite that on the ball. Not that these latter instructors don't necessarily have a grading system—they simply may not think to write it down or share it with the class, making essay writing for you seem more like an exercise in mind reading than anything else. Many college instructors just assume that their idea of a well-written essay is known to everyone, and they don't need to teach you what to do.

Don't wait for a bad grade to find out that your instructor's idea of a good essay is not shared by you. Be proactive about asking your instructors for explicit descriptions of their grading guidelines or even for some examples of very good papers if they have any. If you get a grade you don't understand, reach out to your instructor for specific, constructive feedback so that you can do better next time. Many college instructors won't provide this kind of feedback on their own—you need to ask for it.

Analysis of an Argument Essays

On tests such as the LSAT, GMAT, and GRE, you are also required to write an essay in which you comment on the strength of an argument you are presented with. You don't need specialized knowledge to write this kind of essay, but you *do* need to understand the basic structure of argumentative writing so that you can analyze it effectively.

Argument prompts always contain flawed reasoning. Topics vary greatly, but there is always a clear conclusion made to an argument that is supported by premises, with some flaw in the logic of the argument, and responses must focus on a discussion of those flaws.

It is important that the writer present an opinion only on the structure of the argument, not on the issue. The task is to decide if the argument is persuasive and well reasoned; whether the writer agrees or disagrees with the argument's conclusion is NOT relevant.

Here are the typical pieces of this kind of essay:

1. **Identify the conclusion and premises of the argument**. You shouldn't need to refer to the prompt to get the gist of the argument. In your essay, you should paraphrase and correctly identify the components of the argument, including the conclusion, the premises (or proof) that is offered in support of that conclusion, and any assumptions that the argument makes.

2. **Identify and discuss flaws in the reasoning**. Flaws are descriptions of what's wrong with an argument's reasoning. Argument prompts contain at least two major flaws and frequently have other minor flaws. The flaws frequently involve:

- Unwarranted leaps from the specific to the general or from the general to the specific.

- Questionable comparisons.

- Use of samples that may not be representative

- Faulty interpretation of percentages, averages, or other statistics.

- Confusion of correlation with causality.

- Failure to consider alternative causes or factors.

Flaws are closely related to assumptions. Assumptions are unstated premises; assumptions are what is necessary to link the premises to the conclusion and make the reasoning valid. In addition to pointing out an argument's flaws, test takers should discuss the nature of these flaws and explain why the assumptions are problematic.

3. **Evaluate soundness**. Strong essays go a step beyond discussion of flaws and consider how additional information would affect the conclusion and/or how the argument could be made more sound. They should explain what additional evidence would be needed to evaluate the truth of the assumptions or suggest how additional evidence would strengthen or weaken the argument. The best essays usually offer a prescription for how to make reasoning more sound.

BY METHOD

Bubble-In Answer Sheets

The bubble-in answer sheet is so iconic it's hard to imagine academic life without it. It may seem that the answer sheet has no big role in test taking, but even this seemingly benign piece of paper has a few tricks to using it well. The biggest mistake anyone can make is to misbubble, or put your (possibly correct) answer in the wrong space. If you don't notice you have done this, you could muck up an entire section of a test if not the whole thing. This is a particular danger if you skip around or just skip a question rather then doing all questions in order from first to last.

To keep yourself from misbubbling, don't bubble in your answer after every question. Instead, **bubble by page**. In other words, do all the questions you can on one page, *then* take a moment and carefully bubble in those you answered. When you get near the end of the test or section, though, switch back to bubbling questions as you solve each question. The last thing you want is to run out of time to bubble, leaving questions you solved correctly blank!

Why #2 Pencils?

Modern pencils are made of graphite and clay (there is no lead in a pencil "lead") and graded according to their hardness (H) and blackness (B). The most common pencil is the #2, also known as the HB. This pencil is the best mix of darkness (so the machines can read your answer) and erasability. Nearly all standardized tests require an old-fashioned #2 rather than a mechanical pencil, not because their leads are different (they aren't) but out of concerns that cheaters will stick cheat-sheets into the barrel of a mechanical.

Hand-Written Exams

Hand-written exams seem archaic in the age of laptops and computerized everything, but they will likely remain a fairly big part of school exams as well as parts of some standardized tests. While we've covered the specifics of how to improve your performance on essay or other open-ended/free-response questions, here are a few more tips to keep in mind about any hand-written test:

- **Think, then write**. Having a rough plan of what you are going to say and how you are going to craft it is important—organization and logical flow is usually a crucial component to doing well on many written tests.

- **Get your pencil moving and keep it moving**. Staring at the blank page, "deer-in-headlights" style, for too long, though, is not going to help you. Give yourself a time limit for thinking, then get to writing. If you write yourself into a corner or are unsure how to proceed, don't panic. Leave some room on the page for what it missing, then go on to the next thing. You can always come back if you manage your time well.

- **Neatness counts (sort of).** If your teacher is a stickler for neatness and even includes neatness as part of the grading rubric, then of course you should be as neat as you can. But even when taking tests on which neatness is not a formal criterion you should remember that any grader will prefer to read a neat, easy-to-decipher test than a messy, nearly indecipherable test. If your writing is such a mess that the grader literally can't understand what you've said, then all your brilliant thoughts will be wasted.

- **Edit and proofread as well as you can**, but perfection is probably not attainable. When taking a hand-written test under timed conditions, there are limits as to how perfect your work product can be. Hopefully the person grading your test will take that into consideration, but don't push your luck. Leave some time to edit and proofread, even if it's only a little bit.

Computer Based

Computer-based tests (CBTs) are the wave of the future but are here today. For anyone who likes to write all over their test booklets, switching to a CBT can be a very jarring experience; you may feel that you simply can't do as well because all the behaviors you rely on to take paper tests are not available to you. Fear not! Taking CBT's simply involves adapting some habits you already have and learning a few new ones.

- **If you aren't comfortable testing online, get used to it**. Practice reading tests and articles online and making notes on scratch paper. You can do this every day!

- **Make sure you practice CBT's on a computer whenever possible**. Medium matters: If all you do is practice on paper, then go in and take the test on computer for real, your performance will likely suffer somewhat, since habits and practices you rely on to help on paper tests aren't available to you on the computer.

- **Use scratch paper during the test whenever possible**. If you are given it, use it, particular for multiple-choice tests and anything that requires calculation. If you are given a limited amount of scratch paper, be judicious with how you use it. Conserve space whenever possible.

- **On multiple-choice CBTs, write down answer choices** (A, B, C, etc.) on your scratch paper—as many as you need—and cross out each answer as you eliminate it. Do this even if the questions on your screen aren't labeled with letters. Number the answer sets as well so if you have to skip a question and come back, you will have notes that tell you what, if anything, you have already eliminated on that question. Do this during the pre-test tutorial, if you are given one; this helps you save time once the test starts and you are on the clock.

- **Make sure you know whether skipping questions is allowed or not.** If there is no skipping, you need to be aggressive about eliminating what you can and guessing from the remaining choices. If there is no penalty for wrong answers, then don't leave any question undone. If you are taking a computer adaptive test (CAT), you usually are not allowed to skip questions—you must answer and move on.

- **Use any features built into the system.** Some CBTs allow you to tag questions so you can come back to them, to cross out some answers but then skip the question, or to highlight reading passages. If so, use these features. They are there for a reason and can substitute for many of things you may do on paper tests.

Computer-Adaptive Tests

Computer-adaptive tests, or CAT, are quite different from linear computer-based exams which have more or less the same structure and grading system as paper exams. On CAT exams, a given section begins with a medium-level question. If you get that question right, you get a slightly harder question next. If you get it wrong, you get an easier question next. In this way, the test "adapts" to your performance, and eventually determines your average performance level.

One of the most important things to remember when taking a CAT is that the first one-third of questions on any given section determine your eventual score more than later questions, so it is imperative that you do whatever you can to get those first questions right. Of course, this is not to say that you can afford to miss a bunch of questions at the end of the section, but wrong answers early in a section will simply count against you more.

Open Book

An open-book test is usually taken in class and timed, but you are allowed access to course texts, your notes, and other resources. While this may sound like the best kind of testing ever, think again: Even this test type has its pitfalls.

- **Open book does not mean you don't have any pre-work to do.** When you only have a limited amount of time to write your exam, you will want to have studied enough to be familiar with all your books and resources. That way you will know exactly where to get the information you need. Otherwise, you'll be madly skimming through hundreds or even thousands of pages of material, which you won't have time for. In short, you should study the same amount of time for an open-book test as you would a regular closed-book, "all you have is what is in your brain," test.

- **If anything, an open-book test will demand more from you**: more details, more analysis, and generally a greater command of the material. So what you turn in will be held to a higher standard.

- **Organizing your materials beforehand is crucial,** as is having good class notes that allow you to easily access the information you deemed important enough to write down. If you can write in your books, definitely do so: make notes, underline or otherwise mark important passages. If you can't write in your books, use sticky notes to mark important ages or passages, or just to write your own notes on.

- **Whenever you use direct quotes from other sources, be sure to provide proper attribution.** Direct quotations go in quotation marks. If you choose to paraphrase ideas from another source, that doesn't let you off the hook! You still need to say where the information came from. Writing down someone else's ideas and passing them off as your own is plagiarism, even in an open-book test. Always include the author, source, and page number.

- Lastly, **just because you can directly quote material from other resources doesn't mean that doing so is enough to get a good grade.** An exam that is mostly direct quotes strung together with one or two sentences that are your own is not what your teacher had in mind! A few choice direct quotes (properly attributed to their sources, of course) are fine, and should be used to help support your ideas; just don't over do it. There should be more of your ideas and insight on the page than anyone else's.

Oral

Oral exams are not all that common in high school, except for in language courses, where they are par for the course. Oral exams are more common at the graduate and professional levels, particularly as part of one's candidacy for advanced degrees. These can be some of the most nerve-wracking kind of tests, since they combine your need to actively demonstrate your content knowledge with any presentation anxiety you may feel. But again, this kind of exam can absolutely be prepared for:

- **Practice is crucial** here. Even if you aren't a fan of studying in groups, preparing for an oral exam is the perfect occasion to get together with other students and quiz each other. If you don't have others to help you practice, stand in front of a mirror and practice your responses. Speak out loud, not just in your head.

- **Craft your responses in light of how long the test is.** You want to avoid answers that are much too short or much too long for the time frame of the exam.

- Oral exams are part listening test and part speaking test, so **listen carefully to the questions you are given.**

- **Don't be afraid to ask the examiner to repeat or clarify a question** if need be. If you tend to process written language better than spoken language, you may need to ask your teacher to repeat the question several times or even show it to you in writing.

- **Don't rush to answer** if you need a little time to plan your response. As with any free-response exam question, how you organize your answer can be just as important as how well you demonstrate your content knowledge. Think of the main points you want to express and how you will connect your ideas before you start to speak. Otherwise you may talk yourself in to a corner, lose your train of thought, and never get to your conclusion.

- If this is a formal exam, dress for success. Oral exams can be a lot like job interviews, so it is important to **make a good impression** in general. Be on time, and thank your examiners when the test is over.

SUMMARY

- When it comes to multiple-choice tests, use the format to your advantage. Mine the answer choices for any information that can help you find the correct answer.

- Become familiar with the trap answers common to specific question formats and tests—the more you understand about how test writers try to trap you, the better you will be at avoiding them.

- Use Process of Elimination whenever possible on multiple-choice questions. Doing so puts you in a more critical state of mind, which will make you less likely to jump on trap answers.

- On open-ended questions, always think before you write. How you organize and present your thoughts is just as important as the actual content of your ideas.

- Find a pacing strategy that works for you. Practice finding a perfect balance between accuracy and speed.

6

What to Do (and Not Do) on Test Day

HIGHLIGHTS

- Exam fears
- Postponing or cancelling an exam
- Anxiety solutions
- What you can take with you
- Submitting a complaint
- Cancelling scores

DEALING WITH EXAM FEAR

"Do not turn back when you are just at the goal."

—Publilius Syrus (circa 100 BC)

Part 1: Resisting the Instinct to Run Away

While we don't usually have the luxury in school or college to elect not to take a test, in the world of standardized tests, we often have the option of postponing taking a test if we do not feel ready. Sometimes postponing is the right choice, but often it is not.

For many students, particularly those with high expectations for themselves, anxiety is so great that they consider not taking an admissions test, in spite of weeks or even months spent preparing for it. If you have put all your effort into preparing over the long term, take the exam.

You have prepared long and hard (hopefully with the best material available), you have already spent a few months getting ready for the test, you have paid for a seat reservation for an upcoming test date, and (for most tests) at most could only get a partial refund if you cancel your reservation. Why would you not want to give yourself the opportunity to take the exam, score well, and be done with the test for the rest of your life? No matter how long you put it off, you are never going to feel completely ready; it seems as if there is always one more subject to be studied, one more practice passage to do, etc. And, if something goes badly wrong during the test, you can nearly always void your scores. At the very least, you will have had the experience of actually sitting for the real exam, so that if you do have to take it a second time you will be less anxious.

What If I'm Really Not Ready? (Seriously)

Sometimes you may **not** actually be ready to take the exam. If you bought a book but barely read it, signed up for a course but didn't do all the work, or if you took only a few practice tests are probably not getting the results you could if you put in more effort. And let's be honest: You know if you could have worked more! But contemplate *why* you did not put the effort

into your preparation at this time. In some cases, life circumsta[nces like]
illness or a family emergency interfere with your preparation to su[ch a degree]
that you really couldn't devote yourself to your preparation as you [otherwise]
would have. In other cases, you may have signed up for the test, [without]
understanding how much preparation is involved. Or you may hav[e]
procrastinated and realized too late that the test was upon you.

In any case, you should only put the test off if you can foresee some [future]
time when you really can put in the required effort. Otherwise, you are as [pre-]
pared as you will ever be, and might as well take the test and be done wit[h it.]

But let's say you do everything you could—did *all* the work in that course,
read *all* of those books, did *all* of those practice tests—but do not see significant improvement to reach the score you need. You may just want to take the
test and get it out of the way; if so, go ahead and do so. Or, you may want to
get the test over with, but not unless you can see some improvement. If you
are in this latter group, you still may benefit from sitting for the real exam,
even if you do not score as well as you would like, or even if you intend to
void your scores. As mentioned above, at the very least you will have the experience of seeing a real test. In the best case scenario, your worrying will be
for nothing, and you will score well and be on with the rest of your life! And
if not, you can always take the test again. There is no appreciable stigma to
taking a standardized test twice; many, many test takers do so.

If you have taken a preparation course to get ready for your test, be sure to
read the terms of enrollment and any guarantee policy very carefully. If a
guarantee policy is provided, it often requires satisfactory completion of the
course. If a refund policy exists, the terms of that policy may require not only
satisfactory completion of the course, but also that you take the actual exam
immediately following the program. Definitely contact the test prep company
to find out if these policies are flexible. If you talk to them beforehand, they
are probably more likely to work with you to negotiate a solution that makes
you both happy. They also will appreciate the notice, as well as the opportunity to counsel you in the event that you really *should* be taking the test.

In general, when deciding whether to postpone taking an admissions test, more often than not you should probably go ahead and take it. But make a smart decision regardless of your final choice:

- **Check your application deadlines**. Do you have time to take a later test and still get your completed application in on time?

- **Make a list of the reasons for and against postponing the test**. If you really aren't ready now, do you have the time, resources, and motivation to do it right later? If you really aren't going to be able to do more work than you already have, waiting to take the test probably won't lead to a higher score.

- **Talk to someone, preferably someone with expertise in this area**. If you took a test prep course, absolutely reach out to your instructor. If you have been working on your own, call up a local test prep provider and ask them for advice anyway. The worst they can do is refuse to advise you, but some will probably help you, even if you are not one of their students.

- **If worst comes to worst, you can nearly always take the test and cancel your scores**. Or, if you are taking a test that allows you to only show particular test scores to school you are applying to, you may not need to cancel.

Part 2: Test Anxiety

Guru Says...
Sometimes stress leads you to fixate on the worst that could happen and to make bad choices, so make sure you carefully consider your decision to not take the test.

So you managed to make it to the test—congratulations. Now you are sitting at a desk, pencil at the ready. The test is laid before you. You open to the first page, and...nothing. Your mind is completely blank. You panic. You start to fantasize about how your entire life will collapse in on you. You picture tears and recriminations at the family dinner table ("How will you ever break it to Grandma?"). You may even start reviewing your alternative career options (French fry specialist, homeless person, trophy wife/husband).

You aren't alone—many students suffer from anxiety when in a test-taking situation. A little stress is normal and healthy. But if you have trouble with excessive anxiety interfering with your performance, there are some things you can do. Let's start by learning a bit more about the kind of anxiety you have and how it manifests itself, since these variations affect the kind of solutions that may help you.

Test Anxiety Basics

Anxiety is defined as a physical or psychological response to a perceived danger or threat, with an emphasis on the word "perceived." Anxiety is something that different people experience in different ways. A little anxiety can be a good thing, keeping you sharp and on your toes. But the kind of anxiety that literally impedes your performance is bad. Physiological (physical) symptoms include an upset stomach, restlessness, sweating, sleep problems or insomnia, muscle tension, or headaches. Psychological (cognitive) symptoms may include confusion, irritability, frustration, memory blocks, impaired concentration, or poor judgment.

Causes

Test anxiety has a number of causes. How many of these sound familiar?

1. You worry about how others will view you if you do poorly. You fear disappointing family, or are worried that you won't measure up in comparison to your friends or other students. Your teachers will write you off as not as smart or capable as other students, and maybe start treating you differently.

2. You worry about your own self-image. You tend to assume that doing badly on a test means you are stupid or unworthy. If you are a perfectionist with high expectations, making mistakes is simply unacceptable—you always need to be perfect.

3. You worry about your future and what happens if you don't get the score you need. You fantasize about worst-case scenarios if you fail to reach your goal score. In some cases you may just always be aiming for an A, while in some cases you may actually need a certain score to get a scholarship or admission to the school or program of your dreams.

4. You are just not prepared for a test because you procrastinated when it came to studying, didn't attend class or take good notes, or generally don't have an effective set of study skills.

Test Anxiety Inventory

If you would like to take a real test to understand more about anxiety you may experience and its causes, try the Test Anxiety Inventory (TAI), created by Charles D. Spielberger, a respected expert in test anxiety. In the words of its creator: "The TAI is a self-report psychometric scale, developed to measure individual differences in test anxiety as a situation-specific trait...[R]espondents are asked to report how frequently they experience specific symptoms of anxiety before, during and after examinations. In addition to measuring individual differences in anxiety proneness in test situations, the TAI subscales assess worry and emotionality as major components of test anxiety."

This test costs $9 (this gives you the test and detailed results analysis) and can be taken online at www.mindgarden.com. Since the survey is only 20 questions, it doesn't take long to do. Your results will be e-mailed to you along with some test anxiety management tips.

Solutions

Cognitive restructuring is about controlling the voice in your head that constantly focuses on worst-case-scenario, doomsday thoughts and turning it in to the calm voice of reason. Many test takers defeat themselves by fixating on the negative and convincing themselves that they will do badly. This "bad voice" brings you down, distracting you with negative thoughts: It reminds you of other bad testing experiences; taunts you with threats of exposure to others as "not as smart as you think you are"; tells you that you are a loser if you get a bad grade, and that anything less than perfect is equivalent to failure, or that you are just a loser in general.

> **Words of Wisdom**
> Formulate and stamp indelibly on your mind a mental picture of yourself as succeeding. Hold this picture tenaciously. Never permit it to fade. Do not build up obstacles in your imagination.
> —Norman Vincent Peale (1898–1993), author of *The Power of Positive Thinking*

The solution is not just "thinking positively," but in countering negative thoughts with rationality: "Yes, I didn't do well on that other test, but this is a new opportunity, and I am much more prepared for this one. I don't have to always get an A—I just need to do my best. Worrying is not going to help me do better; it will only distract me from the task at hand, so I need to focus on the test in front of me and not be concerned about what might happen. Besides, I'm good enough, smart enough, and darn it, people like me! (Thank you, Stuart Smalley!)" Successful cognitive restructuring requires repetition and practice, so be sure to use it often. Having a friend or family member help here, providing another rational voice to the one in your head you are trying to cultivate, can be useful as well.

Relaxation techniques: Both the physical and cognitive manifestations of test anxiety can be alleviated with exercises that can help calm your body and mind. You can use just one that works really well for you, or combine them to achieve greater effects. But always keep in mind that you are there to take a test, not to daydream the entire time. Use relaxation techniques before the test and during the test when anxiety is causing you problems (but then get back to the test!). Just spending 30 to 60 seconds relaxing can really help you gain some clarity and control.

Deep Breathing: If you find that you are sweating profusely, your heart is racing, or that you are getting stuck, frustrated, or caught up by negative thoughts, try some simple deep breathing methods. If you can, close your eyes. Inhale through your nose deeply and slowly. Fill your lungs completely. When you can't take in any more air, exhale slowly through your mouth. While you do this, concentrate on the sound of your breath moving in and out, in and out. Do this several times or whenever you feel excess anxiety building up. This is an easy and effective exercise to do throughout the test, and a great way to clear your head between sections or anytime you feel that you are panicking or losing focus.

Progressive Relaxation: Progressive Muscular Relaxation (PMR) is a physical technique for relaxing your body when muscles are tense. PMR involves tensing up a group of muscles so that they are as tightly contracted as possible. Hold them in a state of extreme tension for a few seconds. Then relax the muscles to their previous state. Finally, you consciously relax them again as much as you can. You can apply PMR to any or all of the muscle groups in your body depending on whether you want to relax just a single area or your whole body. Hands, wrists, arms, eyes, necks, and shoulders tend to be focus points for stress in testing situations, so concentrate your relaxation in these places.

Positive Visualization: Replace doomsday visions of failure with something more positive. On the night before your exam (right before you go to sleep is a good time), find a quiet place

Frontline Insights
"As a working adult, I can work 8, 10, even 12 hours a day non-stop. I do this a lot in my current job. When I decided to change careers and take the LSAT, imagine my surprise when, halfway through the test, my shoulders and neck started to ache. After only a few hours, I was aching all over. It was all I could do to finish the test. I never realized how tense I became while taking tests!"
—Carissa T., law student

to relax. Close your eyes and take a few breaths. Then, visualize yourself in the classroom taking the test. See yourself receiving the test, then confidently taking the exam. You are calm, cool, collected, and totally in control. Create this movie in your head, then play it again in the morning, right before you get out of bed. When test time comes you will have already seen yourself confidently taking the test.

During the test, if you are starting to feel anxious, go to your happy place. Visualize yourself in a place that you find relaxing: this could be a tropical paradise, a comfy chair next to fireplace, even a place in your own home in which you can find peace. Try to imagine the place as well as the smells and sounds there—the more complete your image, the better. Breathe.

Desensitization: Taking practice tests do more than just help you build your content knowledge and strengthen your skills. Research has shown that building familiarity with a test with real questions can help desensitize you and reduce the fear that it causes (Szafran 1981). You will know exactly what to expect and how well you can do. You also can look back and say with confidence, "I've done this before; it's not that bad; I can do this."

More effective study skills: Much (though certainly not all) test anxiety comes from a lack of proper preparation. We'll talk elsewhere in this book about ways to improve your study skills, but it is worth contemplating how large a role in your anxiety poor studying plays. The great thing is that study skills are very fixable—the bad thing is that fixing them right before the test won't help. If poor study skills are the source of your anxiety, you'll need some time to implement better practices.

More healthy eating and sleeping habits: When we are busy and stressed, you tend to do gravitate toward personal behaviors that, if anything, exacerbate the situation. The first thing stressed-out, busy people often do is cut back on sleep, which is one of the last things you want to do. Not only does not getting enough sleep make you more susceptible to illness, it can make the symptoms of test anxiety worse. Studies have shown that pulling all-nighters and cramming at the last minute don't help you do better on tests, and in some cases actually make your scores go down.

Similarly, when you are busy, you may skip meals and eat not-so-healthy food (Red Bull, by the way, is not a food), which can result in a lack of energy, sugar crashes, and stomach problems. Drugs, alcohol, and excessive amounts of caffeine can interfere with your ability to think clearly. Though it can be challenging, try to find balance in your life and be sure to prioritize the things that keep you alive: good food, water, and sleep. Remember: these are the basics that keep you alive!

Exercise: Regular exercise helps to mitigate stress and keep you healthy. It can also be a great way to just clear your mind and occupy yourself with something besides studying. Yoga in particular has been shown to help alleviate different kinds of anxiety, stress, even depression.

Professional help: Some students experience test anxiety so severe that they simply cannot function at all: they black out, have panic attacks, or can't physically bring themselves to take the test. Test anxiety alone is not a learning disability, but may (emphasis on the "may" part) be a feature of more generalized anxiety disorders. It also is common among students who do have a diagnosed disability. If your anxiety is this bad, definitely seek out a specialist who has experience treating students with testing anxiety.

BEFORE THE TEST

The Week Before

Testing well is more than the result of what you do during the test itself; there are lots of things you can do the week before that can help you do your best.

Quote Me
If you don't like something change it; if you can't change it, change the way you think about it.
—Mary Engelbreit

- **Visit the testing site.** You want to feel comfortable finding the location before the test—the morning of the test is not the time to get lost or find out that the road you were planning to take is closed for construction! Having a sense of how long it takes to get to the site will help you plan test day. If you can even sit in the room where the test will be held, do so; it will feel more familiar on test day.

- **Check for traffic changes.** Since many standardized tests are given on weekends, make sure there are no road closings or traffic changes that only happen on weekends. Your state's Department of Transportation websites usually list traffic changes and the dates they apply.

- **Check out the parking situation if you are driving yourself.** And if you are testing at a school or college, make sure there isn't a special event going on. You may think there is plenty of parking, but if 50,000 football fans are looking for parking when you are, you'll be out of luck fast.

- **Get up early on the weekend before the real test and take a practice test.** You need to train your mind to be alert in the morning and able to think for the full length of the test. Treat the practice test as the real thing.

- **Get into a pattern of doing 30 to 45 minutes' worth of practice problems each day, from now until the test day.** You're probably really busy, but think of it this way: you can make this tiny sacrifice now, or go through the entire process all over again when you don't get the score you want.

- **When you practice at home, do so under timed conditions.** You need to get the feeling of what it will be like on the day of the test. As always, don't do your homework in front of the television or with the radio playing.

The Night Before

The last thing you want to do the night before a test is add to your stress. Last-minute cramming not only will not help you retain much information, but it will also stress you out more and cut into valuable sleep that you need the next day. Give yourself a break—avoid freaking yourself out with a few simple rules:

- **Determine a cut-off time for studying and stick to it.** Pick a time you will stop working, step away from your books, and do something fun. Go out with friends, exercise, watch a funny movie—anything but studying. Exercise and laughter are great ways to minimize stress. If you are of legal age, don't overdo it with drinking alcohol. One is fine—five is very probably a bad idea.

- **Don't mess with your normal routine**. Eat a normal dinner, and go to bed at a normal time.

- **Make a checklist and get your stuff ready for the next day.** 6:45 A.M. is not a good time to try to remember where you stashed your admission ticket, so pack up while you can still think straight. Lay out everything you need to bring to the test with you, even your clothes. Make sure you plan for any and all environments, especially if you are bound for a testing site you have never been to before. Be prepared for anything from refrigerator-like to sauna-like conditions, so dress in layers so you can bundle up or strip down as needed.

- **Have sweet dreams**. When you finally go to bed, try some of the visualization and relaxation exercises described in the test anxiety section on page 187. Also avoid caffeinated beverages after 4 P.M. or so; caffeine stays in the body for hours—you metabolize half the caffeine you ingest in anywhere from three to 10 hours, so it takes a while to work its way through your system. Caffeine not only keeps you from falling asleep, but it also makes you more likely to be restless, wake up, and not sleep as deeply.

- And don't forget to **set your alarm**! Or even two if you have a tendency to oversleep.

The Morning Of

OK, so it's test day. Get up early enough so you have time to take a shower and eat something—the last thing you need is to start the day stressed because you are running late.

- **Eat smart**. Again, don't mess with success: If you aren't in the habit of eating steak and eggs for breakfast, now is not the time to start. However, if your habit is to eat nothing, make sure you eat *something*. Your brain needs food to function! Avoid anything very full of fat or sugar. The fat will make you sluggish, and too much sugar will eventually make you crash halfway through the test, or at least exacerbate your nervousness. If you always start the day with coffee, though, drink coffee. Just don't drink twice as much as usual.

- **Warm up**. Do a little review in the morning to refresh the material to be tested in your mind. If you have some sample questions to practice on or flashcards to work through, do these over breakfast, and take them with you to the test. You can also look at them before the test starts.

- **Shake your groove thing**. Listen to music to help you get pumped up for the test—this is what the personal music player is made for, after all. Music can help keep some of those negative thoughts from taking over, and even help you find focus. Research has shown that upbeat music can actually boost your mood.

- **Check and double-check**. Double check that list you made last night—make sure you have everything you need. Aren't you glad you wrote it when you were awake?

- **All hail the personal talisman**. If you have a lucky charm, bring it along. If your lucky socks/pants/boxer shorts/bra/t-shirt/pencil/wallet-sized picture of Elvis helps you to find calm in the storm, by all means take it/them with you. As long as they don't bother other people, you should be fine. (Those who don't shower for a week before an important test may want to rethink that particular practice—your neighbors will thank you.)

- **Don't be late!** The test doors will close at a given time. If you are late, you will get shut out of the test and in many cases lose your testing fee. Leave yourself 20 minutes more than you think you'll need to get to the test center, especially if you are going to be parking your car. Be sure to arrive at least 20 minutes before the scheduled test time. If you get there a little too early, you can always listen to music, do a few more questions, or do some breathing exercises.

At the Test Center

- **Don't wait for nature to call**. Use the bathroom before the test starts, even if you think you don't need to. Think about the ocean, Niagara Falls, etc. for inspiration.

- **Avoid hanging out with other people who are visibly freaking out about the coming test.** You've worked so hard to be confident, prepared, and positive! The last thing you need is other people infecting you with their stress or their tragic stories.

- **Count breaks as the test**. Remember that you are considered "at the test" even while on breaks, so no funny business. No calls, no talking about the test with others, no checking your notes or review problems. Proctors will have mentioned this at the beginning of the test, and they are serious. Students have been kicked out of many a test for not following the proper directives during breaks! One notable exception: Food and drink are not allowed in the test room, but you can consume these things outside of the testing room.

- **Forget you own a cell phone**. Most grad tests will not let cell phones in the testing room at all. If you are taking the SAT or ACT, TURN OFF your cell phone before you even set foot in the test center and don't touch it again until the test is over and you have left the testing site. If your phone rings at *any* time during the test, the proctor can (and probably will) remove you from the test and cancel your scores.

Into the Testing Room

Major testing programs have fairly strict rules about what you can and cannot have in the test room with you. This information is easily accessible on their websites as well as with the materials they send you when you register to take the test. Here is a sampling of what can and can't be brought into testing rooms from some of the major tests.

Test	What to Bring	What is Prohibited
ACT	Test center admission ticket, acceptable photo ID, sharpened #2 pencils, a watch, a permitted calculator	No food or drink, any writing instrument other than #2 pencils (no mechanical pencils), personal electronic devices other than permitted calculators, tobacco, reading material, resource materials, scratch paper
SAT	Test center admission ticket, acceptable photo ID, sharpened #2 pencils, a permitted calculator, an acceptable CD player and headphones for Subject Tests with Listening. Also suggested: a watch, a bag for your belongings, a snack and drink (for consumption outside the testing rooms during breaks), extra batteries for your calculator	No cell phones or any other personal electronic device, mechanical pencils, colored pencils, pens, scratch paper, notes, dictionaries, compasses, rulers, listening or recording devices (except CD players for language tests), cameras, timers with audible alarms
LSAT	Test center admission ticket, acceptable photo ID bearing your signature, sharpened #2 pencils. All items must be carried into the test room in a clear plastic Ziploc bag (no larger than gallon size), and may also include your wallet, keys, hygiene products, highlighter, erasers, pencil sharpener, tissues, a beverage and snack for consumption during breaks	No mechanical pencils, pens, electronic timers. Also no weapons or firearms, ear plugs, books, backpacks, handbags, papers of any kind, calculators, rulers, listening devices, cellular phones, recording or photographic devices, pagers, beepers, headsets, and/or other electronic devices

GMAT	Valid ID	No beepers, pagers, pens, calculators, watch calculators, books, pamphlets, notes, blank sheets of paper, rulers, stereos or radios, telephones or cellular (mobile) phones, stopwatches, watch alarms (including those with flashing lights or alarm sounds), dictionaries, translators, thesauri, personal data assistants (PDA's), and any other electronic or photographic devices or potential aids of any kind
GRE CBT

TOEFL | Acceptable ID | No personal items other than your ID. Hats, scarves, jackets and outerwear that are taken into the test room are subject to inspection |
| MCAT | Valid and current government-issued ID | No personal items other than your clothes and a watch. If the test proctor permits you to wear a sweater or jacket into the testing room, it may not be removed in the testing room |

Calculators

Most tests that include mathematics allow you to use a calculator (the GRE is a big exception here), but only certain kinds, and it is your responsibility to know which are acceptable and which are prohibited. Generally, the rules across tests that allow calculators are very similar. You CANNOT use:

- Pocket organizers.

- Handheld or laptop computers.

- Electronic writing pads or pen-input devices.

- Calculators built into cell phones or other electronic communication devices.

- Calculators with a typewriter keypad (keys in QWERTY format).

- Calculators that use paper tape (you can use it if you take the paper out).

- Calculators that make noise (you can use it if you can turn off the sound).

- Calculators that communicate wirelessly with other devices (you can use it if you cover the sensor with tape).

- Calculators that require power cords (you can use them if you remove the cord).

- Calculators with built-in computer algebra systems.

The ACT testing program gets even more specific—here are the particular calculators that are prohibited on the ACT:

It's Up To You

It is your responsibility to know which calculators, if any, you are allowed to use on a test, so be sure to check your registration information carefully.

- Texas Instruments: all model numbers that begin with TI-89 and TI-92, and the TI–Nspire CAS—The TI–Nspire (non-CAS) is permitted.

- Hewlett-Packard: hp 48GII and all model numbers that begin with hp 40G, hp 49G, or hp 50G

- Casio: Algebra fx 2.0, ClassPad 300, and all model numbers that begin with CFX-9970G

DURING THE TEST

If you took our advice, you should already know what to expect on the test you are about to take. Still, listen carefully to the directions read out loud by the test proctor. There may be some new information in them that you need to know. Follow all directives to the letter.

- If this is your first time taking a particular test, listen carefully to all directions, and make sure that when you start the test you read the directions carefully. You may know the content cold, but an unknown format can totally throw you and keep you from answering the right question.

- Take a moment at the beginning of the test or of each individual section to flip through it so you know what is coming. How many questions are there? How may different formats? Do questions start easy and get harder? Are there questions later on in the test or section you may want to do first? Many a student has outright "missed" the last page of section because they didn't know how long it was—be smart and take a quick tour before you start writing.

- At the beginning of each section, focus on what you're supposed to do. Before you start scribbling away, take a few seconds to gather your thoughts. What's your game plan? If you have pacing strategy, jot it down. If you know you tend to panic or rush, write down a little message for yourself to keep you centered, even something as banal as "Don't panic."

- Don't get stuck on any one question. Eliminate any answers you can, then guess from the remaining answers and move on. If you have time at the end of the section and want to come back, circle the question so you'll remember it later.

- During your breaks, try to stay relaxed. Walk around to get your blood moving. Eat that snack. Stay away from people who are freaking out and talking about the test.

ASK AND YE SHALL RECEIVE (MAYBE)

When taking paper exams, proctors will sometimes but not always write the start and stop times on the board and provide a warning a few minutes before the end of a section. At the beginning of the test when the proctor asks if you have any questions, raise your hand and request that this be done. The proctor may say no, but she also may say yes. This is important because any clock in the room, the proctor's time piece, and your watch may be out of sync, and you may think you have more time than you actually do. It's also good to keep track of the proctors—it is common for proctors to give too much or little time, so making them write the time on the board is a good way to hold them accountable as well.

If the test seems hard, stay calm. Remember:

- Many tests have content that is ordered by difficulty, meaning the questions start out easier but get harder toward the end. On the other hand, hard questions may appear anywhere. However, on standardized tests, all questions are worth the same amount. Therefore, ace the easier questions before spending too much time on the difficult ones.

- On a number of standardized tests, one section is experimental and will not count toward your final scores. This is always true of SAT and LSAT; ACT occasionally has an experimental section. If you took one of these tests, drop by PrincetonReview.com a few days after the test and we'll tell you which questions didn't count.

- Most tests are scored on a curve. If it's a difficult test, the curve may be more generous, so don't let the perception of the overall difficulty worry or distract you.

HONESTY IS THE BEST POLICY

Part of the testing "pact" requires that students take tests honestly. If a testing organization suspects that a test taker is cheating in any way, it reserves the right to void that person's test. Cheating behaviors that can lead to a test taker being removed from the test or having his test voided include the obvious:

- Copying from other students.
- Using notes or other resources.
- Gaining access to the test beforehand.
- Copying test material and sharing with other testers.
- Taking the test for someone else.
- Discussing or sharing test content with others during breaks or after the test.
- Taking more time than allowed.
- Going back to previous sections or looking forward to upcoming sections.
- Using your cell phone at any time during the test, including breaks.

In general, you always want to be smart when it comes to taking tests: Follow directions carefully, and don't do anything to draw attention to yourself or that could be construed as disruptive or dishonest.

WHEN TESTING GOES BAD

You have a right to a quiet testing environment and a testing experience that conforms to the rules set by the test maker—this is one of the hallmarks of standardized testing. However, things can go wrong on test day, so it pays to know your rights and how you can lodge a complaint if need be.

The Proctor From Hell

While one can hope that a standardized test is run in an efficient, professional manner, proctors sometimes leave a lot to be desired. Depending on the test you are taking, the proctors may be very experienced or brand new. For tests like the SAT, proctors are low-paid, part-time workers. Proctors at web-based testing centers are more likely to be employees of the center and given a bit more training and held to a higher standard.

It doesn't seem like a tough job. Be at the testing site on time. Read and follow the astonishingly detailed and clear directions provided. Tell time correctly. However, as with most things in life, even proctoring a test is sometimes beyond the capabilities of those employed. The lapses of judgment demonstrated by proctors can be downright mind-boggling. Here are just a few of our favorites reported by teachers and students who actually experienced them:

- The proctor who falls asleep, a.k.a. The Classic.
- The proctor who get so caught up reading in her romance novel that she forgets the time, a.k.a. The Romantic.
- The proctor who "wings it" instead of reading the script provided, a.k.a. The Maverick.
- The proctor who does everything right, at least until he cracks open an ice cold beer during the test, a.k.a. The Big Lebowski.
- The proctor who brings to the test her newborn baby, which proceeds to cry the entire time, a.k.a. The Earth Mother.

- The proctor who stalks around the room, muttering, "I know you are cheating. One word from me and you'll never get into college. Ever." a.k.a. The Creeper.

- The proctor who gives students the wrong version of the test, leaves the room to get test booklets that had already been used, and then has the students finish a different test, a.k.a. The Clueless Wonder.

Nice. Good to know where your testing fees are going, isn't it?

Less-Than-Ideal Testing Conditions

Sometimes it's not the proctor who is the problem, but the environment in which you are asking to test. Some of our favorites include:

- The one where the school that turned its heat off on the weekend, leaving students to take their test in hats, coats, and gloves.

- The one where repairmen came into the cafeteria where students were testing and proceeded to fire up a power sander on a door they were fixing.

- The one where the marching band was rehearsing on the lawn right below the testing room windows.

- The one where a student gets sick, passes out, freaks out, or otherwise causes a ruckus.

How to Lodge a Complaint

If anything happens during the test that you feel has negatively affected your performance, or if you think there is an error on the test, complete the test, but then lodge a formal complaint after the test. Certainly if the problem affected more than just you, encourage all other students who were affected to complain as well. Let's face it: A complaint from 15 people at one site probably indicates a real issue, whereas a complaint from one person is easy for the testing organization to write off as just one person's subjective opinion.

The best you can hope for if there is a problem at your testing site is the opportunity to retest for free, or if you do not test again, you may be able to get a refund for your test fees. A testing organization will not add points to your score because of a testing site complaint. The only exception to this is if the testing organization determines that a test question is actually faulty. In those cases, the question is removed from scoring and all students' scores will be recalculated.

How to Report a Problem

Here are some pointers on how to lodge testing complaints or deal with test-day issues for major standardized tests

SAT & SAT Subject Tests

Complaints about testing day issues must be reported to the College Board no later than the Wednesday after the test.

Problem	Detail	Contact
Canceling Scores	Cancellation includes scores on ALL tests you take at an administration unless your equipment malfunctions. Once your request is received, your scores cannot be reinstated.	**Fax:** (610) 290-8978 **Mail:** SAT Program Score Cancellation P.O. Box 6228 Princeton, NJ 08541-6228
Test Center Complaints	If you have a complaint about the test center or testing conditions, send a letter explaining your complaint. Your scores could be delayed while your complaint is being investigated.	**Fax:** (609) 771-7710 **E-mail:** testcenter@info.collegeboard.org **Mail:** SAT Program Test Administration Services P.O. Box 6200 Princeton, NJ 08541-6200
Test Error or Ambiguity	If you believe there is an error or ambiguity in a test question, continue testing. Report the problem to the supervisor later on test day, then e-mail or write to College Board. Include the test section, test question (as well as you can remember it), and an explanation of your concern.	**Fax:** (609) 683-2800 **E-mail:** satquestion@info.collegeboard.org **Mail:** SAT Program Test Development P.O. Box 6656 Princeton, NJ 08541-6656

(Source: SAT Registration Booklet)

ACT

Problem	Detail	Contact
Canceling Scores		
Test Center Complaints	ACT will examine the situation and determine whether action is warranted, including non-scoring of answer documents or cancellation of scores.	Go online and submit the Test Center Complaint Form found at: www.actstudent. org/forms/centerform.html
Test Error or Ambiguity	If you have a concern about a particular test question from a recent test date, please describe the question and your concerns in as much detail as possible.	Go online and submit the Test Question Inquiry Form at : www.actstudent.org/ forms/inquiryform.html

(Source: www.actstudent.org)

GRE CBT

Problem	Detail	Contact
Canceling Scores	At the end of the test, you will be given the option to cancel your scores. This is the only time you can cancel.	
Reinstating Scores	Canceled scores can be reinstated for a fee of $30 if your request is received at ETS within 60 days after your test date. You may fax or mail a written request to the GRE program.	
Test Center Complaints	Report any problems as soon as possible after the test is over. Complaints should be received no later than seven days after your test date. Allow four to six weeks for a response.	**Fax:** (609) 771-7715 **Mail:** CBT Complaints ETS Mail Stop 29-Q Princeton, NJ 08541

Test Question Inquiries	If you think there is an error in a test question that affects your response, tell the test supervisor as soon as you finish the test, or immediately write to the GRE program.	**Mail:** GRE Test Question Inquiries ETS PO Box 6667 Princeton, NJ 08541-6667

(Source: www.ets.org)

GMAT

Problem	Detail	Contact
Canceling Scores	The only opportunity that you will have to cancel your scores is at the test center. Immediately after you complete the test—but before you view your scores—you will have the option to cancel your scores. You cannot cancel your scores after they are displayed or reported to you. If you cancel your scores, your scores cannot be reinstated, and your cancellation will remain a part of your permanent test record and will appear on all future test reports.	
Test Center Complaints	Address your letter to "Attention: GMAT Complaints" and either fax or mail it.	**Mail:** Pearson VUE 5601 Green Valley Drive Suite 220 Bloomington, MN 55437 **Fax:** (952) 681-3681

(Source: www.mba.com)

LSAT

Problem	Detail	Contact
Canceling Scores	LSAC must receive a signed fax or overnight letter with your request within six calendar days of the test. You can also cancel your score at the test center if you are absolutely certain you want to cancel your score.	
Test Center Complaints	Report any problem to the test supervisor. However, informing the supervisor is not sufficient. You must also follow up your complaint by writing or faxing LSAC. Your complaint, which must include your signature, must be received by LSAC within six calendar days after the administration.	**Mail:** LSAC 662 Penn Street Box 2000-T Newtown, PA 18940 **Fax:** (215) 968-1277
Test Question Inquiries	If, while taking the LSAT, you find what you believe to be an error or ambiguity in a test question that affects your response to the question, report it to the test supervisor as soon as you finish the test and write or e-mail LSAC immediately. For more details, check out the LSAC document "Policies and Procedures Governing Challenges to Law School Admissions Test Questions" available on their website: www.lsac.org	**Mail:** Law School Admission Council Test Development 662 Penn Street, Box 40 Newtown, PA 18940-0040 **Email:** LSATTS@LSAC.org

(Source: www.LSAC.org)

MCAT

Problem	Detail	Contact
Canceling Scores	You have the option to void your MCAT exam if you do not wish your test to be scored. This opportunity occurs at the end of the exam. Voiding your scores on test day means that you will not receive scores. Scores cannot be "unvoided" at a later date.	
Test Center Complaints	If, after taking the MCAT exam, you have a concern regarding test-day procedures or the testing room environment, you should inform the Test Center Administrator on the day of testing and submit your concern in writing within five days of the test date.	**Mail:** MCAT Examinee Services Manager Attention: Test Center Complaints Association of American Medical Colleges 2450 N Street, N.W. Washington, D.C. 20037-1127 **Fax:** (202) 828-4799
Test Question Inquiries	If you discover a question you think is flawed or ambiguous, notify the MCAT Program Office. You have the right to a written response from MCAT exam officials. To ensure this response, we must receive your communication—via fax or regular mail—no later than five days following your test date. You may expect a response within four to six weeks from the date we receive your correspondence.	**Mail:** MCAT Examinee Services Manager Attention: Test Question Challenges Association of American Medical Colleges 2450 N Street, N.W. Washington, D.C. 20037-1127 Fax: (202) 828-4799

(<u>Source</u>: *2007 MCAT Essentials*, available from www.aamc.org)

TESTERS' REMORSE: SHOULD I CANCEL MY SCORES?

Paper Tests

If you're afraid that you didn't do well, don't cancel your score at the test center if given the option. If you are allowed to cancel your scores after taking the test, you usually have a few days to cancel, and you don't want to do something you will regret later. It is hard to be objective when it comes to judging your own performance on a test, so keep a few things in mind:

- Many students feel they did badly when they come out of admissions tests—this is pretty normal, but it doesn't necessarily mean much.

- Valid reasons for canceling are fairly limited. If you totally omitted a whole page or whole section of the test, canceling isn't a bad idea. In the words of Princeton Review Master Tutor Lisa Rothstein, most other valid reasons to cancel involve bodily fluids: vomiting, bleeding, or distracting bathroom urges. In other words, something pretty serious occurs that keeps you from taking the test.

- Talk to someone before you cancel. If you prepped with a tutor or class, definitely contact your instructor if you are considering canceling. For high school tests, check out the boards on www.collegeconfidential.com. For grad tests, do a web search to find test-specific blogs and hear how others felt about the test you took.

- If the schools you are applying to have rolling admissions and you took your test in the early fall, will any increase in score you hope to achieve for a later test administration offset the disadvantage you pick up from delaying your application? Be specific: How many points would you need to make this delay worthwhile and do you have a good strategy for achieving this improvement?

- Know how scores will be used by admissions committees. If admissions committees take the highest score from multiple test administrations, there is little need to cancel your score; you can always take it again and do better, leaving your lower scores behind.

This last point—know how scores will be used by admissions committees—is probably the most important determinant as to whether you should cancel your scores or not. Let's say you took the SAT and bombed the reading but did well on other parts of the test. You don't want to "waste" the good scores you got, so keep your scores and take the test again, focusing your studying on the reading. Admissions committees usually take the highest Math, Reading, and Writing scores from different administrations and combine them, so you want to keep the good stuff you did accomplish this time. However, it is very important that you find out the policies at all schools you are going to apply to, since there is some variety out there. As of June 2008, College Board will reinstate score choice for the SAT, which gives you more control over which scores schools see.

The LSAT is more complicated. Your official LSDAS record will show all scores you have on record, as well as an average score if you have tested more than once. Schools will either (1) use the average, or (2) take the highest score. If they use the highest score, it may be just their policy to do so, but there may be other factors that determine whether highest score will be used. Highest score may be used if you took the test more than once and have a big discrepancy (about 8 points or more) between scores. It may also be used if you are able to convincingly explain why a lower score on your report does not reflect your true test-taking ability; you may have been ill, or had a disruption occur during the test, or simply a track record of testing badly. Again, it is absolutely crucial that you find out how the schools to which you are applying handle multiple scores.

LSAT: A GLIMPSE OF THE FUTURE?

In 2006, the American Bar Association began to require that when reporting statistics on their incoming classes, law schools must report the highest LSAT score on record for all matriculated students. While the new rule allows law schools to continue to treat applicants' multiple scores as they see fit, many predict that more law schools will move to using the highest LSAT score rather than an average score when assessing applications.

Lastly, the ACT has score choice, which allows you to choose which scores from multiple sittings you send to schools. Schools won't mix and match scores from different administrations—they will just take the highest performance from a single test date, which gives you little reason to cancel.

Computer-Based Tests

While paper tests give you a few days to decide whether or not to cancel your scores, you do not have this luxury with computer-based tests. At the end of computer-based admissions tests, you are given the option of canceling your scores. Unfortunately, this is the only time you have to do this, so there is no time to think it over or compare notes with others or get sage advice from other test-takers.

However, some of the same principles apply here as they did above with paper tests. First, note whether the programs you are applying to average multiple scores or consider only the highest score. With the GRE, schools tend not to average, which is great for you. If you feel you could do better, accept your scores and take the test again. With TOEFL, GMAT, and MCAT, there is a decent amount of variety: Multiple scores may all be "considered" and attention paid to any improvement you had, the highest score may be used, the most recent may count, scores may be averaged, or the highest section scores from different administrations may be added together. Since there is no single treatment of scores, you need to do some research.

SHOULD I TAKE THE TEST AGAIN?

On average, most students will improve somewhat if they take a test a second time. But that's an *average*, meaning that some students will get the same score while others will actually see their scores drop. If you honestly believe there is more work you could do to bring your score higher, and you have the time and resources to take the test again, then do so. There is no harm in testing a second time—no application committee will hold this against you.

However, if you choose to retest, note any restrictions that may be in place.

For example, here are some limits on retesting for some major admissions tests:

ACT: You can take the ACT as many times as you like. However, if you take it under special conditions, you will need to wait 60 days between testings.

SAT: You can take the SAT and SAT Subject Tests as many times as you like.

SSAT: You may take all administrations of the SSAT if you like. However, if you take the SSAT with an educational consultant rather than at a regular location, you can only take it once.

ISEE: The ISEE can only be taken once every six months.

GMAT: You may take the GMAT once every 31 calendar days, up to five times in any given 12-month period.

GRE: You may take the GRE as many times as you like.

LSAT: You can take the LSAT up to three times in a two-year period, including tests for which you cancel your score.

MCAT: You may take the MCAT up to three times per calendar year

SUMMARY

- Doing your best on test day involves more than just those few hours you spend taking the test. Good preparation beforehand and smart decisions during and after the test help maximize your test taking know-how.

- If you are thinking about not taking a test, be honest with yourself. If you've prepared, you're probably ready. If you haven't prepared, will you do the work necessary to be ready later? In most cases, you should just take the test, especially if you have the option to cancel scores or if admissions committees just look at your highest scores.

- If you experience test anxiety that interferes with your ability to test well, consider the following:

- Take a Test Anxiety Inventory, which can help determine the source of your anxiety.

- Once you know why you are anxious, take concrete steps to eliminate those causes.

- If your anxiety is so severe that you can't handle it on your own, reach out to a professional.

- The week before the test: Make sure you have a plan of attack. Study every day leading up to the test and do some reconnaissance on the testing site so you know how to get there, how long it takes, and where to park.

- The day before the test: Stop studying and have some fun to help you relax. Lay out all the things you need the next day, and be sure to set your alarm. Get a good night's sleep.

- The day of the test: Give yourself enough time to eat, dress, get your things together, and get to the testing site early.

- At the testing site:

  - Know what you can and can't have in the testing room with you. Turn OFF your cell phone.

  - Follow all directions during the test and be on your best behavior, even during breaks.

  - Don't cancel your scores at the testing site without a very good reason, and never if you have a few days to decide.

  - If your proctor didn't follow the directions, or if there were any disruptions during the test that you feel adversely affected your performance, contact the testing organization as soon as possible.

- If you are thinking of canceling your scores, consider all the factors involved, and whether you even need to.

- Know how schools you are applying to treat multiple scores.

- Feel free to take the test again if you feel you can do significantly better the next time.

Specific Test Information

HIGHLIGHTS

- Specific information about major tests
- Costs of tests
- Online resources
- State-by-state breakdown

HIGH SCHOOL

ISEE (Independent School Entrance Exam)

Website: www.iseetest.org

Created By: Educational Testing Services (ETS) for the Educational Records Bureau (ERB).

Purpose: The Independent School Entrance Examination (ISEE) is a three-hour admission test for entrance into grades 5 through 12. The ISEE has three levels: a Lower Level for students currently in grades 4 and 5 who are candidates for admission to grades 5 and 6, a Middle Level for students in grades 6 and 7 who are candidates for admission to grades 7 and 8, and an Upper Level for students in grades 8 to 11 who are candidates for admission to grades 9 through 12.

Test Description: Breaks are given after the second and fourth sections of the test.

ISEE Lower Level (Candidates for grades 5 & 6)		
Test	**Number of Questions**	**Time Limit**
Verbal Reasoning: Synonyms, Sentence Completions	40	25 minutes
Quantitative Reasoning: Comprehension, Interpretation/Application, Higher Order Thinking	35	35 minutes
Reading Comprehension: Humanities, Science, and Social Studies Passages	36	40 minutes
Mathematics Achievement: Knowledge and Skills, Computation/Comprehension, Applications	35	40 minutes
Essay	1	30 minutes

ISEE Middle Level (Candidates for grades 7 & 8)		
Test	**Number of Questions**	**Time Limit**
Verbal Reasoning: Synonyms, Sentence Completions	40	20 minutes
Quantitative Reasoning: Comprehension, Interpretation/Application, Higher Order Thinking	35	35 minutes
Reading Comprehension: Humanities, Science, and Social Studies Passages	40	40 minutes
Mathematics Achievement: Knowledge and Skills, Computation/Comprehension, Applications	45	40 minutes
Essay	1	30 minutes

ISEE Upper Level (Candidates for grades 9 to 12)		
Test	**Number of Questions**	**Time Limit**
Verbal Reasoning: Synonyms, Sentence Completions	40	20 minutes
Quantitative Reasoning: Arithmetic/ Algebra/ Geometry, Concepts/ Understanding, Applications/Higher Order Thinking, Quantitative Comparison	35	35 minutes
Reading Comprehension: Humanities, Science, and Social Studies Passages	40	40 minutes
Mathematics Achievement: Arithmetic/ Algebra/ Geometry, Knowledge and Skills, Applications, Computation/Comprehension	45	40 minutes
Essay	1	30 minutes

Unscored experimental items included? No.

About Scoring: Students will receive scaled scored between 760–940 as well as percentile scores for each section of the test.

Penalty for wrong answers? No.

Testing Schedule: Students may only test once every 6 months, and students cannot take the test for practice: they must be actually applying to a school. The ISEE is given on multiple dates throughout the school year. Refer to the annual Student Guide (downloadable from the website) for a fill list of locations and dates by metropolitan area.

Testing Fees: Online or mail-in registration is $78—this is for Open or Closed Test sites hosted by member school. Testing is also available at ISEE Testing Offices: small group testing is $125 ($128 in New York City) and individual testing is $140.

Refund for registration cancellation available? Yes—a $15 service fee will be deducted.

Post-test cancellation available? No.

Optional Services & Additional Fees:

Registration via fax or phone: additional charge of $20

Late registration: $98

Walk-in registration: additional fee of $30

Remote location testing: $140 (US) and $160 (international)

Change fees: additional fee of $30 (office testing) or $20 (school testing) will be charged

Score reporting by telephone: $30

Additional score reports (up to six): $15

Handscoring of exam: $25

Rescoring: $15

Contact: For accommodated testing, unlisted test site testing, or understanding score reports:

Educational Records Bureau

220 East 42nd Street, Suite 100

New York, NY 10017

E-mail: isee@erbtest.org

Phone: (800) 989-3721, ex. 312

For school testing, telephone score reports, or extra score report requests:

ISEE Operations Office

423 Morris Street

Durham, NC 27701

Phone: (800) 446-0320 or

(919) 956-8524

SSAT (Secondary School Admissions Test)

Website: www.ssat.org

Created By: The Secondary School Admissions Test Board

Purpose: The SSAT is taken by students seeking admission into private or independent schools. Schools use the scores in different ways: to estimate a student's ability to do work in a private school, to compare a student's performance with other applicants for admission or with the student's present academic record, and to help the student improve skills before college admissions testing. Each school evaluates scores according to its own standards and requirements.

Test Description: There are two versions of the SSAT, an Upper Level (for students currently in grades 8 to 11) and a Lower Level (for those currently in grades 5 to 7). Both tests have the same number of sections, number of items, and timing. However, the sections do not always come in the same order. The Writing Sample could be first or last.

Section	Number of Items	Time
Writing Sample (unscored, but sent with your report to schools)	1	25 minutes
Quantitative (Math)	25	30 minutes
Verbal: Synonyms and Analogies	60	30 minutes
Reading: 6 to 7 passages	40	40 minutes
Quantitative (Math)	25	30 minutes

Unscored experimental items included? No.

About Scoring: Students receive four scores for the test: one for each section of the test (Verbal, Reading, and Math, which combines the two math sections) plus an overall score that combines the Verbal and Math scores. Students also receive a percentile score, which ranks their performance as compared to test takers from the previous three years.

The scaled scores on the Upper and Lower Level tests differ. Upper Level test scores range from 500 to 800 for each section (Verbal, Reading, Math), and from 1500 to 2400 for the total score. Lower Level test scores range from 440 to 710 for each section, and from 1320 to 2130 for the total score.

Penalty for wrong answers? Yes—one-quarter point is deducted for each incorrect answer.

Testing Schedule: The SSAT is given 8 times a year, in October, November, December, January, February, March, April, and June,

Testing Fees:

SSAT National test: $100

SSAT International Test: $180

Later registration: $25 additional fee

Stand-by registration: $55 additional fee

Refund for registration cancellation available? No.

Post-test cancellation available? Yes—students must cancel before 5:00 P.M. EST on the Tuesday following the test date.

Optional Services:

Change of test date or location: $30

Scores via email and up to 10 additional reports: $25 (the "Web Service bundle")

Add or cancel score report: $10

Scores via e-mail: $20

FedEx score reporting: $25

Contact:

SSAT

CN 5339

Princeton, NJ 08543

E-mail: info@ssat.org

Phone: (609) 683-4440

SHSAT (Specialized High School Admissions Test)

Website: Go to schools.nyc.gov, then do a search for SHSAT Handbook

Created By: New York City Department of Education.

Purpose: SHSAT scores are used to determine admission into 8 specialized high schools in the New York City Public Schools: Bronx High School of Science, The Brooklyn Latin School, Brooklyn Technical High School, High School for Mathematics, Science, and Engineering at City College, High School of American Studies at Lehman College, Queens High School for the Sciences at York College, Staten Island Technical High School, and Stuyvesant High School. Students must be residents of New York City.

Test Description: The SHSAT has two sections, one math and one verbal. You do not have to do them in the order they are given—you can go back to a previous section if you want.

Section	Number of Items	Time
Verbal	45 total	75 minutes total (suggested)
Scrambled Paragraphs	5 paragraphs, 6 sentences each	
Logical Reasoning	10 items	
Reading Comprehension	5 passages, 6 questions each	
Math	50 total	75 minutes total (suggested)

Unscored experimental items included? No

About Scoring: SHSAT scores are scaled from 200 to 800, and are reported to schools from lowest to highest. Cut-off scores from year to year vary depending on students' scores, the number of spaces available, and the preferences students gave for which school they want to attend.

Penalty for wrong answers? No.

Testing Schedule: The SHSAT is typically offered to 8th graders the last weekend of October, to 9th graders the first weekend of November, and to any students needing a makeup test on the third weekend of November. Always check the New York City Board of Education website for specific dates for each school year.

Testing Fees: None.

TACHS (Test for Admission to Catholic High School)

Website: www.tachsinfo.com

Purpose: The TACHS is given in the Archdiocese of New York City, the Diocese of Brooklyn/Queens, and other New York counties for admission to the Catholic high schools in those areas.

Test Description: The TACHS lasts two-and-a-half hours and contains about 200 multiple-choice questions divided into four subtests—Reading, Language, Math, and Ability.

Section	Time	Number of Items	Topics Tested
Reading: Vocabulary	10 minutes	20	Definitions
Reading: Comprehension	25 minutes	30	Ability to understand the central meaning of a passage and to recall or locate its details, draw inferences or generalize about what you read.
Language: Spelling, Capitalization, Punctuation, and Usage/Expression	23 minutes	40	Ability to understand the structure of sentences and paragraphs and how they work together to convey ideas, spelling, capitalization, and punctuation
Language: Paragraphs	7 minutes	10	Conciseness, clarity, appropriateness of expression, or organization of ideas.
Math: Concepts, Data Interpretation, and Problem Solving	33 minutes	32	Number relations, problem solving, graphical analysis
Math: Estimation	7 minutes	18	Estimation
Ability: Similarities and Changes	25 minutes	40	Abstract reasoning ability, patterns, visual problems, sequences
Ability: Abstract Reasoning	7 minutes	10	Abstract reasoning ability, problem solving, patterns

Unscored experimental items included? No

About Scoring: You receive one point for every correct answer to the TACHS. These raw points are totaled, then converted to a scaled score. Your score report will include both your scaled scores and your percentile ranking.

Penalty for wrong answers? No.

Testing Schedule: The TACHS is given in October or November. Check the website for specific dates each year.

Testing Fees: $49 includes registration materials, a student handbook, test materials, and the reporting of scores to the three high schools of your choice.

Contact:

TACHS Examination Office

PO Box 64675

Eagan, MN 55164-9522

Registration website: www.tachsreg.com

Phone: (866) 618-2247

HSPT (High School Placement Test)

Website: www.ststesting.com/hsptpg9.html

Created By: Scholastic Testing Service.

Purpose: The HSPT is used by many Catholic schools for admissions and placement. It is taken by 8th graders entering the 9th grade only. It is offered in two different versions, Open and Closed. The Closed HSPT is administered by the school, but scored by STS. Closed HSPT scores are compared to national standard distribution norms, so nationwide percentiles can be computed. The Open HSPT is administered and scored by the school, so STS does not deal directly with student results. The Open HSPT uses old versions of the Closed HSPT.

Test Description: The HSPT consists of five multiple-choice sections: verbal skills, quantitative skills, reading comprehension, math, and language skills. The basic HSPT includes 298 multiple-choice questions and is approximately 140 minutes long, but may be longer depending on the additional sections a particular school chooses to add.

Content	Number of Questions and Timing
Verbal Skills: Analogies, Synonyms, Logic, Verbal Classifications, Antonyms	60 questions, 16 minutes
Quantitative Skills: Number Series, Geometric Comparison, Non-Geometric Comparison, Number Manipulation	52 questions, 30 minutes
Reading: Reading Comprehension, Vocabulary	62 questions, 25 minutes
Mathematics: Concepts, Problem Solving	64 questions, 45 minutes
Language Skills: Punctuation and Capitalization, Usage, Spelling, Composition	60 questions, 25 minutes

Some schools also choose to present one of three optional tests: Mechanical Aptitude, Science, or Catholic Religion.

Unscored experimental items included? No.

About Scoring: HSPT scores are reported on a 200 to 800 scale. Your raw score (the number correct out of the total number of questions) is converted to standard scores that range from 200 to 800. When you get your score report, it will include your scaled scores, national and local percentile rank, grade equivalent, and Cognitive Skills Quotient, which is used to gauge your academic potential.

Penalty for wrong answers? No.

Testing Schedule: The HSPT is offered at various times throughout the year, depending on where you apply. The most common test dates are in the Fall and Spring. Contact the admissions office for the school to which you are applying to determine specific test dates and sign up.

Testing Fees: Find out from the school where you plan to take the exam. Different schools charge different fees for the test.

Contact: To register for the test, contact the school to which you are applying. For information about the test:

Scholastic Testing Service, Inc.

480 Meyer Road

Bensenville, IL 60106-1617

E-mail: sts@mail.ststesting.com

Phone: (800) 642-6787

COOP (Cooperative Admissions Exam)

Website: www.coopexam.org

Created By: CTB McGraw-Hill.

Purpose: Along with the HSPT, a test used for Catholic school admissions and placement, particularly in New Jersey. The COOP is taken by 8th graders entering 9th grade only.

Test Description: The content of the COOP reflects the New Jersey Core Content Curriculum Standards.

Section	Question Type	Number of Questions	Time
1	Sequences	15 to 20	15 minutes
2	Analogies	15 to 20	17 minutes
3	Quantitative Reasoning	15 to 20	15 minutes
4	Verbal Reasoning: Words and Context	12 to 15	15 minutes
5	Verbal Reasoning: Context	8 to 15	15 minutes
6	Reading and Language Arts	45 to 50	40 minutes
7	Mathematics	35 to 40	35 minutes

Unscored experimental items included? No

Penalty for wrong answers? No.

Testing Schedule: The COOP is administered once a year, usually in October or November.

Testing Fees: $40 to register, an additional $10 to take a makeup test.

Contact:

Cooperative Admissions Examination Office MCS Center

4603 Middle Country Road

Calverton, NY 11933

E-mail: support@coopexam.org

Phone: (888) 921-COOP x2667

STATE ASSESSMENTS

The list below provides the name of the tests of adequate yearly progress as required by No Child Left Behind federal legislation as well as other tests given in the 50 states and the District of Columbia

State	Administrating agency	Test name	Also called...
Alabama	Alabama State DOE	Alabama High School Graduation Exam, Alabama Reading and Mathematics Test	AHSGE, ARMT
Alaska	Alaska DOE and Early Development	High School Graduation Qualifying Examination	HSGQE
Arizona	Arizona DOE	Arizona's Instrument to Measure Standards	AIMS
Arkansas	Arkansas DOE	Iowa Test of Basic Skills	ITBS
California	California DOE	Standardized Testing and Reporting, California High School Exit Exam	STaR, CAHSEE
Colorado	Colorado DOE	Colorado Student Assessment Program	CSAP
Connecticut	Connecticut DOE	Connecticut Academic Performance Test, Connecticut Mastery Test	CAPT, CMT
Delaware	Delaware DOE	Delaware Student Testing Program	DSTP
District of Columbia	District of Columbia Public Schools	District of Columbia Comprehensive Assessment System	DC CAS
Florida	Florida DOE	Florida Comprehensive Assessment Test	F-CAT

Georgia	Georgia DOE	Criterion-Referenced Competency Tests, End-Of-Course Tests, Georgia High School Graduation Test, Georgia Alternate Assessment, Georgia Writings Assessments	CRCT, EOCT, GHSGT, GAA
Hawai'i	Hawai'i DOE	Hawai'i State Assessment	HSA
Idaho	Idaho DOE	Idaho Standards Achievement Test	I-SAT
Illinois	Illinois State Board of Education	Illinois Standards Achievement Test, Prairie State Achievement Exam (HS)	ISAT, PSAE
Indiana	Indiana DOE	Indiana Statewide Testing for Educational Progress-Plus	I-STEP+
Iowa	Iowa DOE	Iowa Test of Basic Skills, Iowa Tests of Educational Development	ITBS, ITED
Kansas	Kansas State DOE	Kansas Statewide Assessments	KSA
Kentucky	Kentucky DOE	Commonwealth Accountability Testing System	CATS
Louisiana	Louisiana DOE	Louisiana Educational Assessment Program, Integrated LEAP, Graduate Exit Examination	LEAP, iLEAP, GEE
Maine	Maine DOE	Maine Educational Assessment	MEA
Maryland	Maryland DOE	Maryland School Assessment	MSA
Massachusetts	Massachusetts DOE	Massachusetts Comprehensive Assessment System	M-CAS
Michigan	Michigan DOE	Michigan Educational Assessment Program, Michigan Merit Exam	MEAP, MME
Minnesota	Minnesota DOE	Minnesota Comprehensive Assessments—Series II	MCA-II
Mississippi	Mississippi DOE	Mississippi Curriculum Test	MCT
Missouri	Missouri Department of Elementary and Secondary Education	Missouri Assessment Program	MAP
Montana	Montana Office of Public Instruction	Montana Comprehensive Assessment System	MontCAS

Nebraska	Nebraska DOE	School-based Teacher-led Assessment Reporting System	STARS
Nevada	Nevada DOE	Nevada Proficiency Examination Program	NPEP
New Hampshire	New Hampshire DOE	New England Common Assessment Program	NECAP
New Jersey	New Jersey DOE	New Jersey Assessment of Skills and Knowledge, Grade Eight Proficiency Assessment, High School Proficiency Assessment	NJASK, GEPA, HSPA
New Mexico	New Mexico DOE	New Mexico Standards Based Assessment	NMSBA
New York	New York State DOE	Regents Examinations	Regents
North Carolina	North Carolina Department of Public Instruction	End of Grade Tests (Grades 3 to 8), End of Course Tests (Grades 9 to 12)	EOGs, EOCs
North Dakota	North Dakota Department of Public Instruction	North Dakota State Assessment System	NDSAS
Ohio	Ohio State Board of Education	Ohio Achievement Test, Ohio Graduate Test	OAT, OGT
Oklahoma	Oklahoma State DOE	Oklahoma Core Curriculum Tests[7]	OCCT
Oregon	Oregon DOE	Oregon Assessment of Knowledge and Skills	OAKS
Pennsylvania	Pennsylvania DOE	Pennsylvania System of School Assessment	PSSA
Rhode Island	Rhode Island Department of Elementary and Secondary Education	New England Common Assessment Program	NECAP
South Carolina	South Carolina DOE	Palmetto Achievement Challenge Test	PACT
South Dakota	South Dakota DOE	South Dakota State Test of Educational Progress	DSTEP
Tennessee	Tennessee State DOE	Tennessee Comprehensive Assessment Program	TCAP
Texas	Texas Education Agency	Texas Assessment of Knowledge and Skills	TAKS

Utah	Utah State Office of Education	Utah Performance Assessment System for Students, Iowa Test of Basic Skills	U-PASS, ITBS
Vermont	State of Vermont DOE	New England Common Assessment Program	NECAP
Virginia	Virginia DOE	Standards of Learning	SOL
Washington	Washington State Office of Superintendent of Public Instruction	Washington Assessment of Student Learning	WASL
West Virginia	West Virginia DOE	West Virginia Educational Standards Test	WESTEST
Wisconsin	Wisconsin Department of Public Instruction	Wisconsin Knowledge and Concepts Examination	WKCE
Wyoming	Wyoming DOE	Proficiency Assessment for Wyoming Students	PAWS

COLLEGE ADMISSIONS

PSAT/NMSQT (Preliminary SAT/National Merit Scholarship Qualifying Test)

Website: www.collegeboard.com/psat

Created By: Educational Testing Services (ETS) and administered by the College Board.

Purpose: The most common reasons for taking the PSAT/NMSQT are:

- To receive feedback on strengths and weaknesses on college-level skills.
- To see how your performance compares with others'.
- To enter the competition for scholarships from the National Merit Scholarship Corporation (grade 11 only).
- To help prepare for the SAT.

Test Description: The PSAT is a five section, 2-hour-and-10-minute test. The sections always appear in the same order:

Section	Number of Questions	Time

Critical Reading:
    Sentence Completions
    Passage-based Reading
	24	25 minutes

Math: Multiple-choice only	20	25 minutes

Critical Reading:
    Sentence Completions
    Passage-based Reading
	24	25 minutes

Math:
    Multiple-choice
    Student-produced Response (Grid-ins)
	18	25 minutes

Writing Skills:
    Improving Sentences
    Error Identification
    Improving Paragraphs
	39	30 minutes

The math portion of the PSAT tests arithmetic, basic algebra, algebra II, and geometry.

Unscored experimental items included? No.

About Scoring: Each section of the PSAT—Math, Critical Reading, and Writing Skills—is scored on a scale from 20 to 80. Your overall score combines all three scores and ranges from 60 to 240. You are also provided a percentile score that shows how well you scored in relation to other students in your grade.

In 2006, the average score for 11th graders was about 48 in Critical Reading, 49 in Mathematics, and 46 in Writing Skills. The average score for tenth graders was about 43 in Critical Reading, 44 in Mathematics, and 41 in Writing Skills.

The top 50,000 scorers (11th grade only) on the PSAT receive Letters of Commendation from the National Merit Scholarship Program. Of those 50,000, about 16,000 students qualify as Semi-Finalists chosen from all 50 states.

Cut-off scores for Semi-Finalist status vary from year to year and from state to state. Finally, about 8,000 Finalists will receive some sort of merit scholarship in the form of a National Merit, college-sponsored, or corporate-sponsored award. An additional 1,500 students who didn't make it to the Finalist round will also receive special awards from other organizations.

Penalty for wrong answers? Yes—you lose one-quarter point for each incorrect answer.

Testing Schedule: The PSAT is given twice a year, usually on the Wednesday and Saturday in the third week of October.

Testing Fees: $13 is the basic testing fee. Fee waivers are available for low-income students. Some schools charge an additional fee, while others cover the cost of testing. Talk to your school's guidance office to find out more. If you are a home-schooled student, contact a public or independent high school in your area to take the test there.

Post-test cancellation available? No.

Contact:

PSAT
PSAT/NMSQT Office
P.O. Box 6720
Princeton, NJ 08541-6720
E-mail: psathelp@info.collegeboard.org
Phone: (866) 433-7728 (US) or (212) 713-8105 (international)

National Merit Scholarships
National Merit Scholarship Corporation
1560 Sherman Avenue
Suite 200
Evanston, Illinois 60201-4897
Phone: (847) 866-5100
E-mail: www.nationalmerit.org

National Hispanic Recognition Program

c/o The College Board

11911 Freedom Drive, Suite 300

Reston, VA 20190

E-mail: nhrp@collegeboard.org

SAT

Website: www.collegeboard.com/sat

Created By: Educational Testing Services (ETS) and administered by the College Board.

Purpose: The SAT helps predict success in college and is used for admissions and placement decisions.

Test Description: The SAT consists of 10 sections:

- One, 25-minute Essay
- Two, 25-minute Math sections
    - 20 questions: all problem solving
    - 18 questions: 8 problem solving and 10 grid-ins
- Two, 25-minute Critical Reading section
    - 8 Sentence Completions, Reading Comprehension
    - 6 Sentence Completions, Reading Comprehension
- One, 25-minute Writing section
    - 35 questions: Improving Sentences, Error ID, and Im proving Paragraphs
- One, 25-minute experimental section, which could be Math, Critical Reading, or Writing
- One, 20-minute Math section
    - 16 problem solving
- One 20-minute Critical Reading Section
    - 5 Sentence Completions, 12 to 14 Reading Comprehension

- One, 10-minute Writing section
  - 14 Improving Sentences

Unscored experimental items included? Yes. One of the 25-minute sections will be unscored. This section could be either Math, Critical Reading, or Writing.

About Scoring: Each of the multiple-choice sections of the SAT—Math, CR, Writing—are scored on a scale from 200 to 800. The composite score is the sum of these three scores, and so ranges from 600 to 2400. The essay is scored from 1 to 6 by each of two human graders. Their scores are added together to produce the Essay subscore ranging from 2 to 12. The Grammar subscore ranges from 20 to 80, and represents the test taker's performance on the multiple-choice Writing sections only. The overall Writing score from 200 to 800 is calculated by weighting the Essay and Grammar subscores, scaling them, then weighting them again. Therefore an SAT score report includes five scores in all: Essay subscore from 1 to 6, Grammar subscore from 20 to 80, Math from 200 to 800, Critical Reading from 200 to 800, and Writing from 200 to 800. In addition, students are given percentile rankings.

Average scores based on the performance of the college-bound class of 2007 were 515 for Math, 502 for Critical Reading, and 494 for Writing.

Penalty for wrong answers? Yes—you lose one-quarter point for each incorrect answer.

Testing Schedule: The SAT is given 7 times a year: January, April, May, June, October, November, and December.

Testing Fees: $43 basic registration fee. International students pay an additional $25 to register (only $22 for test takers in India and Pakistan).

Refund for registration cancellation available? Once you've submitted your registration (and received Confirmation or your Admission Ticket) it cannot be canceled and your test fees cannot be refunded. You may, however, transfer your registration to a future test date for fee.

Post-test cancellation available? If you want to cancel your scores on test day, you should ask the test supervisor for a Request to Cancel Test Scores

Form. Complete the form immediately and return it to the test supervisor before leaving the room.

You may decide to cancel your scores after you leave the test center. ETS must receive your request to cancel scores in writing by 11:59 p.m. EST (Eastern Standard Time), on the Wednesday after the test date. You cannot submit cancellation requests by phone or e-mail—your signature is required. You can fax it to (610) 290-8978 with a label that says, "ATTN: SAT Score Cancellation" or mail it to: SAT Score Cancellation, 225 Phillips Boulevard, Ewing, NJ 08618. If you send express mail, address it to: SAT Score Cancellation, P.O. Box 6228, Princeton, NJ 08541-6228. Be sure to include you name, address, gender, birth date, registration number, the test date, the test center number, the name of the test, and your signature.

Change fee: $21

Standby testing fee: $37

International processing fee: $25 ($22 in India and Pakistan)

Scores by phone: $12

Rush reporting service: $26.50 plus $9.50 per report

Additional score report: $9.50

Order additional reports by phone: $10 plus $9.50 per report

Question and Answer Service (a copy of your responses and the test booklet): $18

Student Answer Service (a copy of your responses): $10

Score verification (multiple-choice or essay): $50

Contact: Depending on why you need to contact the folks who bring you the SAT, there are a number of different contacts. Here is the basic customer service information. Other contacts are listed on the College Board website.

College Board SAT Program

P.O. Box 025505

Miami, FL 33102

Phone: (866) 756-7346

SAT Subject Tests

Website: www.collegeboard.com/sat

Created By: Educational Testing Services (ETS) and administered by the College Board.

Purpose: The SAT Subject Tests are designed to measure your knowledge and skills in particular subject areas, as well as your ability to apply that knowledge. Subject Test scores are used for admissions, for course placement, and to advise students about course selection.

Test Description: Subject Tests are hour-long exams. There are 19 in all: Literature, US History, World History, Math Levels 1 and 2, Biology E/M, Physics, Chemistry, Chinese with Listening, French (with and without Listening), German (with and without Listening), Spanish (with and without Listening), Modern Hebrew, Italian, Latin, Japanese with Listening, and Korean with Listening.

Unscored experimental items included? No.

About Scoring: Subscores are reported on a 20-to-80 scale and overall scores on a 200-to-800 scale. Reading and listening subscores are reported for all Language Tests with Listening, and a usage subscore is also reported for the Chinese, Japanese, and Korean tests. Subscores on the Subject Tests are used to compute the total score, but their individual contributions differ between the different tests. For the French, German, and Spanish with Listening tests, the reading subscore counts twice as much as the listening subscore. For the Chinese, Japanese, and Korean tests, subscores are weighted equally.

All scores are accompanied by percentile rankings. Note that percentile rankings vary considerably depending on the test, so don't assume that what is a "good" score on one test is a good score on another. The average scores for college-bound seniors in 2007 are as follows:

English
- Literature: 581

History and Social Sciences
- United States History: 588

- World History: 589

Mathematics

- Mathematics Level 1: 596
- Mathematics Level 2: 639

Sciences

- Biology—Ecological: 589
- Biology—Molecular: 630
- Chemistry: 630
- Physics: 647

Language Tests

- Chinese with Listening: 764
- French: 615
- French with Listening: 618
- German: 604
- German with Listening: 582
- Modern Hebrew: 635
- Italian: 657
- Japanese with Listening: 687
- Korean with Listening: 757
- Latin: 617
- Spanish: 632
- Spanish with Listening: 644

Penalty for wrong answers? Yes—you lose one-quarter of a point for each incorrect answer when there are 5 answers to choose from. You lose one-third of a point when there are 4 answers and one-half of a point when there are 3 answers.

Testing Schedule: SAT Subject tests are given six times a year: October, November, December, January, May, and June. However, not every test is offered on every date, so check the College Board website for the individual schedules for each test. Literature, US History, Math Levels 1 and 2, Physics, Chemistry, and Biology E/M are the only tests offered at every administration.

Testing Fees: $20 basic registration fee plus $8 per test. For language tests with listening, add an additional $20.

Refund for registration cancellation available? No.

Post-test cancellation available? When you cancel your Subject Test scores, all of the Subject Tests taken on that date are canceled. If you begin taking a test and then decide that you are not prepared for it, you should cancel test scores for the day. If you try to erase all your responses to an individual Subject Test, the scores from all tests taken that day are canceled.

If your calculator or CD player fails during a Mathematics Level 1 or Level 2 test, or during a Language Test with Listening, you have the option to cancel just that test. You can still keep scores from other Subject Tests taken the same day. To do this you must report the failure immediately to the test supervisor, fill out and sign a "Request to Cancel Test Scores" form, and return the completed form to the test supervisor before you leave.

Optional Services: See SAT Optional Services above.

Contact: See SAT contact information above.

ACT

Website: www.actstudent.org

Created By: ACT, Inc.

Purpose: According to the test makers, the ACT assesses high school students' general educational development and their ability to complete college-level work. Like the SAT, the ACT is used for both admissions and placement.

Test Description: The ACT consists of four, multiple-choice tests: English, Math, Reading, and Science. There is also an optional Writing section which consists of a single essay. The test is always structured in the same way:

Test	Number of questions and timing	Content Breakdown	What Does it Measure?
English	75 questions, 45 minutes	Usage/Mechanics: 40 questions Rhetorical Skills: 35 questions	Standard written English and rhetorical skills.
Math	60 questions, 60 minutes	Pre-algebra/Elementary Algebra: 24 questions Intermediate Algebra/Co-ordinate Geometry: 18 questions Plane Geome-try: 14 questions Trigo-nometry: 4 questions	Arithmetic, algebra, geometry, trigonometry.
Reading	40 questions, 35 minutes	Four passages: Prose Fiction, Social Studies, Humanities, and Natural Sciences	Reading comprehension
Science	40 questions, 35 minutes	Seven passages: One con-flicting viewpoints, three data representation, and three research summaries.	Interpretation, analysis, evaluation, reasoning, and problem-solving skills in the context of natural science.
Writing (optional)	1 essay, 30 minutes	One topic	Writing skills taught in high school English and first-year college composition courses.

Unscored experimental items included? Occasionally an experimental section will appear on the ACT, usually in June. It is optional and always appears at the end if at all.

About Scoring: Each of the four multiple-choice portions of the test (English, Math, Reading, and Science) is scored on a range from 1 to 36, and your Composite score is the average of those four scores. If you take the ACT plus Writing, you will also receive a Writing subscore ranging from 2 to 12 and a Combined English/Writing score from 1 to 36. This Combined English/Writing score is created by using a formula that weights the English test score two-thirds and the Writing test score one-third to form a combined score. The Writing test is never included in the Composite score.

ACT scores are accompanied by national ranks, which compare your performance with that of recent high-school graduates.

Penalty for wrong answers? No.

Testing Schedule: The ACT is given six times a year: in September, October, December, February, April, and June. The September test is only given in certain states, and the February test is not given in New York.

Testing Fees: $30 for the ACT without Writing, $44.50 for the ACT with Writing. Includes up to four score reports sent to colleges.

Refund for registration cancellation available? Not for the $30 testing fee, but the $14.50 for the Writing test is refundable if you are absent or decide not to take that part of the test.

Post-test cancellation available? No, but with the ACT, you have the option of only sending certain scores to certain schools, so if you have a bad testing experience you can simply not send those scores to any school.

Optional Services:

Late registration fee: $19.00

Standby testing fee: $39.50

International testing fee: $22.00

Test date or test site change: $20.50

TIR (Test information Release) service: $16 (provides you with a copy of your responses and the test booklet—available only in December, April, and June)

Contact: There are different mailing addresses and phone numbers for ACT depending on what you need. Check out the "Contact Us" page on the ACT website for a complete list of contact addresses and numbers.

AP (Advanced Placement)

Website: www.collegeboard.com

Created By: Educational Testing Service (ETS) for the College Board.

Purpose: AP courses provide high-school students with college-level course work, and AP exams provide the opportunity to gain college credit and advanced standing.

Test Description: There are 37 AP exams, which together cover 22 different subject areas:

Art History

Biology

Calculus AB

Calculus BC

Chemistry

Chinese Language and Culture

Computer Science A

Computer Science AB

English Language and Composition

English Literature and Composition

Environmental Science

European History

French Language

French Literature

German Language

Government and Politics: Comparative

Government and Politics: United States

Human Geography

Italian Language and Culture

Japanese Language and Culture

Latin Literature

Latin: Vergil

Macroeconomics

Microeconomics

Music Theory

Physics B

Physics C: Electricity and Magnetism

Physics C: Mechanics

Psychology

Spanish Language

Spanish Literature

Statistics

Studio Art: 2-D Design

Studio Art: 3-D Design

Studio Art: Drawing

United States History

World History

Except for AP Studio Art—which is a portfolio assessment—each AP Exam contains a free-response section (either essay or problem-solving) and a section of multiple-choice questions. The modern language exams also have a speaking component, and the AP Music Theory Exam includes a sight-singing task. Most exams are between 2 and 3 hours in length.

Unscored experimental items included? No.

About Scoring: Final scores for AP exams are presented on a 1 to 5 scale: 1 means "no recommendation," 2 means "possibly qualified," 3 means "qualified," 4 means "well qualified," and 5 means "extremely well qualified." Qualified in this context means qualified to earn credit in that subject. A score of 1 means they are unwilling to make a recommendation. Every participating college sets their own minimum standard for granting AP credit, so just taking an AP exam does not guarantee college credit. Sub-scores are not available (except for Calculus BC and Music Theory) nor are scores analyzed to determine strengths and weaknesses.

The multiple-choice items on an exam are scored by machine, and the free-response items are scored by AP readers who have been trained by the College Board to assess student responses according to a uniform set of rules and rubrics. The scores from the multiple-choice and free-response portions of each test are combined according to a special weighting formula to create a composite score. This composite score is then converted to the 1 to 5 scale. This conversion is done every year by committee and varies a bit year to year to account for the overall performance of students on the exam and any variation in difficulty there may be from year to year.

Penalty for wrong answers? Yes—you lose one-quarter of a point for each incorrect answer when there are 5 answers to choose from. You lose one-third of a point when there are 4 answers and one-half of a point when there are 3 answers.

Testing Schedule: AP exams are given the first two weeks in May. Different exams are given at different times on different days, so check the College Board website to find the specific information for each test. Tests are given at high schools

Testing Fees: Each AP exam costs $84, $8 of which goes to the school to cover administrative costs. The College Board does provide fee reductions for low-income students and expects the schools to forego their admin fee, which brings the cost down to $54.

Refund for registration cancellation available? Yes—if a student registers for a test but does not take it, he may request a refund. Note that the school is charged $13 for unused exams, so the refund is likely not to be a total refund.

Post-test cancellation available? Yes. You must write to the College Board to request that your scores be cancelled. The request must be received by June 15th. Cancelled scores cannot be reinstated.

Optional Services:
Grades by phone: $8.00
Extra grade reports: $15.00
Rush grade reports: $25.00

Free-response booklets: $7.00

Grade withholding: $10 per grade

Contact:

AP Services

P.O. Box 6671

Princeton, NJ 08541-6671

E-mail: apexams@info.collegeboard.org

Phone: (609) 771-7300 or (888) 225-5427 (toll-free in the United
States and Canada)

TOEFL (Test of English as a Foreign Language)

Website: www.toefl.org

Created By: Educational Testing Services (ETS).

Purpose: The TOEFL is used to assess the English skills of non-native speakers of English. If you are a non-native speaker of English at the 11th-grade level or above and wish to attend college or graduate school in the US, you probably need to take the TOEFL.

Test Description: Depending upon your testing area, the TOEFL is administered in either iBT (Internet-based) format or paper-based format (PBT).

The TOEFL iBT test has four sections: Reading, Listening, Speaking, and Writing.

- Reading measures the ability to understand academic reading material.

- Listening measures the ability to understand English as it is used in colleges and universities.

- Speaking measures the ability to speak English in an academic context.

- Writing measures the ability to write in a way that is appropriate for college and university course work.

The TOEFL PBT has three sections: Reading Comprehension, Structure and Written Expression, and Listening Comprehension. It also contains a 30-minute writing portion, known as the Test of Written English.

- Listening Comprehension measures the ability to understand English as it is spoken in North America.

- Structure and Written Expression measures the ability to recognize language that is appropriate for standard written English.

- Reading Comprehension measures the ability to understand non-technical reading material.

- Test of Written English: Students will write an essay in response to a given topic and be evaluated on the development, organization, language, and grammar of their writing.

Unscored experimental items included? On the PBT, yes.

About Scoring: If you take the iBT, more credit is given for correctly answering a hard question than for correctly answering an easy question in the Listening and Structure sections. Therefore, your score on these portions of the test depends not only on how many questions you answer correctly but also on which ones you answer correctly.

At the end of the iBT, you will see your Listening and Reading scores. Your Structure/Writing score and Total score will be reported as a range of scores. Your score from the Structure section is combined with your written essay rating to calculate the Structure/Writing score. Each part accounts for 50 percent of the Structure/Writing score, and the Writing score is also shown separately under the heading, "essay rating."

Your Structure/Writing score will fall within the range once your essay is read and rated. Likewise, your Total score will fall within the range once the Structure/Writing score is known. Scores on any section can range from 0 to 30. The Total score is calculated using a multiple of the scores on the individual parts of the test, and can range from 0 to 300. This is why the Total score does not equal the sum of the Listening, Structure/Writing, and Reading scores.

If you take the PBT, your score report will show three section scale scores and a total scale score. Each correct answer counts equally toward the score for that section. The total PBT score is reported on a scale that ranges from

310 to 677, while the three section scores range from 31 to 68 (for Listening and Structure/Written Expression) and from 31 to 67 (for Reading Comprehension). The TWE score is reported separately, on a scale of 1 to 6. A score between two points on the scale (for example, 5.5, 3.5) can also be reported.

Penalty for wrong answers? No.

Testing Schedule: Both the iBT and PBT tests are given on specific dates. See the TOEFL website for iBT test dates and locations (the list is quite long). The PBT is given six times a year: in August, October, November, January, March, and May.

Testing Fees: The fee for the TOEFL varies a bit depending on where you take the test and on which format you take. The iBT is about $150 and the PBT is $140.

Refund for registration cancellation available? Yes. For the iBT, you can get half of the registration fee refunded to you if you cancel at least three days before your scheduled test date. Otherwise you lose the entire fee. For the PBT, you can receive a partial refund of $65.

Post-test cancellation available? Yes. On the iBT, you are given the option at the end of the test to cancel your scores. This is the only time you may cancel. If you cancel and change your mind, you can reinstate your scores if you do so within 10 days of your test date.

To cancel your PBT scores, you must either complete the score cancellation section of your answer sheet, or contact TOEFL Services. TOEFL Services must receive your request to cancel your scores no later than seven days after the test date printed on your admission ticket.

Optional Services:

Late registration fee: $25

Rescheduling fee: $50

Reinstatement of cancelled iBT scores: $20

iBT Rescore fee: $60 per section (iBT Speaking or Writing)

PBT Rescore fee: $25 for answer sheet rescore, $50 for essay rescore

Contact:

TOEFL Services
Educational Testing Service
P.O. Box 6151
Princeton, NJ 08541-6151 USA
E-mail: toefl@ets.org
Phone: (609) 771-7100 or toll-free (877) 863-3546

OTHER PRE-COLLEGE

CLEP (College Level Examination Program)

Website: www.collegeboard.com/clep

Created By: Educational Testing Services (ETS) and administered by the College Board.

Purpose: CLEP provides students of any age with the opportunity to demonstrate college-level achievement and receive college credit.

Test Description: CLEP exams are given online. There are 34 different tests in all, each 90 minutes long. Except for the English Composition exam, CLEP tests are mainly multiple choice. All tests are scored on a scale from 20 to 80.

CLEP examinations cover material taught in courses that most students take as requirements in the first two years of college. A college usually grants the same amount of credit to students earning satisfactory scores on the CLEP examination as it grants to students successfully completing that course. Many examinations are designed to correspond to one-semester courses; some, however correspond to full-year or two-year courses. Unless stated otherwise in its description, an examination is intended to cover material in a one-semester course. Tests cover a wide array of subjects:

Composition and Literature	History and Social Sciences
• American Literature	• American Government
• Analyzing and Interpreting Literature	• Human Growth and Development
• English Composition	• Introduction to Educational Psychology
• English Literature	• Introductory Psychology
• Freshman College Composition	• Introductory Sociology
• Humanities	• Principles of Macroeconomics
Foreign Languages	• Principles of Microeconomics
• French Language (Levels 1 and 2)	• Social Sciences and History
• German Language (Levels 1 and 2)	• U.S. History I: Early Colonizations to 1877
• Spanish Language (Levels 1 and 2)	• U.S. History II: 1865 to the Present
Science and Mathematics	• Western Civilization I: Ancient Near East to 1648
• Biology	• Western Civilization II: 1648 to the Present
• Calculus	Business
• Chemistry	• Financial Accounting (New in 2007)
• College Algebra	• Introductory Business Law
• College Mathematics	• Information Systems and Computer Applications
• Natural Sciences	• Principles of Management
• Precalculus	• Principles of Marketing

About Scoring: Except for the English Composition test, CLEP exams are scored immediately, so you see your score at the end of the test.

Penalty for wrong answers? Yes—you lose one-quarter of a point for each incorrect answer when there are 5 answers to choose from. You lose one-third of a point when there are 4 answers.

Testing Schedule: Students cannot take the same CLEP exam more than once every 6 months.

Testing Fees: $65 for each online test. Most colleges charge a nonrefundable administration fee that should be sent to the test center directly. The College Board recommends a $15 administration fee; however, each college establishes its own administration fee and may charge a different amount. Students who require a paper version pay $140—only 14 CLEP exams can be offered on paper. General Exams available on paper are English Composition, Social Sciences and History, Natural Sciences, Humanities, College Mathematics. Subject Exams available on paper include Analyzing and Interpreting Literature, College Algebra, Freshman College Composition, Information Systems and Computer Applications, Introductory Sociology, Introductory Psychology, Principles of Management , History of the United States I: Early Colonization to 1877, History of the United States II: 1865 to the Present.

Military personnel are eligible for discounted or free testing. See the website for details.

Post-test cancellation available? No. If you don't want your scores reported, notify the administrator before you complete the exam. You will be asked to verify that you want your score canceled in the testing software. You CANNOT cancel your scores once you've seen your instant score report.

For general information, contact:
CLEP
P.O. Box 6600
Princeton, NJ 08541-6600
E-mail: clep@info.collegeboard.org
Phone: (800) 257-9558

GED (General Educational Development)

Website: www.acenet.edu

Created By: The American Council on Education.

Purpose: The GED certifies that an American or Canadian student has high school-level academic skills.

Test Description: The GED comprises five tests: Language Arts Writing, Social Studies, Science, Language Arts Reading, Mathematics.

Question Type	Number of Questions	Time Allotted
Language Arts, Writing		
Sentence corrections, revisions, and construction questions	50	75 minutes
Essay question	1	45 minutes
Social Studies	50	70 minutes
Science	50	80 minutes
Language Arts, Reading	50	65 minutes
Mathematics		
Multiple-choice and grid-ins (with calculator)	25	45 minutes
Multiple-choice and grid-ins (without calculator)	25	45 minutes

Unscored experimental items included? No.

About Scoring: Each of the five parts of the GED are scored on a scale from 200 to 800, meaning the total possible score ranges from 1000 to 4000. Unlike other standardized tests, the GED is a pass/non-pass test. Minimum passing scores are determined by each jurisdiction that offers the tests.

Penalty for wrong answers? No.

Testing Schedule: GED exams are offered throughout the year—contact your state's GED office for details. See the website for a list of contacts by state.

Testing Fees: Fee levels vary depending on the testing site, but the total to take all 5 tests is about $65 to 70. Additional fees are incurred for rescheduling, retesting, and skipping the test (no show).

Refund for registration cancellation available? No.

Contact:
<u>American Council on Education</u>
One Dupont Circle NW
Washington DC, 20036
E-mail: comments@ace.nche.edu
Phone: (202) 939-9300

<u>GED Program</u>
E-mail: ged@ace.nche.edu
Phone: (202) 939-9490

GRADUATE

GMAT (Graduate Management Admission Test)

Website: www.mba.com

Created By: As of January 2006, the GMAT questions and computer-adaptive format are created by ACT, Inc. The test is administered by Pearson VUE's testing centers and sponsored by GMAC, the Graduate Management Admission Council.

Purpose: The GMAT is used to predict how well an applicant will perform in business school. It is one of the main criteria used to select students for MBA programs.

Test Description: The GMAT is a computer-adaptive test, or CAT. Unlike paper-and-pencil standardized tests that begin with an easy question and then get progressively tougher, the CAT always begins by giving you a medium question. If you get it right, the computer gives you a slightly harder question. If you get it wrong, the computer gives you a slightly easier question, and so on. The idea is that the computer will zero in on your exact level of ability very quickly, which allows you to answer fewer questions overall and allows the computer to more accurately assess your abilities.

The GMAT consists of three parts:

1. Two 30-minute essays to be written on the computer using a generic word-processing program, followed by an optional break

2. A 75-minute, 37-question multiple-choice Math section, followed by an optional break

3. A 75-minute, 41-question multiple-choice Verbal section

Type	Number of Items
Analytical Writing Assessment	
Analysis of an Issue	1
Analysis of an Argument	1
Math	
Problem-Solving	22
Data Sufficiency	15
TOTAL	37
Verbal	
Reading Comprehension	14
Sentence Correction	16
Critical Reasoning	11
TOTAL	41

Unscored experimental items included? Yes. On each of the Math and Verbal sections, one quarter of the questions you encounter will be experimental and will not count toward your score. These 20 questions will be mixed in among the regular questions.

About Scoring: The Verbal and Math portions of the GMAT are each scored from 0 to 60. Your total GMAT score combines the Verbal and Math scores, which are then converted to a score from 200 to 800. Your Analytic Writing Assessment (AWA) essays are graded on a scale of 0 to 6. There are 2 essays, each evaluated by 2 readers (one human and one computer). ETS averages the 4 scores, and rounds to the nearest half point. Your AWA score does not count toward your composite score. In addition, all scores are accompanied by percentile rankings.

Your Math and Verbal subscores, along with your overall score, are ready immediately for viewing when you complete the test. Your writing score is determined separately and available approximately 20 days after the test.

The median GMAT score is approximately 520.

Penalty for wrong answers? No.

Can I skip questions and come back to them? No. You must select an answer to move to the next item.

Testing Schedule: The GMAT is an online test and has no set administration schedule. The test may be taken year-round, but you may take the GMAT test up to 5 times during any 12-month period, but only ONCE during any 31-day period.

Testing Fees: $250 registration fee. You must make reservation with a Pearson VUE testing center to reserve a seat to take the test. There is also a $50 rescheduling fee if change to your scheduled test is made at least 7 days before your test date. If you reschedule within 7 days of your confirmed test date, you will be charged another $250, the full amount for the test.

Refund for registration cancellation available? Yes—if you cancel at least 7 days before your test date, you will receive a refund of $80. If you cancel within 7 days of your confirmed test date, you forfeit the entire registration fee of $250.

Post-test cancellation available? Yes, but you can only cancel at the test center after you have completed the test but before you have seen your scores. You cannot have the scores reinstated at a later date if you cancel.

Optional Services: $45 fee to have the analytical writing assessment re-scored

Contact: Customer service for test takers varies by country. For test takers in the Americas:

E-mail: GMATCandidateServicesAmericas@pearson.com
Phone: (800) 717-GMAT (4628)

For other countries, go to www.mba.com for additional contact information.

GRE (Graduate Record Exam)

Website: www.gre.com

Created By: Educational Testing Services (ETS) under the sponsorship of the Graduate Record Examinations Board.

Purpose: The GRE General Test is a standardized entrance exam used by many graduate schools for admissions and fellowship consideration. Your results indicate how likely you are to succeed in graduate-level studies.

The GRE Subject Tests are intended to measure your knowledge of specific subject matter. Subject Tests are available in eight disciplines: biochemistry, cell and molecular biology; biology; chemistry; computer science; literature in English; mathematics; physics; and psychology.

Test Description: The GRE General Test is a computer-adaptive test (CAT), but is administered as a paper exam internationally and under special circumstances in the U.S. The GRE Subject Tests are given in paper-and-pencil format. The Analytical Writing is always first, but the remaining sections can appear in any order. For the Issue Essay, you are given two topics to write on—choose one. For the Argument Essay, you must write on the single topic presented.

Unlike paper-and-pencil standardized tests that begin with an easy question and then get progressively tougher, the CAT always begins by giving you a medium question. If you get it right, the computer gives you a slightly harder question. If you get it wrong, the computer gives you a slightly easier question, and so on. The idea is that the computer will zero in on your exact level of ability very quickly, which allows you to answer fewer questions overall and allows the computer to more accurately assess your abilities.

Computer-Adaptive GRE General Test		
Question Type	**Number of Questions**	**Time Allotted**
Analytical Writing		
Issue Task	1	45 minutes
Argument Task	1	30 minutes
10-minute break		
Verbal		
Reading Comprehension and Sentence Analysis	30	30 minutes
Quantitative		
Quantitative Reasoning and Problem Solving	28	45 minutes

The GRE General Test includes an optional 10-minute break after the Analytical Writing section and one-minute breaks between the remaining sections of the test. These break times cannot be exceeded.

Paper-Based GRE General Test		
Question Type	**Number of Questions**	**Time Allotted**
Analytical Writing		
Issue Task	1	45 minutes
Argument Task	1	30 minutes
Verbal—2 sections		
Reading Comprehension and Sentence Analysis	38	30 minutes each
Quantitative—2 sections		
Quantitative Reasoning and Problem Solving	30	30 minutes each

Unscored experimental items included? Yes. There will be an unidentified experimental section on the GRE General Test. It will be either Math or Verbal and will be indistinguishable from the real, scored sections.

The GRE will occasionally include a research section. If it appears, it will be the final section on the test, optional, and clearly identified. This section is also unscored, but since it is optional, you can skip it if you want.

About Scoring: On the GRE General Test, you will receive separate Verbal and Quantitative scores; these are reported on a scale from 200 to 800 in increments of 10. Your Analytical Writing section will be listed separately, and is scored on a scale of 0 to 6, in half-point increments. All scores are accompanied by percentile rankings. Here's a look at the average GRE scores for some general graduate fields.

You will be shown your Verbal and Quantitative scores at the end of the CAT, but your essay scores and "official" percentile scores for all three sections will be sent to you a few weeks after the test.

On the GRE Subject Tests, one total score is reported on a 200 to 990 score scale, in 10-point increments, although the score range for any particular Subject Test is usually smaller. Subscores are reported for the Biochemistry, Cell and Molecular Biology; Biology; and Psychology Tests on a 20–99 score scale, in one-point increments.

Intended Graduate Field	Approximate Number of Test Takers	Average Math Score	Average Verbal Score
Life Sciences	117,577	581	462
Physical Sciences	101,085	697	486
Engineering	56,368	719	468
Social Sciences	55,910	565	487
Humanities and Arts	49,882	566	545
Education	43,844	534	449
Business	8,357	592	442

Penalty for wrong answers? On the GRE General Test CAT, no. On the GRE paper-based test and GRE Subject Tests, yes. You will lost one-quarter point for each incorrect response.

Testing Schedule: Because the GRE General Test is a computer-based test, you can take it almost any day. However, you cannot take it more than once per calendar month or more than 5 times within any 12-month period. The paper-based GRE General Test is only offered twice per year. The GRE Subject Tests are given three times per year, in October, November, and April. Check the GRE website for exact dates.

Testing Fees GRE General Test: $140 within the United States, some U.S. Territories, and Puerto Rico. The fee is $170 in all other locations (except China, including Hong Kong, Korea, and Taiwan, where it is $175).

Testing Fees GRE Subject Tests: $130 within the United States, some U.S. Territories, and Puerto Rico. The fee is $150 in all other locations.

Refund for registration cancellation available? You must reschedule or cancel your test no later than 10 full days before your test date (not including the day of your test or the day of your request) or your test fee will be forfeited. Mailed requests must be received no later than 10 full days prior to your scheduled test date. The rescheduling fee is $50. If you cancel your General Test or Subject Test no later than 10 full days prior to your test date, you will receive a refund equivalent to half of the original test fee.

Post-test cancellation available? Yes. You can cancel your scores immediately after you take the GRE General and Subject Tests. This is the only time you can cancel your scores. Unfortunately, you must make the decision to cancel at the testing center before you see your scores. In addition, the fact that you cancelled your scores will be noted on your official GRE score report.

Optional Services:

Score reinstatement: $30 if request received by ETS within 60 days of test date

Writing rescore: $55

Handscoring of paper-based test: $30

Late registration: $25 additional fee

Rescheduling or change of testing location fee: $50

Stand-by testing: $50 (paper test only)

Scores by phone: $12

Q&A review service (Math and Verbal only): $50

Extra score reports: $15

Contact:
GRE-ETS
P.O. Box 6000
Princeton, NJ 08541-6000
Phone: (609) 771-7670 or (866) 473-4373 (toll free in the United
        States, U.S. territories, and Canada)

LSAT (Law School Admissions Test)

Website: www.lsac.org

Created By: The Law School Admission Council (LSAC)

Purpose: According to LSAC, the LSAT is "a half-day standardized test required for admission to all ABA-approved law schools, most Canadian law schools, and many non-ABA-approved law schools. It provides a standard measure of acquired reading and verbal reasoning skills that law schools can use as one of several factors in assessing applicants."

Test Description: The LSAT contains 100 or 101 multiple-choice questions and an unscored writing sample. All sections are 35 minutes long. The multiple-choice sections may appear in any order, but the writing sample is always last. The experimental section is unscored and is not returned to the test taker. A break of 10 to 15 minutes is given between the 3rd and 4th sections.

Section	Number of Questions
Logical Reasoning (a.k.a. Arguments)	24 to 26 questions
Reading Comprehension	4 passages, 26 to 28 questions
Logical Reasoning (a.k.a. Arguments)	24 to 26 questions
Analytical Reasoning (a.k.a. Games)	4 logic games, 22 to 24 questions
Experimental	Any of the three types

Unscored experimental items included? Yes. One section is experimental—it could be either Reading, Arguments, or Games.

About Scoring: The LSAT is scored on a scale from 120 to 180. The median score is approximately 151. Almost 70 percent of all test takers fall into the 140 to 160 score range. Your scores also come with a percentile ranking, which is calculated by comparing your test performance with those of test takers from the last three years. Lastly, LSAT reports include a "score band" of roughly three points above and three points below your score. For example, if your score is 150, your report would include a score band of 147 to 153.

You cannot take the LSAT more than three times in a two-year period.

Penalty for wrong answers? No penalty, so guess away!

Testing Schedule: The LSAT is offered four times per year: February, June, October (or late September), and December. October is the most popular date, but because law school admissions are conducted on a rolling basis, many pre-law advisors recommend testing in June so that you can get your application in sooner when there are more slots available.

Testing Fees: $123 registration fee. Late registration is an additional $62.

Refund for registration cancellation available? Yes—you are refunded $44 if you cancel before your test date.

Post-test cancellation available? Yes. You can either cancel your score at the test center or by writing to LSAC. LSAC must receive your request for cancellation within 6 days of your test date.

Optional Services:
Change test date fee: $32
Scores by phone: $10
Hard copy of score report: $25 if you have an online account

Contact:
LSAC
662 Penn Street
Box 2000-T
Newtown, PA 18940
Phone: (215) 968-1001

PRAXIS I: PPST (Pre-Professional Skills Test) and PRAXIS II

Website: www.ets.org/praxis

Created By: Educational Testing Services (ETS)

Purpose: According to ETS, "[t]he Praxis Series assessments provide educational tests and other services that states use as part of their teaching licensing certification process. The Praxis I tests measure basic academic skills, and the Praxis II tests measure general and subject-specific knowledge and teaching skills." These tests are used as licensure tests for teachers in grades K through 12.

Test Description: The PRAXIS I (PPST) exam is given in both computer-based and paper-based form. Both formats test basic math, reading, and writing skills. The CBT form of the PPST takes approximately 4-and-a-half hours to complete, and consists of four sections. The Reading and Math tests each contain 46 items with 75 minutes of testing time per test. The Writing test consists of 44 multiple-choice questions with 38 minutes of testing time, and one essay question with 30 minutes of testing time.

The paper-based PPST is structured similarly. The Reading and Mathematics consist of 40 multiple-choice questions with 60 minutes of testing time. The Writing test consists of 38 multiple-choice questions and one essay question with two 30-minute sections of testing time.

The PRAXIS II Subject tests measure knowledge of specific subjects that K–12 educators will teach, as well as general and subject-specific teaching skills and knowledge. There are Subject Assessments, Principles of Learning and Teaching (PLT) Tests and Teaching Foundations Tests. All are paper-based tests.

Subject Assessments test content-specific knowledge in more than 100 different subject areas. PLT tests measure your general pedagogical knowledge at four grade levels: Early Childhood, K–6, 5–9 and 7–12. These tests use a case study approach and feature constructed-response and multiple-choice items. Teaching Foundations tests measure pedagogy in five areas: multi-subject (elementary), English, Language Arts, Mathematics, and Science and Social Science. These tests feature constructed-response and multiple-choice items.

About Scoring: The PRAXIS exams are pass/fail tests. Each state has its own cut-offs for licensure, and some require certain combinations of test scores. Your score report will say if you passed or not. Subject tests are scored either on a scale from 100 to 200 or from 250 to 999 depending on the test. PLT and Teaching Foundations tests are scored on a scale from 100 to 200. Median scores vary widely from test to test.

Penalty for wrong answers? No.

Testing Schedule: Computer-based PPST testing is available year-round. Paper-based Subject tests are offered 7 times a year: in September, November, January, March, April, June, and July. PPST paper-based test is only offered in January, April, July, and November. Teaching Foundations tests are only offered in March, June, July, and November.

Testing Fees: Testing fees vary widely depending on test and format. Go to the PRAXIS website for a full list of all test and fees.

Refund for registration cancellation available? Yes. For the computer-based PPST, you can be refunded $20 per test if your request is received at least three days before your testing appointment. For paper-based tests, refunds are available if your request is received by the late registration date.

Post-test cancellation available? Yes. At the end of the computer-based PPST, you have the option to cancel your scores. This is the only time you may cancel. For paper-based tests, you can cancel your scores after the test. Your request must be received no later than one week after the testing date.

Optional Services:

Score verification: $40 for a multiple-choice test, $55 for a constructed-response test, $55 for combined multiple-choice and constructed-response, and $80 for Teaching Foundations.

Paper-based late registration: $45

Paper-based test date or test center change: $45

Contact:
ETS-The PRAXIS Series
P.O. Box 6051
Princeton, N.J. 08541-6051
Phone: (609) 771-7395 or toll-free (800) 772-9476

MCAT CBT (Medical College Admission Test Computer-Based Test)

Website: www.aamc.org/mcat

Created By: AAMC, the Association of American Medical Colleges, develops and maintains the MCAT.

Purpose: According to the AAMC, the MCAT is " designed to assess the examinee's problem solving, critical thinking, writing skills, and knowledge of science concepts and principles prerequisite to the study of medicine." It is required of nearly all U.S. medical colleges.

Test Description: The MCAT is a five-and-a-half-hour-long, computer-based exam split into four sections: Physical Sciences, Verbal Reasoning, Writing, and Biological Sciences.

Section	Number of Questions and Timing	Content Tested
Physical Sciences	52 questions, 70 minutes	Math, physics, general chemistry
Verbal Reasoning	40 questions, 60 minutes	Passage-based reading comprehension
Writing	2 essay questions, 60 minutes	Your ability to formulate and communicate an argument and convey complex ideas
Biological Sciences	52 questions, 70 minutes	Biology, organic chemistry

Unscored experimental items included? Yes.

About Scoring: The Physical Sciences, Verbal Reasoning, and Biological Sciences sections on the MCAT are scored between a 1 and a 15. (1 is the lowest score and 15 is the highest score.) In total, the lowest score you can receive on the MCAT is a 3, and the highest is a 45. The two essays are scored on a J to T scale by one human and one computer grader. Most competitive medical schools look for a combined MCAT score of at least 30 and a Writing score of P or Q. The average score on the multiple-choice portions of the MCAT is 8, and the average Writing score about an N or O.

Penalty for wrong answers? No.

Testing Schedule: The MCAT is given 25 times a year. See the MCAT website for the list of specific dates. To assure your spot at the test date you want, register at least 60 days in advance. You can take the MCAT up to 3 times in one year.

Testing Fees: $210 registration fee. Through the Fee Assistance Program (FAP), low-income students can apply for a fee reduction. If you are granted a reduction, you will pay $85 for the test.

Refund for registration cancellation available? You will be able to cancel the scheduled session, and receive a 50 percent refund on your registration fee by canceling your registration through the web registration system up to seven (7) days before the exam. If you discover that you cannot attend your test session fewer than seven days prior to the scheduled exam date, a refund will not be available.

Post-test cancellation available? You may only cancel your scores at the end of the exam.

Optional Services:

Rescore multiple-choice sections: $50

Rescore essay: $50

Contact:

The MCAT Care Team
Association of American Medical Colleges
Section for Applicant Assessment Services
2450 N St., NW
Washington, DC 20037
E-mail: mcat@aamc.org
Phone: 202-828-0690

OTHER GRADUATE

DAT (Dental Admission Test)

Website: www.ada.org

Created By: The ADA, or American Dental Association

Purpose: According to the ADA's website, the DAT is " designed to measure general academic ability, comprehension of scientific information, and perceptual ability."

Test Description: The DAT is a computer-based exam consisting of four tests: Survey of the Natural Sciences, Perceptual Ability, Reading Comprehension, and Quantitative Reasoning. The DAT is given at Prometric Testing Centers only.

Test	Number of Questions and Timing	Content
Survey of the Natural Sciences	100 questions, 90 minutes	Biology, Organic and Inorganic Chemistry
Perceptual Ability	90 questions, 60 minutes	Visualizing in three dimensions, angle discrimination
Reading Comprehension	50 questions, 60 minutes	Finding, absorbing, and keeping track of information
Quantitative Reasoning	40 questions, 45 minutes	Algebra, Word Problems, Basic Math, Geometry, Trigonometry

About Scoring: You will receive a separate score for Reading Comprehension, Perceptual Ability, Quantitative Reasoning, and each of the science disciplines tested in Survey of Natural Sciences—Biology, Inorganic Chemistry, and Organic Chemistry. In addition, you will receive an Academic Average Score, which combines your scores from all of the sections of the exam except Perceptual Ability. Each of these scores is reported on a 1 to 30 scale (30 being the highest possible score). The national average score is about 16.

Penalty for wrong answers? No.

Testing Schedule: The DAT is computer based, and so has no set dates. Once you send in your registration fee to the DAT program, you then contact Prometric to schedule your test.

Testing Fees: A $175 registration fee comes with up to five score reports sent to colleges.

Refund for registration cancellation available? No.

Post-test cancellation available? No.

Optional Services:

Rescheduling fee: $10

Extra score reports: $5 each

Contact:

ADA Department of Testing Services

211 East Chicago Avenue, Suite 600

Chicago, IL 60611

Phone: (800) 232-1694

OAT (Optometry Admission Test)

Website: www.opted.org

Created By: The OAT is sponsored by the Association of Schools and Colleges of Optometry (ASCO)

Purpose: The OAT is designed to measure general academic ability and comprehension of scientific information and is required of students applying for entrance into an optometry program.

Test Description: The OAT is a computer-based exam consisting of four tests: Survey of the Natural Sciences, Reading Comprehension, Physics, and Quantitative Reasoning. The OAT is given at Prometric Testing Centers only.

Test	Number of Questions and Timing	Content
Survey of the Natural Sciences	100 questions, 90 minutes	Biology, Organic Chemistry, Inorganic Chemistry
Reading Comprehension	40 questions, 50 minutes	Finding and processing information in dense passages
Physics	40 questions, 50 minutes	Vectors, Energy & Momentum, Thermodynamics, Magnetism, Optics
Quantitative Reasoning	40 questions, 45 minutes	Arithmetic, Algebra, Geometry, Trigonometry

Unscored experimental items included? Sometimes, yes—these are referred to as "pretest" questions and are mixed in with the scored items. If they appear on the test, additional time is provided for that section of the test.

About Scoring: You are allowed to take the OAT an unlimited number of times but must wait at least 90 days between testing dates. However, only scores from the four most recent attempts and the total number of attempts will be reported.

OAT scores range from 200 to 400, with the average score about 300. Separate subscores are reported for Biology, Inorganic chemistry, Organic chemistry, Reading Comprehension, and Quantitative Reasoning.

Penalty for wrong answers? No.

Testing Schedule: The OAT is computer based, and so has no set dates. Once you send in your registration fee to the OAT program, you then contact Prometric to schedule your test. Your registration fee is valid for one year, and if you do not test within that year, your fee is not refunded.

Testing Fees: The $195 registration fee includes reports sent to up to five colleges. Fee waivers of 50 percent are available for low-income test takers. Contact the OAT Program for more information on how to apply.

Refund for registration cancellation available? No.

Optional Services:
Rescheduling fee: $10
Extra score reports: $25 each

Contact:
Optometric Admission Testing Program
211 East Chicago Avenue, Suite 600
Chicago, IL 60611-2678
Phone: (800) 232-2159

PCAT (Pharmacy College Admission Test)

Website: PCATweb.info

Created By: PsychCorp, part of Harcourt Assessment, Inc. Endorsed by the American Association of Colleges of Pharmacy.

Purpose: To help identify qualified applicants to pharmacy colleges. The PCAT tests six content areas:

- The Verbal Ability subtest measures general, non-scientific word knowledge and usage using analogies and sentence completion.

- The Biology subtest measures knowledge of the principles and concepts of basic biology, including general biology, microbiology, and human anatomy and physiology.

- The Chemistry subtest measures knowledge of principles and concepts of inorganic and elementary organic chemistry.

- The Reading Comprehension section measures ability to comprehend, analyze, and evaluate reading passages on science-related topics.

- The Quantitative Ability subtest measures skills in mathematical processes and the ability to reason through and understand quantitative concepts and relationships, including applications of basic math, algebra, probability and statistics, pre-calculus, and calculus.

- Two Writing subtests measure the effective use of language conventions and the ability to suggest the solution to a problem in written essays. There is one essay topic in each of two sections that requires you to write a problem-solving essay.

Test Description: The PCAT consists of 240 multiple-choice questions and two Writing topics. The test is 4 hours long, not including time for instructions at the beginning of the test and a break halfway through the test.

Section	Time	Number of Items
Writing: Problem Solving, Conventions of Language	30 min	1 topic
Verbal: Analogies, Sentence Completions	30 min	48 questions
Biology: General Biology, Microbiology, Anatomy, Physiology	30 min	48 questions
Chemistry: General and Organic Chemistry	30 min	48 questions
Break		
Writing: Problem Solving, Conventions of Language	30 min	1 topic
Reading Comprehension	50 min	6 passages, 48 questions
Quantitative Ability: Basic Math, Algebra, Probability & Statistics, Pre-calculus, Calculus	40 min	48 questions

Unscored experimental items included? Yes. Out of each 48 questions on each multiple-choice section, 40 questions count towards your score and 8 are unscored items.

About Scoring: You will receive five scores and percentile rankings, one for each of the multiple-choice sections of the test, ranging from 200 to 600. You will also receive a composite score from 200 to 600, an average of the five separate sections. The national average is about 400.

The Writing score is reported separately, ranging from 5 to 1, with 5 the highest score possible. Scores for only one of the two Writing subtests will be reported to examinees and recipient schools. The other Writing subtest will be experimental, and scores for this subtest will not be reported. The Writing portion of the test is graded by human readers. A Conventions of Language score between 1 and 5 will be assigned by a single reader. The Problem Solving score represents an average of scores assigned by two readers, and may be reported in half-point increments between 1 and 5.

Penalty for wrong answers? No.

Testing Schedule: Offered four times per year in January, June, August, and October.

Testing Fees: A $125.00 registration fee includes one personal score report and score reports sent to up to three colleges of pharmacy or other organizations. This fee is for online or paper registration only.

Refund for registration cancellation available? Yes—50 percent of testing fee will be refunded if request is received by cancellation deadline.

Post-test cancellation available? Yes—scores can be cancelled the day of the test using the No Score Option.

Optional Services:

$35.00—additional charge for registering via paper form

$49.00—additional charge for late online registration

$189.00—additional charge for testing at a location other than a scheduled testing center

$271.00—additional fee for testing outside the US, Canada, and Puerto Rico

$20.00—additional score report

$35.00—fee for handscoring, if requested

$50.00—fee for rescoring, if requested

$21.00—fee for online practice test

Contact:
Harcourt Assessment, Inc.
PSE Customer Relations—PCAT
19500 Bulverde Road
San Antonio, Texas 78259
E-mail: scoring.services@harcourt.com
Phone: (800) 622-3231

NCLEX-RN (National Council Licensure Examination)

Website: www.ncsbn.org

Created By: The NCLEX-RN exam is created by the National Council of State Boards of Nursing.

Purpose: According to the NCSBN, the NCLEX is intended to determine if it is safe for test takers to being practice as an entry-level nurse. A passing score is required to obtain a license to work as a registered nurse.

Test Description: The NCLEX is an application-based, computer-adaptive format exam. The test has a minimum of 75 and a maximum of 265 questions. The number of questions that you are given does not indicate a specific pass or fail result; in other words, only getting 75 questions (the minimum) does not mean you failed. The maximum time allowed is 6 hours, including a tutorial at the beginning of the test and breaks. The questions are primarily multiple-choice with four answers to choose from, but there are also a number of alternate question types. These include multiple-response, fill-in-the-blank, hot-spots, chart/exhibit, and drag-and-drop formats. Unlike other exams, which test separate content areas in different sections, the NCLEX integrates all content across the test.

Unscored experimental items included? Yes—15 test items are unscored, pretest items.

About Scoring: The NCLEX is a pass/fail exam. You will get your results 2 to 4 weeks after the test. You must wait at least 45 or 90 days to retest if you do not pass.

Penalty for wrong answers? No—the NCLEX is a computer-adaptive test, so there is no penalty for wrong answers.

Testing Schedule: Testing is available year-round.

Testing Fees: $200 registration fee. Once your fee is received and you receive an Authorization to Test (ATT) in the mail, you may contact Pearson to schedule your test. Your ATT only lasts so long, so be sure to schedule during the allowed time.

Refund for registration cancellation available? No refunds. If you need to change or cancel a testing appointment, you must contact NCLEX Candidate Services at least one full business day before your scheduled testing window. If you do not, you forfeit your registration fee and your candidate record will indicate you were a no-show for your test when you apply for licensure.

Post-test cancellation available? No.

Optional Services:

Phone registration: $9.50 additional fee

International testing: $150 additional scheduling fee

Contact:
NCSBN
111 E. Wacker Drive, Suite 2900,
Chicago, IL 60601-4277
E-mail: nclexinfo@ncsbn.org
(312) 525-3750 or toll-free (866) 293-9600

8

Appendix A: Disputes with ETS

By Jay Rosner
Executive Director,
The Princeton Review Foundation

Note—We are proud to inform you that a prior version of this article was cited in a decision of the Supreme Court of New York, Appellate Division. The information here was reviewed on April 18, 2005, and is believed to be accurate through that date. We'll try to update this periodically. Please use the information here as an overview and a guideline only. Someone with expertise should analyze the facts of any individual situation before important decisions are made, particularly in questioned or challenged SAT score situations (euphemisms used by ETS when accusing a student of cheating on the SAT). At times ETS changes these policies without notification to anyone outside ETS. So, the current policies of ETS should be reviewed very carefully.

This article is focused upon the SAT's math and verbal (now called "Critical Reading") scores. A writing section was added to the SAT in 2005; to date, there has been no experience with a challenge to a writing section score. Some of procedures described below apply to ETS's GRE and GMAT (the GMAT will be developed by ACT in the future), offered on computer; moreover, those tests have introduced some additional difficulties, including the occasional computer scoring glitch. As for the ACT, their procedures differ in some important respects, although many of the general principles in this article still apply.

I. Introduction & Testing Conditions

Test-takers have wide-ranging interactions with Educational Testing Service ("ETS"). The beginning of the SAT relationship usually occurs when a student mails to ETS a registration form and a check. More and more students are now registering for the test via ETS's web site (www.ets.org). If everything proceeds normally (and it does for the vast majority of test-takers), the test-taker receives an admission ticket by mail before the SAT, takes the test under good testing conditions and receives a score by mail in 3-5 weeks. Scores are usually available by telephone, for an extra fee, 2 weeks after the test, and are now available via the internet.

The relationship between the student and ETS can go awry, but this happens rather infrequently. If an SAT Admissions Ticket (confirming registration for the test) isn't received by the student one week before the test, or if the Ticket is lost, the student should call ETS Customer Service to confirm registration. Usually the pre-registered student's name is on the test center's list; moreover, a student almost always can take the SAT on a stand-by basis, which requires the payment of an extra fee--check the procedures in the SAT Registration Bulletin. After the test the student can figure out what happened with the admission ticket.

Complaints about test center irregularities (noise, mistiming, etc.) range from the trivial to the significant. If test-takers are shorted one minute or less, it's generally not worth taking on ETS over it. Likewise, minor noise or momentary disturbances will be hard to fight; however, on very rare occasions there are significant disruptions to a quiet test situation, and those should be pursued vigorously.

Where significant disruptions or timing discrepancies occur at the test center, the first consideration is whether the student was sufficiently distracted so that a score cancellation should be requested. Some students assume that ETS will add points to their score to reflect the disruption or discrepancy. This will NEVER happen. On rare occasions ETS will schedule a special retest within a few weeks for a group of students, but usually only if a large number of students complain. If a student is unclear as to whether his/her score was impacted, he/she should request to be told the score BEFORE having to decide whether to cancel (this requires an extension of the right to cancel until the score is generated). ETS seldom permits this, but never offers it where it isn't requested.

Most complaints to ETS should be handled by a faxed letter with details and requested resolution (don't wait for snail-mail) along with courteous but persistent telephone follow-up, as one would do with any other business entity. Sometimes test-takers have difficulties with other testing agencies, like ACT or Law Services. Some of their procedures are significantly different from ETS procedures. Try to get advice from someone who is knowledgeable about the testing company with which you are dealing.

II. Questioned Scores, or Cheating Accusations

Delays in receiving test scores sometimes occur. When a student is notified that there is a delay in processing an SAT score, most often (perhaps three fourths of the time) this results in the release (i.e., not canceling) of the score; however, there is also a one in four possibility of the most difficult dispute with ETS--questioned or challenged scores. These are euphemisms for ETS accusing a test taker of cheating, or otherwise unfairly obtaining a test score.

The following will focus on questioned or challenged scores. Again, most other disputes with ETS should be addressed by a letter and telephone follow-up. It is in the area of questioned score disputes that the stakes for the test-taker are the highest, and that ETS has its own arcane procedures which apply.

A student or parent or counselor may wonder exactly what the challenged score was. Sometimes ETS personnel will give the score over the telephone; sometimes they won't. Yet the score is on the first page ("Score Review Summary") of the student's file held by ETS. Just ask for the file (see Section IX below) to find out the questioned score.

III. ETS Attitude Toward Questioned Scores

When a test-taker makes a mistake regarding the SAT, the test-taker pays a price. When ETS makes a mistake regarding the SAT, the test-taker pays a price. There are two ways for a test-taker to lose in this game, and you don't necessarily have to be at fault to suffer some consequences.

Here's the nicest thing I can say about ETS--most people who work there genuinely care about being fair and trying to be responsive to students; however, the most well-motivated of ETS employees are stuck within a system that limits their flexibility. ETS has a "party line," or company attitude, that often dictates what will happen to a test-taker.

Here are some of the significant aspects of ETS's attitude toward questioned scores:

1. ETS requires at least two items of evidence before questioning scores, the most common of which are a large score difference (dramatic improvement from a prior test) combined with similar answers to a test-taker seated nearby.

2. If ETS statistical analysis (which is limited in scope) or their handwriting analysis combines with a large score difference to indicate cheating, ETS employees take the position that they have enough evidence to support a decision of cheating, and that the student actually cheated.

3. ETS employees believe that their system treats students fairly (which it sometimes doesn't).

4. Therefore, in questioned score situations, ETS employees can, on occasion, be arrogant and/or patronizing to the very small percentage of students accused because they (ETS) fully believe that they are correct, that the test-taker cheated and that they (ETS) are bending over backward to be fair and protect the test-taker's rights.

5. ETS asks for evidence from the test-taker, but routinely ignores it (unless it addresses a few, very limited issues such as a hand injury affecting handwriting).

6. The most common evidence submitted by test-takers consists of character reference letters from teachers and other school personnel, which are given virtually no weight in the ETS test security process.

7. Usually the best way to overcome a questioned score accusation is to obtain the ETS file and vigorously attack ETS evidence, which requires a significant degree of expertise.

IV. Types of Questioned Score Situations

There are two basic categories of questioned score situations: group situations and individual situations. Group situations involve the cancellation of scores for an entire group taking the test, and are usually based on test-takers getting access to test booklets before the test begins. Group situations are very complex and relatively rare, and will not be addressed here. Individual situations arise when an individual test-taker has his or her score questioned and threatened with cancellation.

Individual questioned scores come in two types: "unusual agreement" and "disparate handwriting." Of the two types, the former is by far the most common. Unusual agreement refers to unusual agreement of answers, and is an ETS euphemism for cheating by copying or otherwise communicating answers between two individual test-takers. Disparate handwriting is usually a euphemism for sending in an impostor to take one's test.

Because unusual agreement is the far more common basis for questioned scores, it will be the primary focus of the rest of this paper, although some comments will be made about impostor accusations.

V. What to do if the Score Report is Delayed

Often the first indication of questioned scores is that a score report will be delayed. Test-takers usually are in touch with others who have taken the test on the same day, and will find out when other students have received their scores. If a test-taker's score is delayed more that one week, one possibility is that scores are being questioned.

ETS will often send a letter which says, "Your SAT I: Reasoning Test scores are delayed because they are under routine administrative review." As previously stated, perhaps 3/4 of these situations result in a released score, with perhaps only 1/4 resulting in questioned scores. Also, there are other unusual possibilities--on rare occasions, ETS loses an answer sheet or the score report gets mailed to the wrong address or is somehow lost.

If the test-taker receives this "scores are delayed" letter, he/she should call ETS and ask specifically where they are in the review process, and what will happen next. Often the ETS person will reply that there are general processing delays, but the test-taker should ask for specifics. If asked point-blank whether the two items of evidence exist for a score to be questioned, ETS employees will almost always acknowledge it if that is the case.

RULE OF THUMB #1: In calling ETS, always keep careful notes of the dates and times calls are made, write down the name (and correct spelling) of the ETS employee to whom you speak, summarize what was said and try to follow-up with that person in subsequent calls.

VI. ETS Questioned Score Procedure

Step #1 Flagging: The ETS Test Security Office (TSO) reviews a test-taker's score, which has been flagged by large score difference or an inquiry of some type (sometimes an anonymous tip). This review most often occurs before the score is reported back to the student and to the other score recipients (i.e. colleges), but sometimes occurs after a score is reported.

The most common event causing ETS to review a score is that the test-taker has increased his or her score significantly from a score obtained at a prior administration. ETS does computer comparisons of current and prior scores, and "flags" a score for review if the increase is above a certain amount. With SAT scores, if a student increases 350 points or more in combined math + verbal scores, or increases 250 points or more in either math or verbal, the score is flagged for review. This will constitute a questioned score if ETS finds a second item of evidence to support cancellation.

Also, if an outside person (another student, counselor, admissions officer or coach) contacts ETS and says that cheating may have occurred, even if this is done anonymously, ETS will review the score.

If an ETS employee tells you that a score is being questioned, immediately request a letter stating the basis for questioning the score and ask when you can expect to receive this letter. This may help expedite the process by a week or two. Then, seek advice ASAP from someone with expertise.

Step #2 Similar Answers or Handwriting: The TSO looks for handwriting differences in the two test forms of the same individual (current and previous), and does a statistical analysis of similar answers comparing the test-taker's answers with those of everyone seated nearby. If the TSO finds neither handwriting differences nor similar answers, the score is considered valid, and released and reported.

Step #3 "Questioned Scores Letter": The "Questioned Scores Letter" (not to be confused with the "scores are delayed" letter, described above) contains a cursory summary of the evidence supporting canceling the scores, along with a list of options for the test-taker. These options will be discussed below. This letter invites the test-taker to make one submission of additional information that the ETS Board of Review might consider.

Step #4 Copy of the File: The test-taker has the right to request copies of all documents in his/her file. The vast majority of test-takers do not avail themselves of this right. This will be discussed further below. The Board of Review makes its decision based upon evidence in the file, so that it is imperative for a test-taker to see this evidence in order to understand why the ETS TSO is recommending score cancellation. Also, since the test-taker can make only one submission of additional information, it is highly recommended that the test-taker examine a copy of the file before making his/her submission of additional information. It is possible, but not guaranteed, that ETS will permit a second submission to the Board of Review if the first submission was done before a copy of the file was requested.

Step #5 Additional Evidence: The test-taker may choose to submit additional evidence to the Board of Review. It seems that in too many questioned scores situations, the test-taker submits additional evidence, the Board remains convinced that cancellation is appropriate and the test-taker ends up choosing another option. The most common mistake test-takers make is that they submit character reference letters to convince the Board of Review of their innocence. As stated before, the Board gives virtually no weight to these kinds of letters.

Step #6 Board of Review: After additional information is received, the test-taker's file is submitted to the ETS Board of Review. The Board decides whether or not to cancel scores. The Board can release the scores if it chooses (only one member of the three-member panel need "vote" for release of the score and the score will be validated and reported); however, if the Board decides to cancel scores, the TSO sends another "options" letter to the test-taker.

Step #7 Options: The test-taker may challenge the Board's decision to cancel scores either in court or in arbitration, or (sometimes) can ask a university to which he/she is applying to independently evaluate a score cancellation to determine whether the university agrees with the ETS position. Alternatively, the test-taker can take a free retest at a special administration set up by ETS. See comments below on the various options.

VII. Options Given by ETS

Pre-Option: Provide additional information. Although a student usually desires to provide character evidence, this is virtually always ignored by the Board of Review. Usually the only effective evidence is information that attacks ETS's own statistical analysis. One advantage of providing additional information is that the only downside is loss of time; all other options are still available. The primary disadvantage is that the disregarding of the test-taker's evidence can be disheartening. High school seniors need to be particularly careful with delays, as they can adversely impact the college admission process.

Option #1: Free Retest. The disadvantages of retests are several, and usually involve increased pressure and anxiety due to the following factors:

1. A retest is usually taken by the test-taker alone in a room with an individual proctor;

2. A cloud of suspicion surrounds the test-taker;

3. The retest is usually non-disclosed, so it cannot be checked by the test-taker; and

4. The test-taker may have spent weeks or even months preparing for the original test, but then has to achieve a similar level of preparation with only perhaps a week or two notice of the retest.

One advantage of a retest is that it can be arranged rather quickly and scored right away, which is particularly important in admissions deadline situations.

Another very important advantage of a free retest is that a student can score significantly lower (100 points per section, math & verbal) than the questioned test and still receive his/her questioned scores, while retaining the ability to score even higher than the questioned scores. Yet another retest option to be considered (if there is sufficient time) is retaking the test in a more typical, regularly-scheduled public administration, in which case a student would simply ask for a refund of the fee from the questioned test, and a cancellation of that score.

A former president of ETS, Nancy Cole, has stated in a letter that one retest might not be fair, and a student has a basis for arguing for a second retest.

Option #2: Refund. ETS will be happy to resolve the dilemma by refunding the test fee and canceling the questioned scores. This amounts to the test-taker "walking away" from the situation. The test-taker can take the test again at a regularly scheduled administration.

Option #3: Asking a college to review. This option has ETS canceling the scores, but then sending the whole file to a college (not all colleges will even consider doing this) to make its own decision. In past guides to test-takers, ETS discouraged test-takers from choosing this option, implying that it would be a very rare occasion indeed in which a college would accept a score as valid in the face of ETS's having decided that the score was not valid. SPECIAL NOTE TO STUDENT ATHLETES--often student athletes with challenged scores think that if their college accepts their score under this option, then the NCAA will be satisfied. WRONG! If the NCAA requires an SAT score, the NCAA will only take a score that ETS considers valid.

Option #4: Arbitration. While most non-lawyers and lawyers have a positive feeling about arbitration, ETS arbitration is a different kettle of fish. If arbitration is chosen as an option, ETS requires the test-taker to first sign an agreement to arbitrate. This agreement rigs the arbitration in ETS's favor in several ways:

1. It specifies the standard for review, that ETS had substantial evidence to question scores, rather than the more neutral general civil standard of "preponderance of the evidence";

2. It disallows in-person appearances, meaning that the arbitration decision will be decided solely on the submission of documents; and

3. No new evidence can be submitted to the arbitrator that wasn't previously submitted to ETS's Board of Review. A very small percentage (this author estimates 10% or fewer) of students win these arbitrations against ETS.

Option #5: Judicial Review. This is an option many test-takers favor until they are confronted with the enormous cost and time factors involved. Going to court is portrayed as easy to do on television shows, but test-takers never realize that, in this country, only the very wealthy or the seriously physically injured are able to litigate. Furthermore, ETS has won nearly all of its approximately 30 test security cases, except for two that were structured and shaped by the author of this article (with Dalton vs. ETS being the most important case in this field). Finally, many judges are inclined to rule in ETS's favor because to do otherwise can be seen to be improper judicial meddling in affairs better left to testing experts. In the opinion of this author, the best single use of judicial review would be, in certain impersonation situations, to seek a mandatory injunction requiring ETS to submit a test booklet and answer sheet for fingerprint analysis. This might be expensive, but it could generate important evidence for a test-taker where impersonation had been substantiated by the opinion of an ETS handwriting expert.

VIII. Evidence

In theory, evidence in questioned scores situations consists of information that tends either to support or undermine a score cancellation decision. Evidence can come in many forms--everything from the mental state of the student at the exam to prior test scores to an analysis of the correlation between the student's grade point average in school and the test score.

ETS's Board of Review and ETS's TSO both have their own very peculiar ways of considering evidence. Their weighing of evidence can involve a double standard: evidence provided by ETS that favors cancellation of the score is usually given great weight; moreover, evidence provided by the test-taker which supports the validation of the score tends to be given little weight.

Here are some specific examples of the ETS double standard in action:

Proctor vs. proctor—If the proctor submits an irregularity report, ETS weighs it very heavily as evidence of cheating; however, if the proctor notices no cheating and in fact submits an affidavit supporting the student, such evidence is routinely discounted and usually ignored by the ETS Board of Review.

Handwriting expert vs. handwriting expert—The ETS Board of Review virtually never accepts a test-taker's handwriting expert's opinion if it differs from that of the ETS handwriting expert; furthermore, if something is unclear to the Board in the ETS expert's report, the TSO will call for clarification. In the same situation involving the test-taker's expert's report, the Board will conclude that any lack of clarity is a flaw in the report itself.

Whether a student was in the room in general—The ETS Board of Review seems not to be interested in independent proof of whether a test-taker was in the test room in impostor accusation situations where the ETS handwriting expert has opined that the test-taker did not take the test.

Prior test results—ETS views results on its prior tests as valid and reliable, even where the test-taker proves illness or injury as a factor lowering a prior score. Prior tests that happen to be proctored practice tests administered in test preparation courses are routinely disregarded as valid prior test results.

Fingerprint evidence—If a test-taker wants to submit this as proof that he/she took the test, ETS will routinely deny the test-taker access to the original documents. Yet ETS asks the test-taker for a thumbprint to verify authenticity in retest situations. Fingerprint evidence, therefore, is only relevant to ETS if it helps ETS or favors their position, and it is not relevant if it helps or might favor the position of the test-taker. NOTE: in a recent questioned score situation, the mere request to send documents for fingerprint analysis to the fingerprint expert in the Dalton case appeared to be sufficient to get the scores released.

Confirmation that the student increased scores as a result of taking a test preparation course—This is an area of considerable controversy. The author has information from two different test preparation companies that, in the past, their submitting a letter was helpful in getting a student's score released.

However, it was apparent in the Dalton case that detailed information submitted by The Princeton Review was not helpful (the student ultimately won), perhaps because The Princeton Review criticizes ETS and provides students unique assistance like the information in this essay. Consider these contradictory facts: ETS personnel believe that test preparation courses don't improve scores, but the College Board, their partner in the SAT, has set up a for-profit division to provide online test preparation courses!

RULE OF THUMB #2: In calling and/or writing to ETS, it is not helpful to refer to this article, or to The Princeton Review, or to The Princeton Review Foundation. There may still be some ETS employees who have a negative attitude toward our student advocacy positions, and/or us, and you don't need to have that negativity applied to your situation. Make use of the information you read here, but just avoid mentioning this article to ETS.

IX. Getting and Analyzing ETS's Evidence

Anyone desiring to see the evidence in their ETS file needs to be prepared to send a series of letters requesting that evidence. Here's a recommended "First Request" letter:

"First Request" letter in an "unusual agreement" (copying) case, to be faxed to the ETS TSO who signed a "scores are delayed" or "questioned scores" letter:

Please send to me, as soon as possible, a copy of the entire ETS file on (name of test-taker), including copies of the seating chart, (test-taker's) original test booklet and answer sheets for both (test-taker) and Candidate B. Kindly include all the evidence considered by the TSO in deciding to cancel (test-taker's) scores. I make these requests under Standard 8.11 of the Standards for Educational and Psychological Testing of the American Psychological Association. In addition, I request a reasonable extension of your deadline date of _____ so that I will have enough time to review the evidence that you're sending me before I reply to it.

After receiving the above letter, ETS's TSO will respond by sending documents. Which documents? It seems to depend on their mood. Always they send the "Score Review Summary," and what they call their "Response Analysis." The Summary is an overview of the file, and has, on the first page, the scores of the test that are being questioned. This can be significant to many students who are not able to find out over the phone what their questioned scores actually were. Sometimes the Summary will indicate what important information is not in the file--for example, the seating chart may be missing.

The "Response Analysis" shows ETS's analysis of the answers of the test-taker compared to the answers of "Candidate B," the designation of another person from whom the test-taker typically is suspected of copying. This document can be hard to read, understand and interpret, and expert assistance should be sought. Often the most significant information on this document is the number of identical incorrect answers between the test-taker and Candidate B.

Often the file will contain an Erasure Analysis, and an analysis of the variable, or experimental, section. The evidence contained in these parts of the file needs to be evaluated by an expert to assess its strength and possible impact on the decision of the Board of Review.

In copying cases, one of the best methods of establishing the validity of the questioned score is to analyze the answer sheets for items that are dissimilar. Some of the best evidence in proving validity is finding test questions, preferably difficult questions, which the test-taker answered correctly and Candidate B answered incorrectly. Also markings (called scratchwork) in the test-taker's original test booklet that can be tied to the test-taker's answers can be excellent evidence of validity.

If a student decides to retest in a regular testing administration after a questioned score, it is particularly important that there be copious scratchwork in the test booklet that connects to the test-taker's chosen answers.

In mentioning a comparison of answer sheets and a review of the test booklet, it needs to be emphasized that ETS will usually not provide these documents unless specifically requested, and, in many cases, not unless specifically requested several times.

In summary, analyzing the evidence in the test-taker's file held by ETS involves the subtle weighing of many different factors such as matching wrong answers, erasures, the variable section, differing correct answers, scratchwork and any unique circumstances, all of which are interrelated. The test-taker should seek a review of his/her evidence and file by someone with experience and expertise to assist in drawing sound conclusions.

Since 1995 The Princeton Review Foundation has been providing file review assistance and advice free of charge to all students, including those who have taken The Princeton Review SAT course, those who have not and those who have taken another company's course.

9
Sources

ACT, Inc. (2007). *Preparing for the ACT 2007–2008.* Available from
 www.actstudent.org.

American Dental Association (2007). *Dental Admission Testing Program
 2007 Examinee Guide.* Available from www.ada.org.

Andrews, Kevin M,, and Robert L. Ziomek (1998). "Score gains on Re-
 testing with the ACT Assessment." ACT Research Report Series
 98–7. Available from www.act.org.

Arenson, Karen (2007). "Companies Agree to Pay to Settle SAT Error
 Suit." *New York Times,* August 25, 2007.

Association of American Medical Colleges (2007). *2007 MCAT Essentials.* Available from www.aamc.org.

Association of Schools and Colleges of Optometry (2007). *Optometry
 Admission Testing Program 2007 Examinee Guide.* Available from
 www.opted.org.

Bridgeman, Brent, et. al. (2003). *Effect of Fewer Questions per Section on
 SAT I Scores.* College Board Research Report No. 2003-2, ETS
 RR-03-08. The College Board: New York, NY.

Buckleitner, Warren (2006). "College Test Prep Takes a Test: A Review
 of Ten Online SAT Test Preparation Services." *Consumer Reports
 WebWatch.* Available as a PDF from www.ConsumerWebWatch.
 org/pdfs/satprep.pdf.

College Board (2007). *Information for Candidates: College-Level Examination Program.* Available from www.collegeboard.com/clep.

____ (2007) *Official Educator Guide to the PSAT/NMSQT.* Available from
 www.collegeboard.com/psat.

____ (2007). *SAT Progam Handbook 2007-08.* Available from www.col-
 legeboard.com/sat

____ (2005). *The Official SAT Study Guide.* College Board Publications:
 Plano, TX.

____ (2000). "Testing With Extended Time on the SAT I: Effects for
 Students With Learning Disabilities." *Research Notes,* RN-08,
 January 2000. The College Board: New York, NY.

Cooperative Admissions Examination Student Handbook 2007–2008.
 Available from www.coopexam.org. CTB McGraw-Hill: Mon-
 terey, CA.

Crouse, James, and Dale Trusheim (1988). *The Case Against the SAT.*
 University of Chicago Press.

Disability Rights Advocates (2001). "Do No Harm." Available from
 www.dralegal.org.

Educational Testing Service (2007). *The PRAXIS Series Information Bulletin 2007–2008.* Available from www.ets.org/praxis.

___ (2007). *Understanding Your PRAXIS Scores.* Available from www.ets. org/praxis.

___ (2006). *Proper Use of The Praxis Series and Related Assessments.* Available from www.ets.org/praxis.

___ (2002). *GRE: Practicing to Take the General Test 10th Edition.* ETS: Princeton, NJ.

Educational Records Bureau (2007). *ISEE 2007-2008 Student Guide.* Available from www.iseetest.org.

Flippo, Rona F. (2004). *Texts and Tests: Teaching Study Skills Across Content Areas.* Heinemann Publishing: Portsmouth, NH.

Flowers, James L., and Theodore Silver (2006). *Cracking the MCAT CBT Second Edition.* Random House: New York, NY.

Freedman, Miriam Kurtzig (2003). "Disabling the SAT." *Education Next* 3:4, Fall 2003.

Gardner, Howard (2006). *Multiple Intelligences: New Horizons.* Perseus Books: Cambridge, MA.

___ (2003). "Multiple Intelligences After Twenty Years." Paper presented at the American Educational Research Association, Chicago, Illinois, April 21, 2003.

Glenn, David (2007). "College Board Researchers Defend New Essay Component of SAT." *Chronicle of Higher Education*, April 11, 2007.

Glenn, David (2007). "College Board Researchers Defend New Essay Component of SAT." *The Chronicle of Higher Education.* April 11, 2007.

Gould, Stephen Jay (1996). *The Mismeasure of Man.* Revised and expanded edition. W. W. Norton & Co.: New York, NY.

Graduate Record Admission Council (2005). *The Official Guide for GMAT Review, 11th Edition.*

Hancock, Ophelia H. (2004). *Reading Skills for College Students.* Sixth edition. Prentice Hall: Upper Saddle River, NJ.

Herrnstein, Richard, and C. Murray (1994). *The Bell Curve: Intelligence and Class Structure in American Life.* Free Press Paperbacks: New York, NY.

Jacobs, Lynn F. and J. S. Hyman (2006). *Professors' Guide to Getting Good Grades in College.* HarperCollins: New York, NY.

Johnson, Linda Lee (1990). " Learning across the curriculum with creative graphing." *The Reading Teacher.* International Reading Association.

Kravets, Marybeth, and Imy Wax (2007). *K & W Guide to Colleges for Students with Learning Disabilities, 9th Edition.* New York: Random House.

Lemann, Nicholas (1999). *The Big Test: The Secret History of American Meritocracy*. Farrar, Straus, & Giroux: New York, NY.

___ (1997). "The Bell Curve Flattened." January 18, 1997. Available from www.slate.com.

Lewin, Tamar (2003). "Disability Requests Reflect Changes in SAT Procedure." *The New York Times*. November 8, 2003.

Mouton, Stephen. "Accommodations for Learning Disabilities and ADHD." Available from www.iser.com.

Murray, Charles (2007). "Abolish the SAT." *The American: A Magazine of Ideas*. Available from www.american.com.

National Council of State Boards of Nursing (2007). *2007 NCLEX Examination Candidate Bulletin*. Available from www.ncsbn.org.

National Council of Teachers of English (2005). *The Impact of the SAT and ACT Timed Writing Tests: Report from the NCTE Task Force on SAT and ACT Writing Tests*. Available for download from www.ncte.org.

New York City Department of Education (2007). *2007-2008 Specialized High Schools Student Handbook*. Available from schools.nyc.gov.

Nist, Sherrie L. and J.P. Holschuh (2005). *College Success Strategies*. 2nd edition. Penguin Academic Series. Pearson Longman: New York, NY.

Olney, Kathryn (2007). "The Test from Hell." *San Francisco Chronicle*. July 17, 2007.

Perelman, Les (2005). "New SAT: Write Long, Badly and Prosper." June 1, 2005. Available from www.jewishworldreview.com.

Peterson, Ivers (2004). "Extra Time, Math, and the SAT." *Science News Online*. Week of May 8, 2004: Vol. 265, No. 19. Available from www.sciencenews.org.

Princeton Review, The (2007). *Cracking the GMAT 2008 Edition*. Random House: New York, NY.

___ (2007). *Cracking the LSAT 2008 Edition*. Random House: New York, NY.

___ (2007). *Cracking the SAT 2008 Edition*. Random House: New York, NY.

___ (2007). *Cracking the TOEFL iBT 2008 Edition*. Random House: New York, NY.

___ (2006). *Cracking the GRE 2007 Edition*. Random House: New York, NY.

___ (2006). *Cracking the SSAT and ISEE 2007 Edition*. Random House: New York, NY.

___ (2007). *Cracking the GED 2008 Edition*. Random House: New York, NY.

Ravitch, Diane (2000). *Left Back: A Century of Battles Over School Reform*. Touchstone: New York, NY.

Rhoades, Kathleen, and G. Madaus (2003). *Errors in Standardized Testing: A Systemic Problem*. National Board on Educational Testing and Public Policy: Boston, MA.

Rimer, Sara (2007). "For Girls, It's Be Yourself, and Be Perfect, Too." *New York Times,* April 1, 2007.

Roediger, H.L. & Karpicke, J.D. (2006). "Test-enhanced learning: Taking memory tests improves long-term retention." *Psychological Science*, 17, 249–255.

Roffman, Arlyn (2007). *Guiding Teens with Learning Disabilities: Navigating the Transition from High School to Adulthood*. Random House: New York, NY.

Rudner, Lawrence M., and William D. Schaffer (2001). "Reliability." ERIC Document ED458213. ERIC Clearinghouse on Assessment and Evaluation: College Park, MD.

Sacks, Peter (1999). *Standardized Minds: The High Price of America's Testing Culture and What We Can Do About It*. Perseus Books: Cambridge, MA.

Schaeffer, Robert (2006). "Testimony of Robert Schaeffer Before the New York Senate Higher Education Committee." Available from www.fairtest.org.

Schoenbach, Ruth, et. al. (1999). *Reading for Understanding: A guide to improving reading in middle and high school classrooms*. Jossey-Bass, Inc.: San Francisco, CA.

Silverman, Sue William (2002). "I Can't Get no SATisfaction." *The Chronicle of Higher Education*. Vol. 49, Issue 3, pg. B14, September 13, 2002.

Swanson, Sue, and C. Howell (1996). "Test Anxiety in Adolescents with Learning Disabilities and Behavior Disorders." *Exceptional Children*, Vol. 62, 1996.

Szafran, Robert F. (1981). "Question-Pool Study Guides: Effects on Test Anxiety and Learning Retention." *Teaching Sociology*, Vol. 9, No. 1 (October). Pp. 31–43.

Test for Admission into Catholic High Schools Student Handbook 2007. Available from www.tachsinfo.com.

Toch, Thomas (2006). *Margins of Error: The Education Testing Industry in the No Child Left Behind Era*. Education Sector: Washington, DC.

Tovani, Cris (2000). *I Read It, but I Don't Get It: Comprehension Strategies for Adolescent Readers*. Stenhouse Publishers.

Troyka, Lynn Q. and Joseph W. Thweatt (2003). *Structured Reading.* Sixth edition. Prentice Hall: Upper Saddle River, NJ.

Tuckman, Bruce, et. al. (2007). *Learning and Motivation Strategies: Your Guide to Success.* Second edition. Prentice Hall: Upper Saddle River, NJ.

Winerip, Michael (2005). "SAT Essay Test Rewards Length and Ignores Errors." *The New York Times,* May 4, 2005.

NOTES

NOTES

NOTES

NOTES

NOTES

NOTES

NOTES

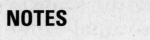

NOTES

Now that you have the tools to do your best on any test, get the advantage on upcoming exams.

Whether Going from High School to College…

ACT or SAT?
Choosing the
Right Exam For You
978-0-375-42924-8
$15.99 / $19.99 Can.

Cracking the ACT,
2009 Edition
978-0-375-42899-9
$19.95 / $22.95 Can.
978-0-375-42900-2 (with DVD)
$31.95 / $35.95 Can.

Cracking the SAT,
2010 Edition
978-0-375-42922-4
$21.99 / $26.99 Can.
978-0-375-42923-1 (with DVD)
$34.99 / $43.99 Can.

Cracking the AP
Calculus AB & BC Exams,
2009 Edition
978-0-375-42885-2
$19.00 / $22.00 Can.
16 AP subjects available

…Or College to Grad School.

Cracking the GRE,
2010 Edition
978-0-375-42932-3
$22.00 / $26.95 Can.
978-0-375-42933-0 (with DVD)
$34.99 / $43.99 Can.

Cracking the LSAT,
2010 Edition
978-0-375-42929-3
$22.99 / $27.99 Can.
978-0-375-42930-9 (with DVD)
$37.99 / $46.99 Can.

Cracking the GMAT,
2010 Edition
978-0-375-42925-5
$22.99 / $27.99 Can.
978-0-375-42926-2 (with DVD)
$37.99 / $46.99 Can.

Visit **PrincetonReview.com** for our complete list of grad school and college test prep books including SAT and AP subject test guides. Also available in bookstores everywhere.